LIFE

OF

EMANUEL SWEDENBORG.

TOGETHER WITH

A BRIEF SYNOPSIS OF HIS WRITINGS, BOTH PHILOSOPHICAL AND THEOLOGICAL.

BY WILLIAM WHITE.

WITH AN INTRODUCTION
BY B. F. BARRETT.

FIRST AMERICAN EDITION.

PHILADELPHIA
J. B. LIPPINCOTT & CO.
1874.

PREFACE.

During the few past years many biographies of Swedenborg have been offered to the public. Dr. Tafel, of Tubingen, in 1839, collected into one volume the testimonies of Swedenborg's personal friends, his letters, and various documents relating to him which were scattered through many volumes. This "Book of Documents" was translated into English, and edited by the Rev. J. H. Smithson, of Manchester, in 1841; and was again reprinted in America and re-edited by Professor Bush, of New York, in 1847. From this "Book of Documents," all the biographies which have appeared, have been more or less indebted. Nathanael Hobart, of Boston, arranged these documents into a connected biographical form, interspersed with judicious remarks of his own, and published it as a "Life of Swedenborg." This "Life" has passed through three editions, and well deserves the success it has attained. In 1849, Elihu Rich published, in London, "A Biographical Sketch of Emanuel Swedenborg." The edition was exhausted in the course of a few months, and the work has not since been reprinted. In the same year, J. J. G. Wilkinson produced his "Emanuel Swedenborg: a Biography," a work which, alike for its artistic excellence as a biography, and the originality and poetic beauty of its thought, has, I believe, no equal in the English language. The comparative silence of our literary critics, in reference to this work, proves that any one who cares to appreciate what is best in the world, had better not be content to trust solely to *their* eyes. From the quotations I have made in the course of the following narrative, the reader will be able to appreciate a few of the good things contained in this Biography by Wilkinson. In 1854, Edwin Paxton Hood published "Swedenborg: A Biography and an Exposition," a work which has been the means of introducing Swedenborg to a large circle hitherto almost ignorant of his existence. In the same year, Woodbury M. Fernald published, in Boston, Mass., "A Compendium of the Theological and Spiritual Writings of Swedenborg," to which an excellent life of the Author was prefixed, compiled in great part from previous biographies. In other forms, many sketches of the life of Swedenborg have been published. The Rev. O. P. Hiller gives an excellent little biography in his volume of "Gems from Swedenborg." Emerson tells the story of his life, in his own way, in "Representative Men;" and a Lecture by George Dawson, on Swedenborg, is now circulating, as a tract, by thousands throughout the land. All these things evidence a growing interest in the greatest teacher of modern times.

The present work does not enter into competition with anything that has before been written. It pretends to nothing but simplicity, and would be ranked as a hand-book, a guide, a directory. If it should lead any to form an acquaintance with the writings of "the most *unknown* man in the world," as Mr. Fernald calls Swedenborg, and I may add, the most abused man in the world, my end will be gained. I believe the day is not far distant when it will be the greatest reproach of these times that the works of Swedenborg lay in our midst, and only a few men cared for them. Happily this number is steadily increasing; and, by and by, we may expect a general acknowledgment of the fact, that Swedenborg was, without exception, the most gifted and extraordinary man that has ever lived.

36 Bloomsbury Street, London, *January*, 1856.

INTRODUCTION.

It is difficult to paint in language the grandest scenes in nature. To him who essays it, words seem powerless and wholly unequal to the task of conveying an adequate description. Any one who has stood by the side of Niagara, and listened to its deafening roar, and felt the grandeur and inspiration of the scene, is never quite satisfied with any written or oral description of that mighty cataract. And the reason is plain. It is not in the power of language, however skilfully employed, to kindle such emotions in the soul as are awakened by the scene itself.

The case is similar in regard to all great geniuses, and especially great authors. It is not easy to describe the loftiest human souls, or adequately to paint their characters in words. And those who are most familiar with their writings, are usually least satisfied with their biographies however vigorously or gracefully written. It is with the most gifted thinkers and writers as with the great Author of the volume of nature; they are best seen and understood in their works. And in any biographies wherein it is attempted to show us such men apart from, or outside of, their writings, it can hardly be otherwise than that they should appear considerably dwarfed. We miss those grand and symmetrical features which reveal themselves on every page of their works, but are to be truly seen no where else. Doubtless it is for this reason, in part, that no Life of SWEDENBORG which has yet appeared, has been entirely satisfactory to those best acquainted with his writings. And for the same reason we doubt if such a Life of him ever will appear.

The present volume, though not in all respects what we wish it were, possesses, nevertheless, some estimable features, which cannot fail to recommend it to the general reader. Among these are its truthfulness, its brevity, its simplicity, and its generally faithful though brief synopsis of the voluminous writings of the great Seer. In introducing it to the American public, we cannot but cherish the hope that it may be the means of disabusing the popular mind of many errors and prejudices in regard to one of the greatest and best of men, and of exciting increased inquiry concerning writings of which the great mass of our people are almost totally ignorant, but which, every year, are attracting more and more the attention of thoughtful and serious minds. There are no writings with which we are acquainted, which will so richly repay the earnest seeker after truth for a thorough and careful study, as the writings of Swedenborg; none that solve so many difficult and perplexing problems; none that appeal so powerfully to the understanding and the heart of every sincere and rational inquirer; none that are so sure to resolve the doubts of every honest doubter; none that shed such a blaze of light upon the Sacred Page, as well as upon "our being's end and aim;" none that bring Scripture, and reason, and science, and the accepted laws of the human soul, into such beautiful and perfect harmony. We say this with confidence, after a thorough study of these writings, and a pretty careful reading of all the reigning systems of theology.

But lest our opinion of this man and his writings should be

deemed somewhat partial, and therefore not deserving of full credit, we introduce here the testimony of a few witnesses who cannot be suspected of any such partiality—of men who never reckoned themselves as Swedenborgians, and were never in any way identified with the Church of the New Jerusalem.

"It has been said by some, and received implicitly without further examination by others, that Baron Swedenborg, after receiving his extraordinary commission, was mad, and became totally deprived of his natural senses; but this insinuation is such a palpable contradiction to truth, and such an insult to common sense, being overruled by every page of his writings, as well as by every act of his life after that period, that we should have thought it altogether unworthy of notice were we not aware that it operates powerfully with many, even at this day, to prejudice them against a character which otherwise they would revere, and against writings from which they would otherwise receive the most welcome instruction, whilst, in the meantime, they can give no reasonable account of their prejudice, nor trace its origin to any better source than the unjust calumny uttered of old against another respectable name—'Paul, *thou art beside thyself*; much learning *doth make thee mad.*'" (Acts xxvi. 24.)—DR. HURD'S *History of the Rites and Ceremonies of all Nations*, p. 705.

"I fully concede indeed to Swedenborg what is usually denied him, namely, an extreme sobriety of mind displayed under all the exceptional circumstances of his career, and which ends by making us feel at last his every word to be almost insipid with veracity. I cordially appreciate moreover the rare destitution of wilfulness which characterizes all his researches; or rather the child-like docility of spirit which leads him to seek and to recognize, under all the most contradictory aspects of nature, the footsteps of the Highest. . . . His books are a dry unimpassioned unexaggerated exposition of the things he daily saw and heard in the world of spirits, and of the spiritual laws which these things illustrate; with scarcely any effort whatever to blink the obvious outrage his experiences offer to sensuous prejudice, or to conciliate any interest in his reader which is not prompted by the latter's own original and unaffected relish of the truth. Such sincere books it seems to me were never before written. He grasped with clear intellectual vision the seminal principles of things, and hence is never tempted to that dreary Socratic ratiocination about their shifting superficial appearances, which give great talkers a repute for knowledge."—*Substance and Shadow.* By HENRY JAMES, pp. 103, 104.

"What appears as Swedenborg's crudities and fantasies, however, are extraneous to his essential system, which has a unity of its own, and an organic connection with Christianity, such as avouches itself the genuine developement of the Christian system. His cosmology, his theology, and his pneumatology are the Christian revelation breaking into more full and rational light from the seals of the letter which had kept and preserved it." (REV. E. H. SEARS, *in the Monthly Religious Magazine for March*, 1865, p. 147.)

And the same writer, speaking of one of Swedenborg's works, in which the "Doctrine of Degrees" is treated of, and whose philosophy, he says, "the reader does not at first get the pith of," adds: "But when he does get it, he sees the amazing sweep of the principle set forth, and its constructive power in theology, and that by missing it every school of materialism has stuck fast to the earth,—Pantheism, babbling of sacred names that mean nothing, the Church glooming among the sepulchres, and modern Spiritualism offering us a future world of sublimated matter; he sees, too, that without the key which this principle offers, they will never get out of that prison-house, but knock their heads eternally against the bars."—*Foregleams of Immortality.* By EDMUND H. SEARS. *Note to p.* 41.

"It is said that Swedenborg was a Fanatic. What then is a Fanatic? One of the profoundest mathematicians of his age; a deep and acute thinker; a subtle logician; a various and versatile scholar; above all, a calm and most quiet bookman and penman, indisposed for every company, and never seen to court the company of the ignorant and the vulgar [who are] ever the resort of the fanatic; a man of few words, until compelled to talk, or talking for a purpose; cool in temperament; never rocked by passion or impulse; always, as far as humanity can be, in equilibrium, weighing all his thoughts and all his actions; perpetually bent upon giving reasons for things; a man of strong inductive habits and powers, and consistent; a whole life of invariable rectitude, and doctrines, and principles, ever above the hour; and ever, from the period of his illumination, the same.—Is this the portrait of a Fanatic? . . . . He was a Titan, and must take his place among the very highest and widest minds of our world; his was truly a Norse intellect; he belonged to the wonderful race of Sea-kings; he was one of the children of Odin, and we know that race—the writers and interpreters of the runes—the utterers of the rythmic charm." (*Swedenborg; a Biography and an Exposition.* By EDWIN PAXTON HOOD, (*Episcopalian,*) pp. 169, 170.)

"I have often thought of writing a work to be entitled, a Vindication of Great Men unjustly branded, and at such times, the names prominent to my mind's eye have been Giordano Bruno, Jacob Behmen, Benedict Spinoza, and EMANUEL SWEDENBORG. I remember nothing in Lord Bacon superior, few passages equal, either in depth of thought, or in richness, dignity and felicity of diction, or in the weightiness of the truths contained in these articles. I can venture to assert, that, as a *Moralist, Swedenborg is above all praise;* and that, as a Naturalist, Psychologist, and Theologian, he has strong and varied claims on the gratitude and admiration of the professional and philosophical faculties."—SAMUEL TAYLOR COLERIDGE, *Literary Remains*, Vol. IV. 423.

"His [SWEDENBORG'S] writings would be a sufficient library to a lonely and athletic student. Not every man can read them, but they will reward him who can. The grandeur of the topics makes the grandeur of the style. One of the missourians and mastodons of literature, he is not to be measured by whole colleges of ordinary scholars. No one man is perhaps able to judge of the merits of his works on so many subjects. It seems that he anticipated much science of the nineteenth century; anticipated in astronomy the discovery of the seventh planet; anticipated the views of modern astronomy in regard to the generation of earths by the sun; in chemistry, the atomic theory; in anatomy, the discoveries of Schlieuting, Monro, and Wilson; and first demonstrated the office of the lungs. Swedenborg styles himself, in the title-page of his books, "Servant of the Lord Jesus Christ:" and by force of intellect, and in effect, he is the last Father in the Church, and is not likely to have a successor. No wonder that his depth of ethical wisdom should give him influence as a teacher. To the withered traditional church yielding dry catechisms, he let in nature again, and the worshipper, escaping from the vesting of verbs and texts, is surprised to find himself a party to the whole of his religion. His religion thinks for him, and is of universal application. He turns it on every side; it fits every part of life, interprets and dignifies every circumstance. Instead of a religion which visited him diplomatically three or four times,—when he was born, when he married, when he felt sick, and when he died, and for the rest never interfered with him,—here was a teaching which accompanied him all day, accompanied him even into sleep and dreams; into his thinking, and showed him through what a long ancestry his thoughts descend; into society, and showed by what affinities he was girt to his equals and his counterparts; into natural objects, and showed their origin and meaning, what are friendly and what are hurtful; and opened the future world, by indicating the continuity or the same laws. His disciples allege that their intellect is invigorated by the study of his books."—RALPH WALDO EMERSON.

"SWEDENBORG was not a man to be carried away by an unbridled imagination; still less did he ever manifest, during his whole life, the slightest symptom of mental aberration. . . . On the other hand, he was in life and disposition so blameless, that no man dare even intimate any suspicion of concerted deception; and posterity have no right to call into question the unsuspected testimony of those who lived in the same age as Swedenborg, and who knew him well. If this mode of judgment be permitted, all historical evidence, even the holiest and most venerable might be reduced to nothing. . . . If it be permitted to say of a man, to whose veracity, intelligence, science, irreproachable conduct, presence of mind, and fidelity to truth, his contemporaries bear testimony—if it be permitted for pos terity to say that such a man had either imprudently deceived himself and the world, or had knowingly dealt in mere falsehood and lies, there is an end to the verification of historical events. . . . He was guided in his researches by a mind clear, acutely analytic, endowed with skill, and well disciplined in mathematics and logic. He endeavored to raise the mind to that height from which the first created germ, acted upon by the creative spirit and power, might be contemplated, and from which the first buds (or principles) of things might be seen growing from the impulsive force which God has implanted in their nature. . . . Throughout the entire course of his learned researches and activity, we every where discover the pious and religious man, who, in all his sayings and doings, was intent upon good. In his inmost soul, he was entirely opposed to all those systems of materialism and naturalism which so wantonly prevailed in his time; and he built his own system on the foundation of an Eternal Esse, and on its creating activities, (from which, as from the only origin and cause, all things are created and preserved). And, throughout the entire course of his labors, he seizes every opportunity of pointing to this first great rational Cause of all things, and, at the same time, he endeavors to show the absurdity of all opposite opinions. Nor did the sensualism of those of his contemporaries which confines itself to the mere surface of things, nor did the more refined Pantheistic abstraction of others, although penetrating more deeply below the surface, find any place in his system and works. There no where appears in the writings of Swedenborg a self-destroying contradiction, nothing abrupt, disjointed, or unconnected, or arbitrary, or illogical, such as is accustomed to accompany the phenomena of dreams, or the effusions of an unregulated fancy; but every thing that he writes is so connected and uninterrupted, as to present a perfect whole.—REV. PROFESSOR VON GŒBRES, (*Roman Catholic*,) "*On Swedenborg and his Views.*"

"EMANUEL SWEDENBORG occupies a prominent position among the master minds of humanity. . . . It is not our province or purpose to decide the question of his Seership, but we may be permitted to remark that to all impartial and reflecting minds his historical appearance presents a problem that still awaits solution. The smile of incredulity begins to die upon the lips of the conscientious sceptic, and the opprobrious terms—dreamer and madman—are yielding to the more courteous epithet—mystic. In vain will you ransack the archives of his family or personal history for a trace of insanity. Equally fruitless will be your endeavor to trace any symptoms of incoherence or raving in his methodical pages. If he must needs be mad, there is a rare method in his madness; and if the world insists on his being a visionary it must admit that his visions are something anomalous, in their systematic and mathematical form. But we have yet to learn that visionaries and dreamers can write a cool business-like style, and pen dry and well-digested folios. Nor is it a common thing to find a madman deficient in the sallies of the imagination, and remarkable for strong common sense. Such is the problem and anomaly presented by this remarkable man, whose gift of Seership is attested by such characters as Kant and the sister of the great Frederick. . . . Swedenborg's philosophy, as developed in his scientific as well as theological works, may be characterized as a very decided system of empirical realism, distinguished for an almost diophanic introvision into the human heart for consummate simplicity and consistency. He regards the science of Correspondence as the key of knowledge—a divine philosophy, unlocking the treasures of the spiritual as well as the natural worlds, and sending thought at a bound from the zoophite to the Seraphim. The material world is the ultimate and pedestal of the universe, filled with various collations corresponding to others in the higher ascending spheres of the universe. Thus nature is, in truth, a revelation, and a divine book, whose letters the groves, hills, and rivers, the firmament and the lamps of heaven, are hieroglyphic representatives of corresponding spiritual realities. . . . It is refreshing, in the eleventh hour of the eighteenth century—the age of Atheism, Libertinism, Freemasonry, and Rosicrusianism, to meet a man who united a healthy, plain, and practical view of life, man, and nature, with the sublimest, and at the same time the most scientific, handling and treatment of things, spiritual and eternal. In the eyes of a discriminating posterity, Emanuel Swedenborg will obtain an elevated rank in the illustrious brotherhood of the luminaries of the Church."—TENNEMANN'S *Manual of the History of Philosophy.*

Such is the testimony in regard to this man and his writings, offered by independent and serious minds, who cannot be suspected of any undue bias in his favor. Not one of these witnesses was ever identified with what is popularly known as the New Church, whereof Swedenborg is held to be the divinely appointed herald. Let the candid reader ask himself, What conceivable motive could have induced them to extol unduly the virtues of this man, or to overestimate the wisdom and worth of his writings. B. F. B.

PHILADELPHIA, *February* 12th, 1866.

CONTENTS.

2 *

CHAPTER IX.

CHAPTER X.

CHAPTER XI.

CHAPTER XII.

CHAPTER XIII.

CHAPTER XIV.

CHAPTER XV.

CHAPTER XVI.

CHAPTER XVII.

CHAPTER XVIII.

CHAPTER XIX.

LIFE AND WRITINGS

OF

EMANUEL SWEDENBORG.

CHAPTER I.

His Birth and Parentage—His first ideas of Religion, and his Scholastic Life.

AUTHORS are never wiser than when they trust to time for justice. The poor thinker, neglected by his age, unseen amid the glare of mere show and pageantry, need not fret himself. Time will roll on, the false and meretricious will sink into forgetfulness, while his true words will become accepted, and his thoughts the stars by which wise men guide their course across the dark ocean of life.

It was the lot of Emanuel Swedenborg to be cast on a shallow, sceptical, and perverse age. Living a life of the utmost purity, and teaching truths which we esteem it our great felicity to know, he had but poor thanks so far as fame and disciples went. But the dawn of his day of justice is approaching. His name, which in past times has too often been used to point a sarcasm at whatever is visionary and transcendental, has of late years been slowly rising into estimation. Here and there, one eminent man after another has spoken some brave words in honor and admiration of the great Swede. Slowly, but surely, his writings are claiming attention; his disciples, though still few, are quietly earnest and enthusiastic, and ever and anon there is seen in the newspaper or periodical, the name of Swedenborg mentioned with respect, if not with reverence. Considerable curiosity exists in large circles to know more of him, of what he did, what were his doctrines, and the nature and number of his books. To satisfy, in some measure, these queries and if possible to incite a desire for an intimate personal acquaintance with the writings of Swedenborg, is the purpose of the present work.

Emanuel Swedenborg was born at Stockholm, on the 29th Jan., 1688. The year is a memorable one, as being that in which outraged England drove the faithless Stuarts from the throne. His father's name was Jesper Swedberg, and his mother's, Sarah Behm; both descended from families of worth and usefulness in Sweden. His father, at the time of his birth, was chaplain to a regiment of cavalry. After passing through several offices, one of which was a professorship of theology in the University of Upsal, Jesper Swedberg was, in the year 1719, elevated to the bishoprick of Skara in West Gothland. His character stood high in Sweden. Simple, patriotic, and honest, he was, without being brilliant, a learned and industrious man. He wrote much, and published occasionally, as the following extract from his diary proves: "I can scarcely believe that anybody in Sweden has written so much as I have done; since, I think, ten carts could scarcely carry away what I have written and printed at my own expense, and yet there is much, yea nearly as much, not printed." Of the professions of his sons, he wisely remarks; "I have kept my sons to that profession to which God has given them inclination and liking: I have not brought up one to the clerical office, although many parents do this inconsiderately, and in a manner not justifiable, by which the Christian Church and the clerical order suffer not a little, and are brought into contempt." Writing in his diary forty years after Emanuel's birth, he says: "Emanuel, my son's name, signifies 'God with us,' a name which should constantly remind him of the nearness of God, and of that interior, holy, and mysterious connection, in which, through faith, we stand with our good and gracious God. And blessed be the Lord's name! God has, to this hour, been with him; and may God be further with him, until he is eternally united with Him in his kingdom."

Of Swedenborg's childhood we have little record. In a letter which, late in life, he addressed to Dr. Beyer, he remarks; "With regard to what passed in the earliest part of my life, about which you wish to be informed: from my fourth to my tenth year, my thoughts were constantly engrossed by reflections on God, on salvation, and on the spiritual affections of man. I often revealed things in my discourse which filled my parents with astonishment, and made them declare at times, that certainly the angels spoke through my mouth. From my sixth to my twelfth year, it was my greatest delight to converse with the clergy concerning faith; to whom I often observed, that charity or love is the life of faith; and that this vivifying charity or love is no other than the love of one's neighbor; that God vouchsafes this faith to every one; but that it is adopted by those only who practise that charity. I knew of no other faith or belief at that time, than that God is the Creator and Preserver of Nature; that He endues men with understanding, good inclinations, and other gifts derived from these. I knew nothing at that time of the systematic or dogmatic kind of faith, that God the Father imputes the righteousness or merits of the Son to whomsoever, and at whatever time, He wills, even to the impenitent. And had I heard of such a faith, it would have been then, as now, perfectly unintelligible to me."

This confession very vividly shadows forth the future man. We see how earnestly his sound, practical mind perceived and clung to the real and substantial in theology. His experience of the doctrine of justification by faith alone, finds parallels in the lives and experience of many eminent men. It was not until after many years' preaching, that the fact of the existence of such a doctrine was presented to the mind of Dr. Chalmers, to whom also it was quite unintelligible; yet, overcome by the sphere of learning and prestige with which the doctrine was environed, Chalmers yielded assent to it, and fancied, as thousands do, he believed what by no possibility he could ever understand. Swedenborg was too single-eyed in his pursuit of truth to be led aside by authority, however imposing; and often, in the following narrative, we shall have to observe with what independence, yet with what humility and simplicity, he recorded the truths which it was his mission to reveal.

This excellent son of good Bishop Swedberg received the best education that the times and his country could afford. In his twenty-second year, at the University of Upsal, he took his degree of Doctor in philosophy. The dissertation which he wrote for his degree was afterwards published. It consisted of a selection of sentences from Seneca, Publius Syrus Mimus, and other Latin writers, enriched by comments of his own, and notes illustrating the obscurities of the Latin text. This work was so highly thought of, as to occasion a poetic eulogy, written in Greek, to be inscribed to its author. Swedenborg dedicated this, his first literary production, to his father, in a prelude full of veneration and love. Its length alone prevents our gratifying the reader with the perusal of this beautiful tribute of filial affection.

Among his many virtues, it should not be accounted the least, that Swedenborg was a loving, dutiful son.

The same year he published, in a work of his father's, a Latin version of the twelfth chapter of Ecclesiastes, which proved, in a high degree, his mastery of the Latin language.

In 1710, was finished the strictly scholastic period of Swedenborg's life. He had now reached manhood, and must live as a man among men. His youth manifests less precocity than solid and regular development of mind. The record of his life at this time, evidences a common-sense appreciation of life and its duties, an honest love of virtue, and a desire to be useful in his day and generation. The sequel will show that his day of life was not unworthy of its dawn.

CHAPTER II.

Travels—Becomes Author—Is crossed in Love.

HAVING completed his university education, Swedenborg entered on his travels. In his journal, he thus briefly describes a four years' absence from Sweden.

"In the year 1710 I set out for Gottenburg, that I might be conveyed, by ship, thence to London. On the voyage, my life was in danger four times: first on some shoals, toward which we were driven by a storm, until we were within a quarter of a mile from the raging breakers, and we thought we should all perish. Afterwards we narrowly escaped some Danish pirates under French colors; and the next evening we were fired into from a British ship, which mistook us for the same pirates, but without much damage. Lastly, in London itself, I was exposed to a more serious danger. While we were entering the harbor, some of our countrymen came to us in a boat, and persuaded me to go with them into the city. Now it was known in London that an epidemic was raging in Sweden, and therefore all who arrived from Sweden were forbidden to leave their ships for six weeks, or forty days; so I, having transgressed this law, was very near being hanged, and was only freed under the condition that, if any one attempted the same thing again, he should not escape the gallows.

"At London and Oxford I tarried about a year. Then I went to Holland and saw its chief cities. At Utrecht I tarried a long time, while Congress was sitting and ambassadors were gathering there from nearly all the courts of Europe. Thence I went into France, and passed through Brussels and Valenciennes to Paris. Here and at Versailles I spent a year. At the end of this time I hastened, by public coach, to Hamburg, and thence to Pomerania and Greifswalde, where I remained some time, while Charles the Twelfth was coming from Bender to Stralsund. When the siege began, I departed in a small vessel, together with a lady named Feif, and by Divine Providence was restored to my own country after more than four years' absence."

While traveling he was not idle; for we find that in 1715, while at Greifswalde, he published an oration on the return of Charles XII. from Turkey, and a small volume of Latin prose fables. On his return to Sweden, he issued, at Skara, a little book of poems, written for the most part during his journeyings. These have been republished at various times; but, as poems, much cannot be said of them. Wilkinson, in his "Biography of Swedenborg," remarks: "These poems display fancy, but a controlled imagination. If we may convey to the English reader such a notion of Latin verses, they remind one of the Pope school, in which there is generally some theme, or moral, governing the flights of the Muse." Indeed, it was well that Swedenborg was but slightly endowed with the poetic faculty. Much of his future mission lay in fields which require the coolest and calmest of minds to describe; the sight and contemplation of which, would have sent a Shaksperian or Byronic temperament into extatic frenzies.

Swedenborg, himself the son of a bishop, was connected with high and influential families in Sweden. One of his sisters was married to Eric Benzelius, afterwards Archbishop of Upsal; and another to Lars Benzelstierna, governor of a province. Other members of the family held high and responsible offices in the kingdom. A young man thus situated would find little difficulty in settling for life in a sphere of usefulness adapted to all his tastes. While on his travels on the Continent he wrote letters to Eric Benzelius, detailing every novelty in mathematics, astronomy, and mechanics, which came under his observation; besides sending home models of all such inventions as he thought might be useful to his country. These letters and services won for him considerable notice; and on his return to Sweden, he assumed the editorship of a new periodical work, entitled "Dædalus Hyperboreus." Among the contributors to this magazine, was the celebrated mathematician, Christopher Polheim, who has been called the Swedish Archimedes. Swedenborg's connection with Polheim seems to have led to his appointment to the office of Assessor of the Board of Mines, which he held with distinguished honor for many years.

In the year 1716, Polheim invited him to go with him to Lund, on a visit to Charles XII., who had just escaped from Stralsund. He was very kindly received by the King, and obtained from him his official appointment as Assessor. He was to assist Polheim in his undertakings, to have a seat in the College of Mines, and to give his advice, especially when any business of a mathematical nature was on hand.

Charles seems to have at once discerned the rare abilities of Swedenborg, and with a desire of uniting him in still closer bonds of amity with his favorite Polheim, he advised Polheim to give him his daughter in marriage. To this proposal Swedenborg appears to have been in nowise averse. He lived with Polheim, at once as his coadjutor, and as his pupil in mathematics; and having thus constant opportunities of seeing the fair Emerentia, Polheim's second daughter, had become enamored of her graces. In one of his letters, he remarks: "Polheim's eldest daughter is promised to a page of the king's. I wonder what people say of this in relation to myself. His second daughter is, in my opinion, much the handsomest." The attachment, however, was not mutual, and the lady would not allow herself to be betrothed. Her father, who deeply loved Swedenborg, caused a written agreement to be drawn up, promising his daughter at some future day. This document, Emerentia, from filial obedience, signed; but, as ladies generally do, when forced to love in this way, took to sighs and sadness, which so affected her brother with sorrow, that he secretly purloined the agreement from Swedenborg. The paper was soon missed; for Swedenborg read it over frequently, and, in his grief at its loss, besought Polheim to replace it by a new one. But as Swedenborg now discovered the pain which he gave to the object of his affections, he at once relinquished all claim to her hand, and left her father's house. This was his last, as it was his first endeavor after marriage. In after years, when jocosely asked whether he had ever been desirous of marrying, he answered: "In my youth I was once on the road to matrimony." And on being asked what was the obstacle, with his characteristic simplicity he said: "She would not have me." Considering the studious and abstracted life which he eventually led, it is not to be regretted that he remained unwedded. That he was no harsh despiser of the sex, we know well from his writings; and that his life was in agreement with his books, we also know. The loveliest descriptions of female grace and beauty we have ever met with, are contained in his works, chiefly in his treatise on "Conjugal Love." M. Sandell, a member of the Royal Academy of Sciences in Sweden, who pronounced a magnificent eulogium on his fellow-member, Swedenborg, shortly after his death, says: "Though Swedenborg was never married, it was not owing to any indifference toward the sex; for he esteemed the company of a fine, intelligent woman as one of the most agreeable of pleasures; but his profound

3 *

studies rendered expedient for him the quiet of a single life."

Swedenborg seems to have had much intercourse with the King. In one of his letters, he says: "I found his Majesty very gracious to me; more so than I could expect. This is a good omen for the future. Every day I laid mathematical subjects before his Majesty, who allowed everything to please him. When the eclipse took place, I had his Majesty out to see it, and we reasoned much thereupon. He again spoke of my 'Dædalus,' and remarked upon my not continuing it; for which I pleaded want of means. This he does not like to hear of; so I hope to have some assistance shortly." But assistance did not come, and "Dædalus" went the way of many such undertakings. Talking of mathematics one day, Charles remarked that "he who knew nothing of mathematics, did not deserve to be considered a rational man;" a sentiment which Swedenborg thought "truly worthy of a king." *

* The following account of Charles XII., written by Emanuel Swedenborg, was printed in the "Gentleman's Magazine," for September, 1754. It is a portion of a letter which Swedenborg wrote to M. Nordberg, while the latter was engaged in writing his "Life of Charles XII.," in which work the letter appeared at full length. It is too long to be quoted here; the following extracts contain the pith of it. It may be proper to observe, that it was written by the author prior to his being called to the sacred office which occupied the last twenty-nine years of his life. This accounts for his speaking of the celebrated Swedish hero with so much greater respect than he is known to have afterwards entertained for his memory.

"Having been frequently admitted to the honor of hearing his late most excellent Majesty, Charles XII. discourse on mathematical subjects, I presume an account of a new arithmetic invented by him, may merit the attention of my readers.

"His Majesty observed then, that the denary arithmetic, universally received and practiced, was most probably derived from the original method of counting on the fingers; that illiterate people of old, when they had run through the fingers of both hands, repeated new periods over and over again, and every time spread open both hands; which being done ten

Charles XII. was now engaged in the siege of Frederickshall, and Swedenborg's aid was called in. He very ingen-

times, they distinguished each step by proper marks, as by joining two, three, or four fingers. Afterwards, when this method of numeration on the fingers came to be expressed by proper characters, it soon became firmly and universally established, and so the denary calculus has been retained to this day. But surely, were a solid geometrician, thoroughly versed in the abstract nature and fundamentals of numbers, to set his mind upon introducing a still more useful calculus into the world, instead of ten, he would select such a perfect square, or cube number, as by continual bisection, or halving, would at length terminate in unity, and be better adapted to the subdivisions of measures, weights, coins, etc.

"Thus intent on a new arithmetic, the hero pitched upon the number eight, as most fit for the purpose, since it could not only be halved continually down to unity, without a fraction, but contained within it the square of 2, and was itself the cube thereof, and was also applicable to the received denomination of several sorts of weights and coins, rising to 16 and 32, the double and quadruple of 8. Upon these first considerations, he was pleased to command me to draw up an essay on an octonary calculus, which I completed in a few days, with its application to the received divisions, coins, measures, and weights, a disquisition on cubes and squares, and a new and easy way of extracting roots, all illustrated with examples.

"His Majesty having cast his eye twice or thrice over it, and observing, perhaps from some hints in the essay, that the denary calculus had several advantages not always attended to, he did not at that time seem absolutely to approve of the octonary: or, it is likely he might conceive, that though it seemed easy in theory, yet it might prove difficult to introduce it to practice. Be this as it may, he insisted on fixing upon some other that was both a cube and a square number, referrible to 8, and divisible down to unity by bisection. This could be no other than 64, the cube of 4, and square of 8, divisible down to unity without a fraction.

"I immediately presumed to object that such a number would be too prolix, as it rises through a series of entirely distinct and different numbers, up to 64, and then again to its duplicate 4,096, and on to its triplicate 262,144, before the fourth step commences; so that the difficulty of such a calculus would be incredible, not only in addition and subtraction, but to a still higher degree in multiplication and division; for the memory must necessarily retain in the multiplication table, 3,969 distinct products of the 63 numbers of the first step multiplied into one another; whereas only 49 are necessary in the octonary, and but 81 are required in the denary arith-

iously planned rolling machines, by which two galleys, five large boats, and a sloop, were conveyed from Stromstadt to

metic; which last is difficult to be remembered and applied in practice, by some capacities. But the stronger my objections were, the more resolute was his royal mind upon attempting such a calculus.

Obstructions made him eagerly aspire
All to surmount, and nobly soar the higher.

He insisted that the alleged difficulties might be overbalanced by very many advantages.

"A few days after this I was called before his Majesty, who, resuming the subject, demanded if I had made a trial. I still urging my former objections, he reached me a paper written with his own hand, in new characters and terms of denomination, the perusal of which, he was pleased, at my entreaty, to grant me; wherein, to my great surprise, I found not only new characters and numbers, (the one almost naturally expressive of the other) in a continued series to 64, so ranged as easily to be remembered, but also new denominations, so contrived by pairs, as to be easily extended to myriads by a continued variation of the character and denomination. And further casting my eye on several new methods of his for addition and multiplication by this calculus, either artificially contrived, or else inherent in the characters of the numbers themselves, I was struck with the profoundest admiration of the force of his Majesty's genius, and with such strange amazement, as obliged me to esteem this eminent personage, not my rival, but by far my superior in my own art. And having the original still in my custody, at a proper time I may publish it, as it highly deserves; whereby it will appear with what discerning skill he was endowed, or how deeply he penetrated into the obscurest recesses of the arithmetical science.

"Besides, his eminent talents in calculation further appear by his frequently working and solving the most difficult numerical problems, barely by thought and memory; in which operations others are obliged to take great pains and tedious labor.

"Having duly weighed the vast advantages arising from mathematical and arithmetical knowledge in most occasions of human life, he frequently used it as an adage, that *he who is ignorant of numbers is scarce half a man.*

"While he was at Bender, he composed a complete volume of military exercises, highly esteemed by those who are best skilled in the art of war."

Iderfjol, overland; a distance of fourteen miles. Under cover of these vessels, Charles was enabled to transport his heavy artillery under the very walls of Frederickshall; but it availed little, for at the siege of this town, on November 30, 1718, (old style,) this inveterate warrior received the fatal blow which ended his troublous and eventful career. He was struck in the head with a cannon ball, and though death must have been instantaneous, he was found with his right hand firmly grasping the handle of his sword; so prompt was he to put himself in an attitude of defence.

> "His fall was destined to a barren strand,
> A petty fortress and a dubious hand;
> He left a name at which the world grew pale,
> To point a moral or adorn a tale."

In 1719 the Swedberg family were ennobled by Queen Ulrica Eleonora, and Swedenborg from that time took his place with the nobles of the equestrian order, in the triennial Assemblies of the States. This distinction conferred little else than a change of name. He was neither a Count nor a Baron, as has very commonly been supposed.

Emanuel Swedenborg was rapidly winning for himself the name of a deep thinker and a ready writer. In 1717 he published "An Introduction to Algebra," under the title of "The Art of the Rules." It was highly praised for its clearness, and the order and force of its examples. The first portion of the work, however, was all that was published. The second, containing the first account given in Sweden of the differential and integral calculus, still remains in MS. His second publication this year was, "Attempts to find the Longitude of Places by Lunar Observations." Both works were written in Swedish.

In 1719 four works proceeded from his increasingly fertile pen. "A Proposal for a Decimal System of Money and Measures;" "A Treatise on the Motion and Position of the

Earth and Planets;" "Proofs derived from Appearances in Sweden, of the Depth of the Sea, and the greater Force of the Tides in the Ancient World;" and "On Docks, Sluices, and Salt Works."

His work on the Decimal system of coinage and measures was republished in 1795. Swedenborg's ideas on this and most other subjects were far ahead of the times in which he lived. In one of his letters he thus alludes to the discouragements he met with on this account. "It is a little discouraging to me to be advised to relinquish my views, as among the novelties the country can not bear. For my part, I desire all possible novelties; aye, a novelty for every day in the year; for in every age there is an abundance of persons who follow the beaten track, and remain in the old way; while there are not more than from six to ten in a century who bring forward innovations founded on argument and reason."

CHAPTER III.

Travels again—Publishes five Scientific Pamphlets and "Miscellaneous Observations"—Returns Home and enters on the duty of his Assessorship—Writes his "Opera Philosophica et Mineralia," and goes abroad to publish it.

In the spring of 1721, Swedenborg visited Holland a second time, and chose Amsterdam as a place of publication for the following five little works:—"Some Specimens of a Work on the Principles of Natural Philosophy, comprising New Attempts to Explain the Phenomena of Chemistry and Physics by Geometry;" "New Observations and Discoveries respecting Iron and Fire, and particularly respecting the Elemental Nature of Fire, together with a new construction of Stoves;" "A New Method of finding the Longitude of Places, on Land or at Sea, by Lunar Observations;" "A New Mechanical Plan of constructing Docks and Dykes;" and "A Mode of Discovering the Powers of Vessels by the application of Mechanical Principles."

The titles of these pamphlets prove that their author was no ordinary man. But the publication of them was not his only object in this visit to the continent. It was his desire to improve his practical knowledge of mining, to enable him the better to fulfill his duties as Assessor. For this purpose he left Amsterdam for Leipsic, passing through Aix-la-Chapelle, Liege, and Cologne, and visiting the different mines and smelting works which lay in his route. At Leipsic he published, in 1722, "Miscellaneous Observations connected with the Physical Sciences," Parts I. to III.; and at Hamburg, in the same year, Part IV., principally on minerals, iron, and the stalactites in Beaumann's cavern. The reigning Duke of Brunswick, Louis Rudolph, most hospitably received Swedenborg, defrayed his traveling expenses, and on his departure, testified his admiration of the young savant by presenting him with a gold medallion, and a weighty silver goblet. In return for these favors, Swedenborg dedicated Part IV. of his "Miscellaneous Observations" to him.

In speaking of the foregoing works, it is difficult, in the few words to which we must limit ourselves, to do them the justice which their originality and daring speculation deserve. As Wilkinson remarks, "the fortress of mineral truth was the first which he approached, and with the most guarded preparation. His method was furnished by geometry and mechanics; the laws of the pure sciences were to be the interpreters of the facts of chemistry and physics. The beginning of nature, says he, is identical with the beginning of geometry; the origin of natural particles is due to mathematical points, just as is the origin of lines, forms, and the whole of geometry: because everything in nature is geometrical, everything in geometry is natural. Carrying out this theory, he seeks to define the laws of chemical essence and combination, by the truths of mathematics." Mr. Strutt, the translator of these works into English, says: "This extraordinary attempt to bring invisible things to light, has been thoroughly justified by the success which has attended Dalton's hypothesis, in an age better prepared for its application; and by the equally remarkable fact that the definitions given of solids, acids, and alkalies, have gradually approximated very near indeed to those which result from Swedenborg's hypothesis. We say nothing here of a latent connection between the principle on which it is founded, and some of the results obtained by Berzelius, whose fame, as a chemist, is as wide as the civilized world." It need only be added that M. Dumas, the French chemist, ascribes to these works by Swedenborg, the origin of the modern science of crystallography. He says, "It is to him we are indebted for the first idea of making cubes, tetrahedrons, pyramids, and the different crystalline forms, by the grouping of spherical particles; and it is an idea which has been renewed by several distinguished men, Wollaston in particular."

After an absence of fifteen months, Swedenborg returned to his home in Stockholm, at midsummer, 1722. He now for the first time entered fully upon the duties of his Assessorship; having deferred doing so until his knowledge of metallurgy had become sufficiently practical and extensive. At this time he published an anonymous pamphlet "On the Depreciation and Rise of the Swedish Currency." The currency seems to have been a favorite subject with Swedenborg; and in his senatorial capacity, it engaged much of his attention. The pamphlet seems to have been much thought of, for we find that it was republished at Upsal in 1771. There are few productions of this kind that will endure a revival forty-nine years after their first publication.

The tenor of Swedenborg's life for eleven years after this, seems to have flowed quietly on in the regular fulfilment of the duties of his office. It may be supposed that he had become tired of writing and publishing scientific works, and that for a time he wished to rest from this kind of labor. His abilities were appreciated by his countrymen, for we find that he was solicited to accept the Professorship of mathematics in the University of Upsal, in 1724. He declined the honor. It appears that he had a distaste for the unpractical and merely speculative character of the pure mathematician. We find him writing to his brother-in-law in this strain:—"I wonder at Messieurs the mathematicians having lost all heart and spirit to realize that fine design of yours for an astronomical observatory. It is the fatality of mathematicians to remain chiefly in theory. I have often thought it would be a capital thing, if, to each ten mathematicians, one good practical man were added, to lead the rest to market: he would be of more use and mark than all the ten." In 1729, Swedenborg became a member of the Royal Academy of Science at Stockholm.

Discontinuing the pamphlet style of publication, Swedenborg now centered his thoughts upon the production of a much larger and more laborious work than he had hitherto attempted. It was entitled "Opera Philosophica et Mineralia." In order to secure its proper publication, he went abroad, for the third time, in May, 1733. After spending five months in Germany, seeing everything note-worthy, he commenced the printing of his work at Leipsic, in the month of October. In the course of the year 1734, the whole was finished in three handsome folio volumes, enriched with numerous copper-plates, and an engraved likeness of the author. At this time he was again a visitor at the court of the Duke of Brunswick, who munificently defrayed the cost of his expensive publication. The volumes were published at Leipsic and Dresden.

At the same time he issued a little work called "A Philosophical Argument on the Infinite, and the Final Cause of Creation; and on the Mechanism of the Intercourse between the Soul and the Body." It may be regarded as a supplement to the foregoing.

His work being finished, he left Leipsic for Cassel, and passing homewards through Gotha, Brunswick, and Hamburg, arrived at Stockholm in July, 1734. It is to be remembered that in this journey he had still the duties of his office in view. He visited mines everywhere, studied their modes of working, and sought continually to make himself useful to his country.

It now becomes necessary to speak of his great volumes of philosophical and mineral works.

CHAPTER IV.

Opera Philosophica et Mineralia.

In attempting to give the reader an idea of the contents and aims of this great work, within the compass of a few paragraphs, one feels extreme difficulty in knowing where or how to begin. It starts so many topics, is so full of the deepest scientific truth, speculates so boldly, and reaches to such heights of subtle thought, that we must necessarily confine ourselves to a very superficial view, and the enumeration of a few of its prominent features.

As before said, the work occupies three large folio volumes. Of the second and third of these, it does not lie in our province to say much. Both are strictly practical works; one on iron, and the other on copper and brass. They are evidences of Swedenborg's ardent devotion to the duties of his office; and as a testimony to the worth of the books themselves, it need only be said, that portions of them have been repeatedly reprinted, and that they are held in high estimation by those who study metallurgy as a science, or follow it as a profession. The publication of the secrets of trade and manufacture in these volumes, was not relished by the narrow-minded and selfish. Of such the author observes:—"There are persons who love to hold their knowledge for themselves alone, and to be the reputed possessors and guardians of secrets. People of this kind grudge the public everything, and if any discovery, by which art and science will be benefited, comes to light, they regard it askance, with scowling visages, and probably denounce the discoverer as a babbler who lets out mysteries. But why should such secrets be grudged to the public? Why withhold from this enlightened age? Whatever is worthy to be known, should by all means be brought to the great and general market of the world. Unless we do this, we can neither grow wiser nor happier with time." These are true, liberal, and noble words.

But it is the first volume which is the greatest and most important of the three. It has recently been translated into English by the Rev. Augustus Clissold, and published in two considerable octavos. It is entitled "Principia; or the First Principles of Natural Things, being New Attempts toward a Philosophical Explanation of the Elementary World." In this volume an attempt is made to explain the generation of the elements, the creation of matter, and the nature of the occult forces playing within nature. To pronounce an absolute opinion upon such a work would be highly hazardous; for positive science at present, affords no sufficient data to test many of its highest reasonings. So far, however, as such tests have been granted, they serve to manifest the fact that among speculative natural philosophers, Swedenborg is second to none. Gœrres, an eminent German philosopher, speaking of the "Principia," remarks:—"It is a production indicative of profound thought in all its parts, and not unworthy of being placed by the side of Newton's mathematical 'Principia of Natural Philosophy.'" We will now adduce a few proofs of the truth of this assertion.

Humboldt, in his "Kosmos," remarks: "That great and enthusiastic although cautious observer, Sir William Herschel, was the first to sound the depths of heaven, in order to determine the limits and form of the starry system we inhabit." The discovery of the place of our sun and system in the Milky Way, is certainly due to Herschel, but Swedenborg has a prior claim to the honor. In the "Principia," written four years before Herschel was born, the statement of our sun's position in the heavens was explicitly made, with the method by which the fact was observed. But this is not all. The changes observed in the planetary orbits, seemed at one time to warrant the belief in a final destruction of all things through the falling of creation into chaos. After awhile, however, La Grange brought forward his beautiful theory, by which was established the doctrine, that though the solar system is liable to certain mutations in the form and eccentricity of its orbits in very long periods, yet in consequence of a certain relation which prevails in the system, between the masses, orbital axes, and eccentricities, in time all orbits return again to what they originally were, oscillating between very narrow limits. This discovery of a cyclar return, confirmed by the most eminent astronomers, is pronounced by Professor Playfair to be, "next to Newton's discovery of the elliptical orbits of the planets,—without doubt the noblest truth in physical astronomy." This discovery has also to be claimed for Swedenborg. In his "Principia," the fact of this cyclar mutation and return of the planets to order, is repeatedly stated, and with great accuracy and plainness. Want of space alone forbids several quotations in proof. It need only be noted that the "Principia" was published forty-four years before La Grange announced his famous theory. Again, the doctrine of the translatory or progressive motion of the stars along the Milky Way, and their streaming out at the northern end, and in at the southern; diverging at the northern end in every direction, while at the southern end they converge at every point,—one of the most magnificent truths of modern astronomy,—is clearly set forth in this wonderful work of Swedenborg's, years before the full fact had dawned upon the scientific world. Again, the sublime doctrine of the cosmical arrangement of the stars, or of the clustering of stars into distinct systems, forming starry systems, as planets do solar systems, generally attributed to Kant, Mitchell, and one or two others, was promulgated by Swedenborg in the "Principia," when Kant, the first of the acknowledged propounders of the theory, was a boy of ten years of age. The first enunciation of the nebular hypothesis, is also to be referred to Swedenborg's "Principia." Indeed La Place, to whom the hypothesis is generally attributed, indirectly owed some of his ideas on the subject to Swedenborg. La Place owned that Buffon was the first that suggested the theory of the origin of the planets and their satellites from the sun. Now Buffon was acquainted with Swedenborg's "Principia," as is evident from the fact that an eminent London bookseller recently sold a copy of the "Principia" containing Buffon's autograph.* It need only be added, that, fifteen years before Buffon published his theory, and seventy-five years before La Place offered his own to the public, Swedenborg had propounded his version of the nebular hypothesis in the "Principia." It is true that La Place and Swedenborg differ on several points; but recent science and experiment have tended to prove that, wherein they differ, Swedenborg's theories are the most accurate.

While advancing these high claims for Swedenborg, in astronomical science and theory, it is but right to remove from the public mind an erroneous idea, which, like his titles of Baron and Count, has no foundation in fact. We allude to his common repute as the announcer of the existence of the seventh planet, Uranus, discovered by Herschel in 1781. That he announced the existence of this planet long before its actual discovery, has been stated innumerable

* The bookseller referred to was Mr. Bohn, of Henrietta street, Covent Garden.

times, at home and abroad; and Emerson in his lecture on the Mystic, takes opportunity to be witty in regretting that he did not discover the eighth. The mistake has arisen from Swedenborg's talking of a seventh planet in "The Worship and Love of God," a book of his yet to be noticed. Now the belief in the existence of a seventh planet was entertained by most of the astronomers of his day, and even so far back as Kepler, in 1584. Swedenborg, in speaking as he did, only expressed a general idea. Astronomers observing the wide space between the orbits of Mars and Jupiter conjectured that some planet must roll between. The after discovery of numerous asteroids between these orbits, gave some show of truth to their conjectures. It was of this supposed planet between Mars and Jupiter, and not of Uranus, (afterwards discovered by Sir William Herschel,) that Swedenborg spoke.

In magnetism, as in astronomy, the "Principia" is no less rich in original thought and discovery. It was not until the close of the eighteenth century that the position of the magnetic equator was discovered to be different from that of the geographical. After observations confirmed the fact that the mean latitudinal positions of the magnetic poles and equators, are identical with those of the earth's ecliptic and ecliptical poles. This fact, over which there has been much congratulation, was set forth in the "Principia" many years before it was confirmed by actual observation. Again, the fact that the southern magnetic pole has a longer axis from the center of the magnetic equator, than the northern, and hence occupies a higher latitudinal position; and, as a consequence, that the revolution of the north magnetic pole is quicker than that of the southern; also that the south magnetic pole possesses a greater attractive force than the north,—facts not suspected till the investigations of Hansteen in 1819, and only fully confirmed by observation very recently,—were all proclaimed in the "Principia" nearly a century before positive science had embraced them in her domain. Swedenborg also takes precedence of all other discoverers in the announcement of the identity of the magnetic streams forming the aurora, and those influencing the magnetic needle. So full is the "Principia" of truths respecting magnetism,—which the world generally supposes to be a novelty of the present day—that we could not imagine a greater pleasure or surprise awaiting any one devoted to the prosecution of magnetic science, than the perusal of this commonly supposed old-fashioned and antiquated "Principia" of speculative science.

We will now say a few words on the great chemical truths which the "Principia" revealed. In 1734, not a whisper had been breathed regarding the composite nature of the atmosphere. The earliest date which can be assigned for the practical discovery of the two-fold nature of atmospheric air, is 1772–4, the date of Priestley's celebrated experiments. But we find in the "Principia," that Swedenborg sets forth the following facts:—that pure and dry atmospheric air is a compound of two constituents; that these constituents are combined in unequal proportions; that the element greatest in quantity is the extinguisher of combustion; and lastly, that the element greatest in quantity is a constituent of water as well as of air. The merest tyro in science will, at a glance, perceive the importance and extent of ground which these propositions cover, and how profound must have been that genius, which, in the midst of the deepest scientific darkness, could draw from nature these deep and choice truths. But this was not all. Water as well as air yielded to him the secret of its constitution. In Swedenborg's day, the whole world thought and spoke of water as an element, and even after the composite nature of air was revealed, water maintained its elemental character up to 1783, when the discovery was almost simultaneously made by Watt, Priestley, Cavendish, and Lavoisier, that water, like air, is a result of the combination of two gases. Now in the "Principia," written fifty years before, we are expressly told that pure water is a compound substance, and the particulars and quantities of the two elements in its composition are correctly given. There are many other truths in modern science which the "Principia" anticipates; such as the atomic theory, and the identity of electricity and lightning; but we must draw to a close. Enough has been said to show the high merits of the book, and to prove how worthy it is of the study and attention of all true lovers of science.

The publication of the "Principia" gained for its author great reputation, and his friendship and correspondence were eagerly courted by all the philosophers of his day. In December, 1734, the Academy of Sciences at St. Petersburg appointed him one of their corresponding members. The Pope honored the work by placing it in that noble catalogue of books, the Index Expurgatorius, in 1739.

It may be very pertinently asked, how it happens that a work abounding in such important doctrines and theories should be so little known. The neglect is easily accounted for in the great subsequent fame of its author as a religious visionary. His later reputation effectually out-shone that which he so deservedly won in his younger days; and few, even of his own disciples, until recently, thought of lifting from the dusty shelves those great books of scientific theory, which, of themselves, established for their author a place among the greatest of men. The "Principia," as its translator truly says, "is a book for the future;" and taking these words in their full import, it would be hardly possible to pronounce a higher panegyric.

CHAPTER V.

Doings and Travels.

FROM 1734 to 1736, Swedenborg remained at home. In July, 1735, his father died; and a year after, Swedenborg went abroad, as he states in his diary, "for a sojourn of three or four years, to write and publish a certain book." During his absence he resigned half of his official salary to his substitutes. His father having left him some money, he was the better able to do so. He journeyed through Denmark, Hanover, and Holland, and arrived at Rotterdam during the fair. Observing the amusements of the people, mountebanks, shows, etc., he took occasion to moralize thus upon the character and prosperity of the Dutch. "Here at Rotterdam, it has suggested itself to me to inquire why it is that God has blessed a people so barbarous and boorish as the Dutch, with such a fertile and luxuriant soil; that He has preserved them, for so long a course of years, from all misfortune; that He has raised them up in commerce above all other nations; and made their provinces the mart and emporium of the wealth of Europe and the world. On consideration, the first and principal cause of these circumstances appears to be, that Holland is a republic, which form of government is more pleasing to God than an absolute monarchy. In a republic, no veneration or worship is paid to any man, but the highest and lowest think themselves equal to kings and emperors; as may be seen from the characteristic bearing of every one in Holland. The only one whom they worship is God. And when God alone is worshiped, and men are not adored instead of Him, such worship is most acceptable to Him. Then again, in Holland, there is the greatest liberty. None are slaves, but all are as lords and masters under the government of the most high God; and the consequence is, that they do not depress their manliness either by shame or fear, but always preserve a firm and sound mind in a sound body; and with a free spirit, and an erect countenance, commit themselves and their property to God, who alone ought to govern all things. It is not so in absolute monarchies, where men are educated to simulation and dissimulation; where they learn to have one thing concealed in the breast, and to bring forth another upon the tongue; where their minds, by inveterate custom, become so false and counterfeit, that, in divine worship itself, their words differ from their thoughts, and they proffer their flattery and deceit to God himself, which certainly must be most displeasing to Him. This seems to be the reason why the Dutch are more prosperous in their undertakings than other nations." Then, with rare discrimination, he adds, "but their worshiping mammon as a Deity, and caring for nothing but gold, is a thing which is not compatible with long prosperity." The silent and uninfluential place which Holland now fills in Europe, places the seal of truth on these quiet lines.

The Roman Catholic Church seems to have attracted much of his attention in his travels, and the grossness and sensuality of its priesthood were strongly remarked upon. "The monks," says he, "at Roye, are fat and corpulent, and an army of such fellows might be banished without loss to the State. They fill their bellies, take all they can get, and give the poor nothing but fine words and blessings; and yet they are willing to take from the poor all their substance for nothing. What is the good of bare-footed Franciscans?"

In Paris, he spent a year and a half. There also he was amazed at the clerical riot and corruption. "It is found," he observes, "that the tax which they term the dixièmes, yields annually thirty-two millions sterling; and that the Parisians spend two-thirds of this amount over their own city. One-fifth of the whole possessions of the kingdom is in the hands of the clerical order. If this condition of things last long, the ruin of the empire will be speedy." He little dreamed of the fearful verification which these words would receive.

His journal in Paris reveals the fact of his hearty enjoyment of sight-seeing and amusements. Visits to churches, monasteries, palaces, gardens, museums, and theatres, evidence with what zest he drank the cup of life, and with what interest he looked upon men and their affairs. In this respect we do well to compare Swedenborg with many whom the world in its ignorance associate with him. At no period of his life was he a cold self-righteous ascetic, looking abroad upon men with a bitter and accusing scowl. At no time did he insult his Maker with upbraidings that his fate was to live in an evil world, and with a wicked generation. He received life with thankfulness, partook temperately of all its lawful pleasures, did his duty, and took care while living with the world to keep himself unspotted from its evil. This social discipline was one of the Divine means by which he was fitted for the full performance of his future mission.

We are not informed of the nature of the work which he at this time went abroad to write and publish. From his manuscripts, however, it appears that he was preparing materials and disciplining his mind for his great work, the "Animal Kingdom," by writing short papers on various physiological subjects. Many of these papers have been translated and published under the title of "Posthumous Tracts."

Leaving Paris in March, 1738, Swedenborg directed his steps toward Italy, and after visiting its principal cities, arrived at Rome on the 25th September. Mr. Rich, in his "Biography of Swedenborg," remarks,—"This visit should be a memorable one, for it brought the church of the past and the future into a singular communion with each other; —Rome in the still atmosphere and fading light of autumn, with all its trophies of Pagan art, and its hoary traditions; and Swedenborg, the predestined Seer of the last ages, whose eye was just kindling with the light of inspiration. We should lose all faith in the instinctive prescience of the human spirit when great events are at hand, if we might not believe that a presentiment of something in the shadowy distance, connecting his future with the strange mystery of the city, did not cross, for a moment, the mind of Swedenborg, when he entered the once holy and revered metropolis of the faith."

After a sojourn of five months, Swedenborg left Rome on the 15th of February, 1739, varying his homeward route. His journal from the 17th of March, 1739, when he was at Genoa, is a blank, and his after wanderings we can only conjecture. "It is most probable," says Wilkinson, "that he deposited the manuscript of the "Economy of the Animal Kingdom," at Amsterdam, on his way from Leipsic to Sweden, in 1740; that he lived in his own country from 1740 or 1741 till 1744, and in the latter year went again to Holland, and from thence came to England, where we meet him in 1745."

In 1740–41, Swedenborg published at Amsterdam his "Economy of the Animal Kingdom;" and in 1744–45, the "Animal Kingdom," Parts I. and II. at the Hague, and Part III. in London.

CHAPTER VI.

The "Economy of the Animal Kingdom," and the "Animal Kingdom."

In the "Animal Kingdom," Swedenborg referred solely to the human body, it being the microcosm, or representative of all inferior systems. In the "Economy of the Animal Kingdom," he treats of the blood, and the organs which contain it; the coincidence of the motion of the brain with the respiration of the lungs; and of the human soul. The method pursued in this work is admirable. A careful series of extracts, containing facts from the best anatomists, is prefixed to each chapter, and thence is deduced the author's theory. It would be very difficult indeed to present, in an abstract, the substance of these quotations, and without this, (which would be inconsistent with our limits,) the theories could not be fairly understood or appreciated. His demonstration of the coincidence of the motion of the brain with the respiration of the lungs, is well worthy of notice. Wilkinson, speaking of this in his "Biography of Swedenborg," says: "Let any reader think for a moment of what he experiences when he breathes, and attends to the act. He will find that his whole frame heaves and subsides at the time; face, chest, stomach, and limbs, are all actuated by his respiration. His sense is, that not only his lungs but his entire body breathes. Now mark what Swedenborg elicited from this fact. If the whole man breathes or heaves, so also do the organs which he contains, for they are necessarily drawn outwards by the rising of the surface; therefore they all breathe. What do they breathe? Two elements are omnipresent in them, the blood-vessels and the nerves; the one giving them pabulum, the other life. They draw then into themselves blood, and life or nervous spirit. Each does this according to its own form; each, therefore, has a free individuality like the whole man; each takes its food, the blood, when it chooses; each wills into itself the life according to its desires. The man is made up of manlike parts; his freedom is an aggregate of a host of atomic, organical freedoms. The heart does not cram them with its blood, but each, like the man itself, takes what it thinks right.

"But, furthermore, thought commences and corresponds with respiration. The reader has before attended to the presence of the heaving over the body; now let him *feel his thoughts*, and he will see that they too heave with the mass. When he entertains a long thought he draws a long breath; when he thinks quickly, his breath vibrates with rapid alternations; when the tempest of anger shakes his mind, his breath is tumultuous; when his soul is deep and tranquil, so is his respiration; when success inflates him, his lungs are as tumid as his conceits. Let him make trial of the contrary: let him endeavor to think in long stretches at the same time that he breathes in fits, and he will find that it is impossible; that in this case the chopping lungs will needs mince his thoughts. Now the mind dwells in the brain, and it is the brain, therefore, which shares the varying fortunes of the breathing. It is strange that this correspondence between the states of the brain or mind, and the lungs, has not been admitted into science; for it holds in every case, at every moment. In truth it is so unfailing, and so near to the center of sense, that this has made it difficult to regard it as an object; for if you only try to think upon the breathing, in consequence of the fixation of thought, you stop the breath that very moment, and only recommence it when the thought can no longer hold, that is to say, when the brain has need to expire. Now Swedenborg, with amazing observation and sagacity, has made a regular study of this ratio between the respiration and the thoughts and emotions; he shows in detail that the two correspond exactly, and moreover that their correspondence is one of the long-sought links between the soul and the body, whereby every thought is represented and carried out momentaneously in the expanse of the human frame. It is difficult to give a more plain or excellent reason of the tie between the body and the soul, than that the latter finds the body absolutely to its mind; while on the other hand, the living body clings to the soul, because it wants a friendly superior life to infuse and direct its life."

The "Animal Kingdom," written after the same plan as the "Economy," treats of the organs of the abdomen, of those of the chest, and of the skin. Swedenborg, in setting forth his plan of operation, in which he announces his intention to examine, physically and philosophically, the whole anatomy of the body, and lastly of the soul, and of its state in the body, says: "From this summary or plan, the reader may see that the end I propose to myself in the work, is a knowledge of the soul, since this knowledge will constitute the crown of my studies. This, then, my labors intend, and thither they aim. To accomplish this grand end, I enter the circus, designing to consider and examine thoroughly the whole world of microcosm which the soul inhabits; for I think it vain to seek her anywhere but in her own kingdom. I am, therefore, resolved to allow myself no respite, until I have run through the whole field to the very goal, or until I have traversed the universal animal kingdom to the soul. Thus I hope that by bending my course inward continually, I shall open all the doors that lead to her, and at length contemplate the soul herself, by the Divine permission."

One of his manuscripts repeats this design in these words: "I have gone through anatomy with the single end of investigating the soul. It will be a satisfaction to me if my labors be of any use to the anatomical and medical world, but a still greater satisfaction if I afford any light towards the investigation of the soul."

In striving to compass such high spiritual knowledge, by merely natural means, he necessarily failed. In one of his books, written several years after, when a brighter light had dawned upon his mind, he says: "Many in the learned world have laboured in investigating the soul, but as they knew nothing of the spiritual world, and of the state of man after death, they could not do otherwise than construct hypotheses, not respecting the soul's nature, or its operation on the body. Of the soul's nature, they could have no other idea than as of something most pure in ether, and of its continent as of ether. Now having such a conception of the soul, and yet knowing that the soul acts on the body, and produces everything in it that has relation to sense and motion, therefore they labored, as we before observed, to investigate the soul's operation on the body, which some said was effected by influx, and some by harmony. But these means discovered nothing in which the mind desirous of seeing the ground of things, can acquiesce." We have in these sentences the cause of the fruitlessness of his own labors at this period, in their highest aims. They formed, however, a part of that providential discipline which was fitting him for his future office.

Fruitless though these works necessarily were, in their highest aim, yet in lower ends they are treasure-houses of thought and suggestion. Taking for his basis the dry facts of the anatomists, he proceeds to clothe them with life and comeliness. He shows how part is bound to part in the human system, and fills the cold details of science with a warm and human interest. Emerson well says: "The 'Animal Kingdom' is a book of wonderful merits. It was written with the highest end, to put science and soul, so long estranged from each other, at one again. It was the anatomist's account of the human body in the highest style of poetry; and nothing can exceed the bold and brilliant treatment of a subject usually so dry and repulsive."

It was hardly possible for books to be ushered into the world to die more quietly than did these physiological treatises. Slightly noticed in a few catalogues and reviews of that day, they were laid on the shelf, and reposed in dust and forgetfulness for a full century. Called to other thoughts and higher labors, their author was arrested midway in his plans; and ceasing to exist behind his books, and by his life, conversation, and activity, to keep up the public interest, the world soon forgot their existence. But their worth has been their preservative; and now we behold their resurrection, and slow, but certain, growth into acceptance and fame. Translated by Wilkinson, and enriched by him with prefaces which Emerson describes as "throwing all the contemporary philosophy of England into the shade," they are now placed before the world, and, in their excellence serve to manifest the profound understanding and genius of their author.

In 1745, Swedenborg terminated his long series of scientific works, by the publication, in London, of "The Worship and Love of God." This book is an embodiment, in a story, of its author's scientific doctrines. In a connected narrative, it treats of the origin of the earth, the birth, infancy, and love, of Adam; and of the soul in its state of integrity, in the image of God. It is a book of which little need be said, as it was probably written as much for an exercise of fancy, as with any serious intent. Cast into shade, as it is, by the brighter light of his after knowledge, it remains to mark the point of intellectual development at which Swedenborg had at this time arrived; and in this respect it will always have a strong interest to those who delight in tracing the growth and education of his mind.

CHAPTER VII.

His Life, as a Man of Science, ends.

THE biographer of Swedenborg can feel no difficulty in distributing under proper heads the principal events of his life. It divides itself so distinctly into two parts, at this juncture, that, between his past and his future there is what he himself would call a "discrete degree."

In 1745, when the merely scientific phase of Swedenborg's life closed, he had arrived at the mature age of fifty-seven years. As we have seen, he had, from early manhood, united an active and practical, with a deeply philosophic, life. An earnest student of nature, he had never become so engrossed in thought as to forget the end of all thought—the improvement and the happiness of mankind. His long series of scientific works had gained him a wide-spread reputation, and wherever he went, he was hailed as a friend and brother by the thoughtful and philosophical. In Sweden, as before said, he was well connected; and had he been desirous to live at home, and immerse himself in the cares and politics of his country, he might have reached the highest offices and honors which royalty could confer. At the age of fifty-seven, with Swedenborg's attainments, success, and fame, a worldly man might have been content. Such a one would, probably, have taken his ease, reposed upon the past, and have been content with the competence of comfort and reputation which he had attained. But Swedenborg was a man of a very different character. Love of ease formed no part of his constitution, and if he had not been led by the hand of Providence to the contemplation of the spiritual world and its glorious realities, he would, to the end of his life, have remained a zealous and single-eyed seeker after the truths of the natural world.

The annals of science do not furnish an instance of any one who surpassed Swedenborg in that humility of spirit, and that simple desire for truth, which is the crowning grace and glory of the true philosopher. Although, at times, he propounded views which he knew were antagonistic to the ideas of some of the leading savans of his time, yet we never find him getting angry or attempting to scold the world into belief with him. He simply lays down what he believes to be the truth; and with the most charming modesty trusts for its acceptance among men, to its agreement with reason and facts. Full of this trustful spirit we find him saying in the "Principia:" "In writing the present work, I have not aimed at the applause of the learned world, nor at the acquisition of a name or popularity. To me, it is a matter of indifference whether I win the favorable opinion of every one, or of no one; whether I gain much or no commendation. Such things are not objects of regard to one whose mind is bent on truth and true philosophy. Should I, therefore, gain the assent or approbation of others, I shall receive it only as a confirmation of my having pursued the truth. I have no wish to persuade any one to lay aside the principles of those illustrious and talented authors who have adorned the world, and in place of their principles to adopt mine. For this reason it is, that I have not made mention so much as of one of them, or even hinted at his name, lest I should injure his feelings, or seem to impugn his sentiments, or to derogate from the praise which others bestow upon him. If the principles I have advanced have more of truth in them than those which are advocated by others; if they are truly philosophical, and accordant with the phenomena of nature, the assent of the public will follow in due time, of its own accord; and in this case should I fail to gain the assent of those whose minds, being prepossessed by other principles, can no longer exercise an impartial judgment, still I have those with me who are able to distinguish the true from the untrue, if not in the present, at least in some future age. Truth is unique, and will speak for itself. Should any one undertake to impugn my sentiments, I have no wish to oppose him; but in case he desire it, I shall be happy to explain my principles and my reasons more at large. What need, however, is there of words? Let the thing speak for itself. If what I have said be true, why should I be eager to defend it? Surely truth can defend itself. If what I have said be false, it would be a degrading and silly task to defend it. Why then should I make myself an enemy of any one, or place myself in opposition to any one?" And again, in the "Economy," he remarks: "Of what consequence is it to me that I should persuade any one to embrace my opinions? Let his own reason persuade him. I do not undertake this work for the sake of honor or emolument; both of which I shun rather than seek, because they disquiet the mind, and because I am content with my lot; but for the sake of truth, which alone is immortal." These are long extracts, but they are well worthy of citation, alike for their own intrinsic truth and beauty, and for the illustration they afford of the spirit and sentiments of their author.

The little thought he gave in after years to his scientific writings, and the little care he seemed to have lest the world should forget them, is very evident from his subsequent writings, in which they are scarcely alluded to. Some of the friends he made in the latter portion of his life, appear to have had very faint ideas of the extent of his achievements in natural science. Count Hopken, a very intimate friend of his, for many years, remarks: "Swedenborg made surprising discoveries in anatomy, which are recorded somewhere in certain literary Transactions." Thus it appears that he was entirely ignorant of the existence of Swedenborg's great work, the "Animal Kingdom." What stronger proof could be given than this, of the sincerity with which the foregoing extracts were penned, in which he commits his works to the care of the God of truth, in humble acquiescence in whatever verdict his justice might pronounce.

Great and manifold were the merits of these scientific works; yet we should, perhaps, do well to look upon them, as their author seems to have done, as school-boy exercises. Through the severe training and development of the whole powers of his mind, by the composition of these works, his Divine Master was fitting him to gaze upon the awful realities of the spiritual world, and to become a worthy exponent of the hidden wisdom of the Holy Scripture.

It must, necessarily, be a matter of interest with many to know what were the religious opinions of Swedenborg at this period of his history. Occupying himself so intensely with natural science, it was hardly to be expected that theology could receive much of his attention. Among his posthumous papers, however, we find a little treatise on faith and good works, in which he comes to the wise conclusion that "there is no love to God if there be none to the neighbor;" or that "there is no faith if there be no works;" and therefore, that "faith without works is a phrase involving a contradiction." Throughout all his scientific writings we find a simple and open assent to the primary truths of religion, and a constant endeavor to confirm some truth of religious doctrine by the natural facts which came under his notice. His religious views up to this time were generally such as the Christian world held, with here and there a quiet dissent as to particular points, and a strong tendency to eschew the merely theoretical and mystical belief, for the practical and active. We have his own testimony to the fact, that dogmatic and systematic theology formed no part of his otherwise extensive reading; and thus he came to the study of the Word of God unperverted by the sophisms of creed-makers. Of the gentle and earnest piety of his soul, we have striking proof in his "Rules of Life:"

1. Often to read and meditate on the Word of God.

2. To submit everything to the will of Divine Providence.

3. To observe in everything a propriety of behaviour, and to keep the conscience clear.

4. To discharge with fidelity the functions of my employment, and the duties of my office, and to render myself in all things useful to society.

More need not be said on this head than that he kept these vows.

We now close the first book of Swedenborg's life, and open the second. Emphatically his was a double life. So rich in thought and action were both parts, that either would have been reckoned sufficient to render him a remarkable man. The one life was an orderly and regular growth out of the other: the first was a providential preparation for the second. Carefully disciplined by thought and investigation in the outer world, through a long series of laborious years, the curtain which separated the seen from the unseen was, for him, drawn aside, and his prepared eyes saw in clear sunlight those mysteries of life and spirit, which the best and wisest of men have most ardently desired to see. Let us, then, leave Swedenborg the Man of Science, and turn to him as the Servant of the Lord Jesus Christ, the worthy exponent of the spiritual sense of the Word of God, and the announcer of the New Era in which reason and faith are to be at one, and men everywhere friends and brothers.

CHAPTER VIII.

His Spiritual Sight opened, and the Conditions of his Seership.

WE will now proceed, without circumlocution, to lay before our readers, in all its fullness, the claim which Swedenborg made, at this period, to open intercourse with the spiritual world, under the sanction and protection of the Lord. This assumption runs through the whole of his after life, and without a clear idea of its nature and conditions, we shall be unable rightly to appreciate aught else that follows. In one of his letters, he says, "I have been called to a holy office by the Lord himself, who most graciously manifested himself to me, his servant, in the year 1743, when he opened my sight to a view of the spiritual world, and granted me the privilege of conversing with spirits and angels, which I enjoy to this day. From that time, I began to print and publish various arcana that have been seen by me, or revealed to me; as respecting heaven and hell, the state of man after death, the true worship of God, the spiritual sense of the Word, with many other most important matters conducive to salvation and true wisdom." Again, in the preface to his work entitled, "Arcana Cœlestia," he writes: "Of the Lord's Divine mercy, it has been granted me now for several years to be constantly and uninterruptedly in company with spirits and angels, hearing them converse with each other, and conversing with them. Hence it has been permitted me to hear and see stupendous things in the other life, which have never before come to the knowledge of any man, nor entered his imagination. I have there been instructed concerning different kinds of spirits, and the state of souls after death; concerning hell, or the lamentable state of the unfaithful; concerning heaven, or the most happy state of the faithful; and particularly concerning the doctrine of faith which is acknowledged throughout all heaven."

We are aware that these pretensions will be received by many with ridicule, and by some with contempt, arising from a distaste for spiritual subjects; while by a few they will be treated with respectful attention. All that we ask, is, a little patience; and to readers of every class, we would say,—Do not be hasty; do not prejudge the matter; condemn not till you are conversant with the whole circumstances of the case. Swedenborg's claim, we admit, does appear startling; but to greet its announcement with the laugh of scepticism, and to deny its validity, as many do, without an attempt at examination, is anything but philosophical—is anything but righteous.

No reader of this sketch can have failed to perceive the high philosophical genius, and perfect truthfulness of Swedenborg; and all must agree with us in believing that wilful deception was an impossibility with such a man. No explanation of what Swedenborg himself calls the opening of his spiritual sight, can be offered, that is more transparently ridiculous than that of imposture. The degree of vehemence with which some have preferred this charge against him, may be taken as an accurate index of their ignorance of the man, or of their inability to discern a truthful and earnest spirit.

No denial of the possibility of such spiritual vision as is claimed by Swedenborg, can be accepted from the Christian. Such denial is alone the privilege of the professed materialist. We all know how much of our loved and common faith rests on claims that are quite as startling as those of Swedenborg. From the visions of Abraham to those of John in Patmos, the whole Scriptural narrative is interwoven with supernatural incident. Now, how is it that we yield such ready faith to whatever is related in Scripture, however marvelous, and have so much wonder to spare over the unbelieving Jews? The Rev. O. Prescott Hiller, in a short memoir of Swedenborg, prefixed to a collection of "Gems" from his writings, has some very apposite remarks on this subject. He says: "Swedenborg states that there are three heavens; so does Paul, for he speaks of the 'third heaven.' Swedenborg affirms, calmly, that his spiritual senses were opened and elevated in such a manner that he might have a perception of that state of existence, and see and hear what is there. So does Paul. Swedenborg states that he had, in spirit, been permitted to behold the Lord: so does Paul:—'Have I not seen,' said he, 'Jesus Christ our Lord?' (1 Cor. ix. 1.) Thus parallel are the cases. But, exclaims the prejudiced observer: 'Paul! Paul! Paul was an apostle! Paul was one of the founders of the Christian Church! Paul lived eighteen hundred years ago! There are no visions now-a-days! The case is entirely different!' To these exclamations it may be replied: Your last remark is but a begging of the question under consideration. We affirm that though indeed unfrequent, yet there are occasionally spiritual visions in these times, as well as in former, and that there is good and very strong testimony that a remarkable case of the kind exists in the instance of this philosopher, Swedenborg, not by any means on account of his own declaration merely, but from the nature of the truths and statements brought forth by him, of which our own minds, enlightened, we trust, by reason and God's Word, are the judges. The burden of proof—it may be continued in answer—falls upon you to show by what law of Divine order, by what change in the character and structure of man's mind, a spiritual vision can not exist now, as well as in the time of Paul,—in the eighteenth or nineteenth, as well as in the first century. The truth is, antiquity has a wonderful charm for the mind, and a great power over it: 'distance lends enchantment to the view.' It is not difficult to believe anything, however wonderful, to have taken place in that misty and mysterious region, the distant *past;* but now in these dull, common times, to believe such strange things to be capable of happening, seems absurd. But do you not suppose that those times, to the men then living, appeared as dull and common-place as our times to us? Did not the regardless rain fall on Paul's head, as well as on yours and mine? and this very sun and moon light his steps as well as ours? Did not Paul, do you think, rise often in the morning with a heavy heart, and after breakfast, go forth to his duties, or sit down to write his epistles, sad and oppressed in spirit, dejected at the thought of the heavy responsibilities upon him, and awed with the idea that he must address the Athenians to-morrow? And when at length he stood before them and began, did they not ask: 'Who is this?' Think you that gaping crowd knew anything about any great and celebrated Paul, whose name has become so familiar to our ears? They had not heard of such a person. 'And some said, What will this babbler say? others, He seemeth to be a setter forth of strange gods; because he preached to them Jesus, and the resurrection. And when they heard of the resurrection of the dead, some mocked; and others said, We will hear thee again of this matter. Howbeit certain men clave unto him, and believed; among whom was Dionysius the Areopagite, and a woman named Damaris, and others with them.' (Acts xvii. 16–34.) Here we have a picture of human nature, as it was, and as it still is. A new person comes forward, a stranger, unheard of before, and utters strange ideas, something new and unusual, something different from what men have been accustomed to hear, and think of, and believe; most of the hearers jeer and mock, and turn away, calling him a babbler; some are rather pleased at some things they have heard, but the interest has not taken sufficient hold of them to make them anxious to pursue the subject farther just now, and they go away and forget what they have heard; a few, whose minds were in a receptive state, whose hearts had been prepared, perhaps, by torturing doubts, and secret meditations, and by trials and sufferings of spirit—these at once perceive and seize upon the truths they have heard, clasp them to their bosoms as something long looked for, as precious treasure, and go away rejoicing in their new faith, and resolved to sell all they have and follow the Lord. Gradually the truth spreads; these few tell what they have heard to others, their friends, who they know have been troubled with similar doubts and difficulties. By and by these believers meet together and form a little congregation, and appoint the ablest of their number to preach to them in regard to these new truths, both for their own fuller instruction and for the information of strangers. Years roll away. It becomes an established religious society. Similar societies in neighboring cities league with them; and they form a General Church, which begins to have a name—the 'Christian Church.' Ages roll on, and this becomes a vast establishment, extending over whole nations, and reaching to distant quarters of the globe. This Paul, who was once a nameless preacher, 'a babbler,' and 'mad,' is now looked back upon with the utmost veneration; his words are oracles of truth; whatever he affirmed, whether in regard to himself or others, is implicitly believed. Custom, general acceptance, the belief of ages, undoubting confidence in the opinions of our parents and friends, all go to render the mind perfectly ready to believe those things. Faith is now an easy and natural thing, and we wonder at those strange and hard-hearted unbelievers of Paul's own time, who had the glorious opportunity of listening to him with their own ears. 'Oh! that we could have enjoyed such an opportunity,' exclaim many, 'how gladly would we have listened!'

"But these persons know not what they say, nor the nature of the human mind. If they are so anxious to have such an opportunity, so ready to be tested, and to show that they would have discernment enough to see genuine truth, though heard for the first time, and to acknowledge a great teacher and apostle, though yet unknown to the world—that opportunity is now before them. A Paul is again preaching to the Athenians and to the world. A great teacher is again uttering new and sublime truths. The Lord Himself has come a second time, not in Person, but in Spirit; not as the 'Word made flesh,' as before, but as the essential Word, by the opening of the interior truth—the *spiritual sense*—which it contains. Those who believe, that, had they been on earth, they would have acknowledged the Lord at His First Coming, or would have readily received the teachings of His Apostles, have now the opportunity of making trial of their faith; of showing whether they are able to overcome the inveteracy of custom, the natural opposition of prejudice, the fear of public opinion, the love of the world and its powers and pleasures, (all which difficulties the first Christians had to encounter,) whether, in the face of all these, they can, looking for the truth with a single eye, discern it now at its feeble dawn; and, advancing steadily and earnestly towards it, be among the first to hail the rising day."

What more can be said on the subject? The Christian has no choice but to acknowledge, or refute, Swedenborg's claims on the ground of their own intrinsic merit.

Swedenborg was gifted with peculiar powers of respiration. From early childhood, when on his knees at prayer, and afterwards when engaged in profound meditation, he found that his natural respiration was for the time suspended. As we have seen in his work on the "Animal Kingdom," his attention to the correspondence between thought and respiration had been of long continuance,—probably from the fact that his own system supplied him with such constant illustrations of its nature. This power of suspended respiration under deep thought, common to all men, was preternaturally developed in Swedenborg. At this period he discovered the use to which these peculiar powers of his were to be applied; for he writes: "My respiration has been so formed by the Lord, as to enable me to breathe inwardly for a long period of time, without the aid of the external air; my respiration being directed within, and my outward senses, as well as actions, still continuing in their vigor, which is only possible with persons who have been so formed by the Lord. I have also been instructed that my breathing was so directed, without my being aware of it, in order to enable me to be with spirits, and to speak with them." Those who have studied mesmerism and clairvoyance know many facts that confirm and illustrate this position of Swedenborg's with regard to respiration; and it is quite evident that the Hindoo Yogi are capable of a similar state. There is this great difference, however, between such instances and the case of Swedenborg, that his powers were natural, and continuous in their exercise, and not sought after and induced by himself; while theirs are only occasional, and are frequently brought about by artificial means.

Swedenborg's intromission into the spiritual world was a gradual process; and for this reason the date of his illumination is variously given, ranging between 1743 and 1745. It appears, however, that he came into the full exercise of his spiritual seership while living in London.

Of late years it has become common to talk of Swedenborg as a clairvoyant, to associate him with mesmeric subjects, and make him a kinsman of French and American spiritualists, such as Cahagnet, and Andrew Jackson Davis. This mistake is made through ignorance. It is a law of the spiritual world that every man is associated with his like. Supposing, therefore, that any man's spiritual sight were opened, he would come into conjunction only with spirits like himself; that is, with those who would echo his own ideas and opinions, and repeat his own feelings. It is evident, then, that in such a case the nature of the revelations are entirely dependent upon the character of the revelator, and in all cases must be suspiciously received by the lover of truth. Now Swedenborg claims to have been under the special protection of the Lord, and to have received the doctrines he promulgated directly from Him, and not in any case from spirits. Of course, every one will decide for himself as to how far he can receive this assertion; but it is well that all should be informed of the precise character of Swedenborg's claim, and of his own testimony as to the source of his information. In his Diary, written about this time, he says, that "spirits narrate things wholly false, and lie. When spirits begin to speak with man, care should be taken not to believe them; for almost everything they say is made up by them, and they lie; so that if it were permitted them to relate what heaven is, and how things are in heaven, they would tell so many falsehoods, and with such strong assertion, that man would be astonished; wherefore it was not permitted me, when spirits were speaking, to have any belief in what they stated. They love to feign. Whatever may be the topic spoken of, they think they know it, and form different opinions about it, altogether as if they knew; and if man then listens and believes, they insist, and in various ways deceive and seduce."

Any one who has paid attention to the phenomena of

spirit-rapping, and to the communications received through clairvoyants from the world of spirits, and has observed the very Babel of contradictions uttered by these "mediums," will be able to appreciate the truth of the passage we have quoted, as well as our desire to draw a broad and distinct line between such and Swedenborg.

It is a very natural question, and one often put by those unconversant with the nature of spiritual intercourse, how it happens that such a man as Swedenborg, sitting quietly in his chair, could see and speak with angels and spirits, and travel through vast spaces in the spiritual world. It is thus: Space and time are attributes of matter alone. Their appearances do, indeed, exist in the spiritual world, but not as the fixed and mensurable things of our material sphere. Did not our subject forbid digression, it would be easy to bring this truth down to the comprehension of every one, by reference to a few items of experience which must at some time have fallen to the lot of all. We are all, as to our minds, in constant, though insensible, communion with spirits; and from them we receive thoughts and feelings of every kind. A good man and a wicked man may be, as to the body, in the same room, while between their minds there may be the wide gulf that separated Dives and Lazarus. Now if the spiritual sight of these two men were opened, where would they be? One would be in heaven, and the other in hell; and that, too, without either moving from the place where he stood. It was in virtue of this principle of the spirit's perfect independence of space, that Swedenborg, under the Divine guidance and protection, was led through spiritual societies of all kinds: and in his various works we have the record of the wondrous things thus heard and seen.

Again, it may be asked: What is the nature of this spiritual sight so often referred to? In the words of Paul, we answer: "There is a natural body, and there is a spiritual body;" and, as a consequence, there is a natural sight, and there is a spiritual sight. The natural body lives from the spiritual body, and derives its form and parts from it. The natural body is the instrument of the spiritual body, and through it as a medium, it is enabled to exist in this lower world, and in constant contact with matter. Now it is possible for the spiritual body to be raised partially above the natural body, without causing death, or the entire withdrawal of its life from the natural body. This partial withdrawal of the spiritual body, and the enjoyment of sight in the spiritual world, is what is meant by the opening of the spiritual sight. Time forbids us to draw upon the innumerable illustrations of this fact which the history of the past and the experience of the present, in conjunction with the Word of God, afford. Let one instance from the Bible suffice. In 2 Kings, vii. 8–17, we read that Elisha, compassed about with horses, chariots, and a great host, sent by the king of Syria to seize him, was on a mountain with his servant, who, full of terror, exclaimed: "Alas! my master, how shall we do? And he answered, Fear not, for they that be with us are more than they that be with them. And Elisha prayed and said, Lord, I pray thee *open his eyes*, that he may see. And the Lord *opened the eyes* of the young man, and he *saw:* and behold, the mountain was full of horses and chariots of fire round about Elisha." Here is a case quite to the point. The natural eyes of the young man were already open; for how otherwise could he have seen the Syrian host, and have been afraid? Elisha prayed that his eyes might be opened. What eyes? Why, clearly, the eyes of his spiritual body; which done, he was enabled to perceive the heavenly guardianship which was extended over his master. Every one will now understand what we mean, when we shall have occasion to speak of the opening of man's spiritual sight.

Having thus defined the conditions of Swedenborg's spiritual vision, and cleared away some questions which, if answered, would have impeded our narrative, we will now proceed with our history.

CHAPTER IX.

Prepares for his New Office—Resigns his Assessorship—His "Adversaria"—His "Spiritual Diary"—The Death of Polheim.

CALLED to a high and holy office, Swedenborg set about preparing himself for the fulfilment of its duties. Leaving London in the beginning of July, 1745, he took ship for Sweden, where he arrived on the 7th of August. On this voyage, his spiritual intercourse was suspended. He lived quietly at home during 1746; probably in the performance and enjoyment of the settled routine of his Assessorship, and in earnest meditation on the heavenly arcana now fully opened to his view. In 1747, in order that he might be more at liberty to devote himself to the mission to which the Lord had called him, he asked leave of King Frederick to retire from his Assessorship, and that he might enjoy, during life, as a retiring pension, half of his official salary; requesting, at the same time, that no addition to his rank or title might be conferred upon him. The King yielded to his wishes; but in consideration of his long and faithful service of thirty-one years, continued to him the whole of his salary.

Meanwhile, he learned Hebrew, and read the Bible through several times in its original languages. Like all true students, he read and thought with pen in hand; and as the hidden and Divine wisdom of the Word was opened to him, he embodied in "Adversaria," or notes, the truths thus revealed. These Adversaria extend over the historical books of the Old Testament, and several of the prophets. They have all been printed of late years, from their author's original Latin manuscript, by that indefatigable and learned Newchurchman, Dr. Tafel, of Tübingen. They have not yet been translated into English, probably because they were not published by Swedenborg himself, and are only to be regarded as preparatory studies for future works. They also abound with indistinct views on many subjects, which subsequent knowledge rendered clear. As records of their author's spiritual progress, as well as for the many valuable facts which they contain, it is to be hoped that the day is not far distant when the "Adversaria" will appear in an English dress. We cannot spare anything which serves to illustrate the mental history of such a man as Swedenborg.

In 1747, he ceased writing his "Adversaria," and commenced a Spiritual Diary, which he continued for twenty years. This Diary, written also in Latin, (as all his theological works were,) has been lately published by Dr. Tafel in ten closely printed octavos. Two volumes have been translated and published in England and America, and the remainder will probably soon follow. It will hardly be necessary for us to go into a detailed account of the principles and facts scattered throughout its long and miscellaneous record. We shall meet with all the leading ideas in noticing the books published by himself, and laid before the world as matured and finished productions. It may be said, however, that the "Diary," as a work, is perfectly unique; for in no literature can we find its counterpart. We have in it, for twenty years, an almost daily record of Swedenborg's spiritual states and temptations; his interviews and conversations with angels, spirits, and devils; and accounts of their pleasures, punishments, and thoughts. No one who makes an intimate acquaintance with this "Diary," will ever after allow a shadow of doubt to cross his mind as to the candor and truth of Swedenborg; for in every page, he will perceive that quiet and solemn earnestness which belongs alone to the upright and honest in heart. In its whole range of experience, he will detect no vanity, shuffling, double-dealing, or anything inconsistent with his published works; but all as straightforward, open, and unreserved, as truth itself. Although written in the quietude of his own study, and for his own eye and use alone, he could not have been more ingenuous and sincere had the whole universe been looking down upon its pages.

On the page of history, the "Diary" throws some wondrous light. In it, we read of interviews with many of the famous men of ancient and modern times. From some names which the world has learned to revere, the mask of excellence is quite torn away, while the infamy of others is proved to have been but judgment from appearance, and from scandal. Any one who is infected with the spiritual disease of hero-worship, should read the "Spiritual Diary." He will there discover that the most dazzling intellect fades into moping idiocy and insanity, when it lacks the sterling heart, and honest aim; and that goodness alone is the life and soul of true wisdom. He will also learn why it is so.

We would here say a word upon a jest started by Emerson, (and which has re-appeared under many forms,) to the effect that all the souls with whom Swedenborg held converse, talked Swedenborgese. In reply, we would ask, how they could speak in any other way? Swedenborg did not profess to be a mimic; and if Cicero or anybody else spoke with him in the spiritual world and in the spiritual language, Swedenborg, in translating the speech into his own simple diction, would, of course, seize the substance, and care nothing for the form. That the language was not Cicero's, might be true; but if the ideas were, what matter? The subject would hardly be worth mentioning, did we not see the jest receiving a wide currency; but a few words of common sense are all that are necessary to take the life out of it.

There is no work with which we are acquainted, that can give its readers a better idea of the reality of the future life, than the "Spiritual Diary." No other book, we know, can so stir up a man to set his mind, or spiritual house, in order here, so that he may be spared the turmoil and sorrow which otherwise he will encounter beyond the tomb. In its pages, the life after death is portrayed in all its stern reality; not as a vague dream, or a shadowy vision, of which the mind can form no fixed idea. We read of the awful states induced in the other life, by evil habits contracted in this; from loose speech, jesting upon sacred subjects, indulgence in idleness and luxury, down to blacker crimes. We learn from sight, as it were, how evil is its own torment, and how goodness is its own sweet and rich reward; and in view of the momentous issues of what we too often regard as the trifles of life, we feel impelled to make our peace and heaven here, that we may bear them with us into the Hereafter. Such high uses does the "Spiritual Diary" subserve.

The "Diary" is, however, a work not suited for an early student of Swedenborg. The principles upon which it is written, not being understood, a young reader could hardly fail to form erroneous ideas from it, and misjudge the work itself. It is only after some acquaintance with the spiritual laws expounded in Swedenborg's theological writings, that it can be read with profit. Incidents, which, at first sight, might appear ridiculous and irrational, are brought within the pale of reason and belief when the laws upon which they are founded are understood; and as effects, not causes, constitute the burden of the "Diary," the need of this caution will be apparent. When, however, the laws of spiritual life are understood, the "Diary" becomes a work of peculiar and most profitable instruction.

While Swedenborg was living in Sweden, in 1751, his old friend and coadjutor, Polheim, died; and Swedenborg was favored with a view of *both* sides of his grave. Writing in his "Spiritual Diary," he says: "Polheim died on Monday, and spoke with me on Thursday. I was invited to the funeral. He saw the hearse, the attendants, and the whole procession. He also saw them let down the coffin into the grave, and conversed with me while it was going on, asking me why they buried him, when he was alive. And when the priest pronounced that he would rise again at the day of judgment, he asked why this was, when he had already risen. He wondered that such a belief should prevail, considering that he was even now alive; he also wondered at the belief in the resurrection of the body, for he said he felt that he was in the body: with other remarks." Such a relation will seem strange, very strange to many. But have patience. When the laws and principles upon which such phenomena take place, are comprehended, all their strangeness and improbability will straightway disappear.

CHAPTER X.

The Arcana Cœlestia.

It was about the middle of 1749, that Swedenborg made his first appearance as a theologian, by the publication of the first volume of the "Arcana Cœlestia." At the beginning of 1750, we find his publisher, John Lewis, of Paternoster Row, announcing the issue of the second volume, in cheap numbers, both in English and Latin. The issue continued in volumes till 1756, when the work was completed in eight good sized quartos. His publisher states in one of his advertisements, that though he is "positively forbid to discover the author's name, yet he hopes to be excused for mentioning his benign and generous qualities." He avers that "this gentleman, with indefatigable pains and labor, spent one whole year in studying and writing out the first volume of the 'Arcana,' was at the expense of £200 to print it, and advanced £200 more for the printing of the second; and when he had done this, he gave express orders that all the money that should arise in the sale, should be given towards the charge of the propagation of the gospel. He is so far from desiring to make a gain of his labors, that he will not receive one farthing back of the £400 he has expended; and for that reason his works will come exceedingly cheap to the public."

The "Arcana Cœlestia" is an exposition of the books of Genesis and Exodus, with intervening chapters which describe the wonders of the future life. At the outset, it will be necessary to state that Swedenborg believed the Bible to be the Word of God. "Well, what Christian does not believe so?" it may be asked. Few expressions pass more glibly over the lips of religious people, than the short phrase, "the word of God;" but how many take time to consider its infinite meaning? The Word of God—a production of the infinite Father of all, the Creator and Sustainer of the universe,—must be infinitely superior to any human composition; and, like God's other volume, the book of nature, must yield up fresh wonders to every investigator; and the more it is searched into, the more real unceasing beauties of wisdom and design, till at length the strained intellect of man finds its truest wisdom lies in the deepest humility and adoration. Thus logically thinking, we experience a serious reverse when we turn to the opinions expressed regarding the Word by even its most reverential commentators. At no period of history has the Bible been submitted to more earnest study than in these times; but the results have been in the highest degree meagre and unworthy, when placed in comparison with the same exercise of mind on the subjects of natural creation. We have most elaborate and minute criticisms on the sacred text; we have treatises on the animals, the insects, and the vegetables mentioned in the hallowed record; we have books filled with descriptions of domestic life among the Jews, their customs, and their language; the prophecies have been subjected to all manner of ingenious interpretation, but after all, with the poorest spiritual results, and such as can in no wise excite a deeper respect, or a warmer love, for God's holy Word, than was entertained centuries ago, when such learning was a rarer thing. Yet if we believe that God inspired this Book, can we for a moment suppose that it should have no other end than the narration of the history of a petty people, and the enunciation of dark prophecies, which the acutest of men pronounce impenetrable mysteries, and which the daring and the foolish turn to all manner of profane purposes in political soothsayings? If the Bible be indeed the Word of God, it must contain within itself much more than the majority of Christians suppose; otherwise it presents a most startling anomaly when viewed in comparison with the other Divine work, the natural universe.

The assumption, then, with which Swedenborg starts, is, that the Scripture is in very truth the Word of God; that every syllable and expression therein are His; that Moses, David, the prophets, and the Evangelists, were simply the inspired penmen, who wrote implicitly according to Divine dictation.

He teaches, moreover, that the Word does not belong to men alone, but is the possession likewise of the angels of heaven, to whom it wears different forms according to the degree of their love and intelligence. In general, it may be said to have three senses, or meanings; first, a celestial sense, apprehended by the celestial or highest angels; secondly, a spiritual sense, apprehended by a lower range of angelic minds, the spiritual; and thirdly, a natural sense, with which we are all familiar, written down to the comprehension of the lowest, most worldly, and sensual of men—the Jews. These three senses make one by correspondence; although diverse, they are still harmonious, and connected by one divine life.

The Word, moreover, we are taught, has worn different garments, or varied natural senses, at different eras. The first church, Adam, or the primeval race of men, did not possess a written Word, but were gifted with a perception of spiritual essences. Nature was literally spread before them as an open book. To them, Nature was the expression of the Divine Wisdom; and they saw in every beast of the forest, in every flower of the field, and in every scene of creation, evidence of the Divine presence, and material emblems of spiritual and heavenly things. As men declined from purity, and, together with their innocence, lost their wisdom and their powers of celestial perception, a written Word became necessary, accommodated to the changed state of the new spiritual church called Noah. In time, this Word had also to be withdrawn, for its purity and language transcended the apprehension of a falling and sensualised world. Yet this Ancient Word, Swedenborg tells us, is not lost, but still exists in Tartary, probably as an unvalued treasure, which may be restored to the church in due season. To this Ancient Word, we have two allusions in the Jewish Scriptures; the first in Numbers xxi. 14, where we read: "Wherefore it is said in the book of the *Wars of Jehovah;*" and the second in Joshua x. 13: "Is not this written in the book of *Jasher?*" The book of the Wars of Jehovah, and the book of Jasher, forming parts of the Ancient Word, became unintelligible from being written in high correspondential and emblematic language; and uninteresting because not associated with the personal and worldly interests of men. The Jewish Scriptures were then written. The Divine Wisdom clothed itself in such words, histories, and laws, as the earthly-minded Jews could love and reverence, and thus be kept, in some measure, in connection with heaven, and in the possession of the most general and leading truths of religion. The Gospels, added in the course of time to the Jewish Word, served still further to preserve the church in union with heaven and the Lord. But now we see that mankind having in the course of centuries re-ascended to a higher degree of intellectual life, begin to be dissatisfied with the Scriptures, to arraign the truth of science against them, to wonder how it is possible that such writings can be the Word of God, and to ask, with Emerson, "What have I to do with jasper and sardonyx, beryl and chalcedony, what with arks and passovers, ephahs, heave-offerings, and unleavened bread; what with chariots of fire, and ephods; what with lepers and emerods; what with dragons crowned and horned, behemoth and unicorn?" But the Lord anticipates all man's wants; and, caring above all things for his spiritual well-being, never permits him to live without a witness of His love and designs towards him. By His Word, the Lord reveals himself to man; and without it, man could know nothing of God, of heaven and hell, and of a life after death. How necessary then it is that man be preserved from falling into contempt of its teachings; and yet if it contains no other than a literal sense, what can a Christian say in reply to such questionings as those above quoted? and what tenable theory can be advanced to meet the objections of the sceptic drawn from geology, astronomy, and many other sciences which clash with the letter of Scripture? In the "Arcana Cœlestia," we find a solution of all such doubts in the clear manifestation of the Divine authorship of the Word, through the revelation of its spiritual sense, whereby reason and faith are perfectly conjoined; and man, while here below, is fed with angels' food.

But it is not to be concluded from this that Swedenborg in any way slights or undervalues the literal sense of the Word. Far from it. He says: "The literal sense of the Word is the basis, the continent, and the firmament of its spiritual and celestial senses; and hence in it the divine truth is in its fulness, its sanctity, and its power; therefore the doctrine of the church should be drawn from the literal sense, and confirmed thereby." From this, every one will see that no mysticism can be sheltered under a belief in the spiritual sense of the Word; for, from the literal sense, determined by the severest criticism, all doctrine must be drawn, and all creeds tested. Swedenborg also teaches, that by means of the literal sense, men enjoy conjunction with the Lord; for His divine spirit is with all who read his Word devoutly. To promote this divine communion, the letter of Scripture has been so framed as to possess a universal interest. The child reads the Bible, and is delighted with its charming stories; the simple cottager loves it and prizes it as he prizes no other book; the poet draws from it his richest inspirations; and the man of learning, who has gathered knowledge from all times and lands, turns to its hallowed page, and in the light of its divine wisdom sees himself but a child in knowledge.

Though the Scriptures are thus marvellously adapted, in the literal sense, to the tastes, feelings, and necessities of men of all grades and states, yet, as before said, many portions of them do, in our days, require to be vindicated from the charge of being inconsistent with science—from the charge of insignificance, and dealing in petty details. They need, in fine, to be elevated from mere history, poetry, and obsolete law, into practical use and connection with the daily life and conduct of every man and woman; so that they may be to us, in very deed, the Word of God, as truly as they were to the Jews three thousand years ago.

Let us now see how, in the "Arcana Cœlestia," all this is effected.

"From the posterity of the most Ancient Church, Moses received what he wrote concerning the creation, the Garden of Eden, etc., down to the time of Abraham," writes Swedenborg. Describing the method by which the people of that church expressed themselves, he adds: "When they mentioned earthly and worldly things, they thought of the spiritual and celestial things which they represented; so that they not only expressed themselves by representatives, but also *reduced their thoughts into a kind of series, as of historical particulars,* in order to give them more life; and in this they found their greatest delight." Understanding this fully, we shall not be surprised to learn that the first eleven chapters of Genesis are *purely allegorical;* written not as a description of the creation of the material world, and its fortunes, but as a description of the internal life of the earliest people, of the development of their minds up to celestial perfection, and then of their gradual declension from purity, their love of the evil and the false, and finally the destruction of their souls, symbolized by the deluge overspreading the face of the whole earth. These chapters were thus written by the Lord in accommodation to the tastes of the men of the Ancient Church, who, as we read, had "their greatest delight in the expression of spiritual and celestial things in a series of historical particulars;" just as, in after times, He clothed His Wisdom in Jewish history and law, so that He might be with the Jews, and preserve within them some small remains of spiritual life. What a relief to the mind, torn and troubled with the thousand doubts which science has cast upon the early chapters of Genesis, is the acceptation of the truth of their entirely allegorical signification! And how plainly, in their spiritual sense, do we find testimony of their divine authorship! It should not be forgotten that the doctrine of the symbolical nature of these chapters, was set forth by Swedenborg long before science had demonstrated that their merely literal sense was wholly irreconcilable with the facts of nature; thus quite independently of any external pressure or necessity. It must be known to every one that geology—the science which, above all others, has brought the most weighty objections against the six days' creation, and the deluge of the whole earth by a flood which covered the tops of the highest mountains,—is a new science. At the time when Swedenborg wrote, it was entirely undeveloped. The reconciling of the literal sense of these chapters with the facts of geology, has perplexed more minds, and engaged more intellect, than did ever perpetual motion and the squaring of the circle. The amount of speculation which has been expended upon this theme, is immense, as every one at all acquainted with the religious history of the last fifty years is aware; and still the labor is vigorously prosecuted. We have no inclination to undervalue the motives that prompt to it. For all sincere lovers of the Word of God we entertain the deepest respect, and rejoice to think that their faith in the Bible remains unshaken amid such fiery trials. Yet if Christians were wise and unprejudiced, they would turn to Swedenborg's "Arcana Cœlestia," and there find all that heart or mind could wish. Its readers, who have been many, (and yet, when compared with the wide world of Christendom, insignificantly few,) have had, during all these seasons of doubt, the fullest peace; and have been ready to welcome every truth of science, however militating against the literal sense of the early chapters of Genesis; and all the while have remained such lovers of the Word as none but believers in its spiritual sense can be. We believe that the religious world will, in process of time, when all methods of reconciling the letter of Scripture with geology shall have manifestly failed, finally turn to Swedenborg; and when the heavenly truth glowing in his pages shall beam upon their opened sight, they will wonder why they did not read his luminous volumes sooner.

From the Call of Abram, the Word is to be looked upon as a narration of historical events. Yet while, as history, it possesses a great charm and interest to every mind, from its matchless and beautiful simplicity, we cannot see what claim it could have to the title of the Word of God, did it not contain within itself, as Swedenborg abundantly demonstrates, a spiritual sense, universally applicable to men in all states, times, and situations. In the highest or celestial sense, the Word refers solely to the Lord, and is a description of his nature and attributes, of his assumption of corrupt humanity, and the process of its glorification. Man being formed in the Lord's image and likeness, whatever treats of Him, is, in a secondary sense, or in a lower degree, descriptive of man, his nature and regeneration. This secondary application of the Word forms its spiritual sense, which when understood, transforms Genesis and Exodus from mere history and dull ceremonial law, into a Divine revelation of the laws of spiritual life, pregnant with practical benefit to all men, because applicable to every incident and thought of life.

Time and space would alike fail were we to attempt to give the most general outline of the multitude of spiritual truths which are unvailed in the course of the exposition of Genesis and Exodus; and not of these two books alone, but of passages from all parts of the Word, which are drawn upon to illustrate and confirm the truth of the interpretation. As Wilkinson says, "Consider, gentle reader, twelve goodly 8vo volumes [in English,] written with such continued power that it seems as if eating, drinking, and sleeping, had never intervened between the penman and his page, so unbroken is the subject, and so complete the sense. Add to the other health and harmony of this unflagging man, a memory of the most extraordinary grasp, which enabled him to administer the details of an intellect ranging through all truth on the one hand, and through the whole field of Scripture illustration and text upon the other. Then take into account the unity of the work from first to last; the constant reference that binds all parts of it together, and shows the caution with which each strong affirmation is at first set down. Observe also the felicity of phrase, the happiness of mind, the easy greatness, which shine along and dignify those serious pages. Remark also, that the author does not deal in generalities, but sentence for sentence, and word for word, he translates his text into spiritual meaning, and criticises and supports himself with nearly every parallel text in the sacred writings."

The earnest reader of the "Arcana" will never question the reality of Swedenborg's mission. He would as soon question the reality of the world, or his own existence. This is a strong assertion, a stranger to the work will perhaps say; but it is only a stranger to these wondrous volumes that will say so; for every one at all familiar with them will agree with us. We never take down a volume of the "Arcana" to read, without feeling more and more assured that Swedenborg was an anointed servant of the Lord. The depths of spiritual experience he reveals, his insight into the inmost recesses of the heart, his explanation of the causes of thoughts, and the origin of our various desires and inclinations, of lowness of spirits, of pleasant and dull moods, in short, of all spiritual trials and temptations, with the heavenly ends they are permitted to serve, together with a thousand other matters which it concerns us all to know, are of such a nature that we cannot but feel that such knowledge must have been derived from a Divine source, and that unless his stand-point had been most peculiar, and providentially appointed, it would have been impossible for him to have written as he has. To speak of the "Arcana" as it deserves, would, to one unacquainted with it, appear like exaggeration, while every reader would feel that we had fallen far short of the truth in many points. No criticism, however reverential, can adequately express the innumerable and marvellous excellencies of the work; and should this feeble testimony to its worth excite any one to read and *study* it,—and it is a work which should be studied, if read at all,—we know that he will say, as the Queen of Sheba said of Solomon, "It was a true report that I heard of thy acts and of thy wisdom. Howbeit I believed not the words, until I came, and mine eyes had seen it: and behold the half was not told me."

We have not spoken of those chapters which come between the expositions of Scripture, because the subjects therein treated of will recur in notices of his other books. They serve to diversify the work, and to relieve the mind tasked with the deep thought involved in the spiritual expositions, by the contemplation of some of the leading facts of the future life.

The "Arcana Cœlestia" was translated into English by the late venerable John Clowes, a clergyman of the Established Church in Manchester, and a most cordial receiver and preacher of the doctrines of the New Church. It is published in twelve octavo volumes, with an index prepared by Swedenborg himself, which forms a thirteenth volume. This index has been greatly extended by Elihu Rich, filling two large octavos. Several editions of the "Arcana" have also been published in America; and the sale, considering the size and cost of the work, has been in both countries very considerable. It is a work which will in coming days run through many cheap editions; and when that time shall come, many will wonder why such a treasury of spiritual wisdom lay so long in our midst, and yet men thought so little of it. But the world is approaching Swedenborg as fast as steady progress will permit.

CHAPTER XI.

Anecdotes.

Of Swedenborg's external life, during the composition of the "Arcana Cœlestia," we know little. From his "Spiritual Diary," we incidentally learn that he was in Stockholm on the 23d of July, 1756. A revolution had been attempted, and the leaders of the conspiracy, Count Brahe and Baron Horn, were executed on that day. Swedenborg writes of Brahe thus:—"Brahe was beheaded at ten o'clock in the morning, and spoke with me at ten at night; that is to say, twelve hours after his execution. He was with me almost without interruption for several days. In two days' time, he began to return to his former life, which consisted in loving worldly things; and after three days, he became as he was before in the world, and was carried into the evils that he had made his own before he died." (S. Diary, 5099.)

Robsahm, a friend of Swedenborg's, probably alludes to this circumstance, when he writes: "One day as a criminal was led to the place of execution to be beheaded, I was by the side of Swedenborg, and asked him how such a person felt at the time of his execution. He answered: 'When a man lays his head on the block, he loses all sensation. When he first comes into the spiritual world, and finds that he is living, he is seized with the fear of his expected death, tries to escape, and is very much frightened. At such a moment no one thinks of anything but the happiness of heaven, or the misery of hell. Soon the good spirits come to him, and instruct him where he is, and he is then left to follow his own inclinations, which soon lead him to the place where he remains for ever.'" It appears that whatever happens at the hour of death, is carried into the other life, and the state is continued for some time. Thus we read in the "Spiritual Diary" of a person who had been reduced by melancholy to despair, until being instigated by diabolical spirits, he destroyed himself, by thrusting a knife into his body. "This spirit came to me," writes Swedenborg, "complaining that he was miserably treated by evil spirits. He was seen by me, holding a knife in his hand, as though he would plunge it into his breast. With this knife he labored very hard, as wishing rather to cast it from him, but in vain."

It soon became widely known that Swedenborg had intercourse with spirits; and many and various were the demands made upon him, for information of one kind and another. The Queen of Sweden asked him whether his spiritual intercourse was a science or art that could be communicated to others. He said: "No, it is the gift of the Lord." "Can you then," said she, "speak with every one deceased, or only with certain persons?" He answered, "I can not converse with all, but only with such as I have known in this world, with all royal and princely persons, with all renowned heroes, or great and learned men, whom I have known, either personally, or from their actions or writings; consequently with all *of whom I could form an idea;* for it may be supposed that a person whom I never knew, and of whom I could form no idea, I neither could or would wish to speak with."

The Prince of Prussia was brother to the Queen of Sweden, and shortly after his death, Swedenborg being at court, the Queen perceiving him said: "Well, Mr. Assessor, have you seen my brother?" He answered, "No." Whereupon she replied: "If you should see him, remember me to him." In saying this, she did but jest. Eight days afterwards, Swedenborg came again to court, but so early that the Queen had not left her apartment called the white room, where she was conversing with her maids of honor, and other ladies of the court. Swedenborg did not wait for the Queen's coming out, but entered directly into her apartment, and whispered in her ear. The Queen, struck with astonishment, was taken ill, and did not recover for some time. After she was come to herself, she said to those about her: "There is only God and my brother who can know what he has just told me." She owned that he had spoken of her last correspondence with the prince, the subject of which was known to themselves alone.

The following is narrated by J. H. Jung Stilling:— "About the year 1770, there was a merchant in Elberfeld with whom, during seven years of my residence there, I lived in close intimacy. He spoke little; but what he said was like golden fruit on a salver of silver. He would not have dared for all the world to have told a falsehood. His business requiring him to take a journey to Amsterdam, where Swedenborg at that time resided, and having heard and read much of this strange individual, he formed the intention of visiting him. He therefore called upon him, and found a very venerable looking, friendly old man, who received him politely, and requested him to be seated. Explaining his errand, and expressing his deep admiration of Swedenborg's writings, he desired that he would give him a proof of his intercourse with the unseen world. Swedenborg said: 'Why not? Most willingly.' The merchant then proceeded to tell that he had formerly a friend, who studied divinity at Duisburg, where he fell into a consumption, of which he died. Visiting this friend a short time before his decease, they conversed together on an important topic. The question he then put to Swedenborg, was: 'Can you learn from the student what was the subject of our discourse at that time?' Swedenborg replied: 'We will see; what was the name of your friend?' The merchant told his name, and Swedenborg then requested him to call in a few days. Some days after, the merchant went again to see Swedenborg, in anxious expectation. The old gentleman met him with a smile, and said: 'I have spoken with your friend; the subject of your discourse was *the restitution of all things.*' He then related to the merchant, with the greatest precision, what he, and what his deceased friend, had maintained. The merchant turned pale; for this proof was powerful and invincible. He inquired further: 'How fares it with my friend? Is he in a state of blessedness?' Swedenborg answered: 'No, he is not in heaven; he is still in the world of spirits, and torments himself continually with the idea of the restitution of all things.' He ejaculated: 'My God! What! in the other world?' Swedenborg replied: 'Certainly; a man takes with him his favorite inclinations and opinions, and it is very difficult to be divested of them. We ought, therefore, to lay them aside here.' The merchant took his leave, perfectly convinced, and returned to Elberfeld."

An ambassador from Holland, named Martville, died at Stockholm. After his death, a considerable sum of money was demanded of his widow in payment of a debt. She felt certain the debt had been paid, but was unable to find the receipt for the money. Being advised to consult Swedenborg, who, she was told could converse with the dead whenever he pleased, she adopted the advice, more from curiosity than from a belief in his powers. The lady called on Swedenborg and told him her trouble; and he promised if he met her husband in the spiritual world, he would inquire of him about the matter. Eight days afterwards Martville appeared to his wife in a dream, and mentioned to her a private place in his cabinet, where she would not only find the receipt, but also a hair pin set with twenty brilliants, which had been given up as lost. This happened about two o'clock in the morning. Full of joy, she arose and found them in the place designated. She returned again to rest, and slept till nine o'clock. About eleven Swedenborg was announced. His first remark, before Madame had time to speak, was, that he had, during the preceding night, seen several spirits, and among others her late husband. He had wished to converse with him, but Martville excused himself on the ground that he must go to discover to his wife something of importance. This account, attested by the lady herself, was noised through all Stockholm. It may be added that Madame desired to make Swedenborg a handsome present for his services, which he, of course, declined.

Sometimes Swedenborg's announcements of the states of the departed alarmed his auditors. We read of a case of this kind which took place on a voyage from Gottenburg to London. The vessel staying at Oresound, the Swedish Consul invited the officers of the custom house, together with several of the first people of the town, all anxious to see and know Swedenborg, to dine with him at his house. Being all seated at table, and none of them taking the liberty of addressing Swedenborg, who likewise was silent, the Consul thought it incumbent on him to break silence, and asked Swedenborg, as he could see and speak with the dead, whether he had seen Christian VI., King of Denmark, after his decease. To this he replied in the affirmative; adding, that when he saw him the first time, he was accompanied by a bishop or other prelate, who humbly begged the King's pardon for the many errors into which he had led him by his counsels. A son of the deceased prelate happened to be present at the table: the Consul therefore fearing that Swedenborg might say something further to the disadvantage of the father, interrupted him, saying: "Sir, this is his son!" Swedenborg replied: "It may be, but what I am saying is true."

Such anecdotes might be greatly multiplied, but space forbids. No one, perhaps, has a lower idea of the worth of these stories, as testimonies to Swedenborg's veracity, than the writer; yet they could not well be omitted from an account of his life. Gossip spread them far and wide in his own day, as is evidenced by the various forms in which they have come down to us; and any biographer would fail in his duty did he not show how the common world of men dealt with, and regarded Swedenborg. These anecdotes also in some degree manifest what a kind, affable, simple, and honest man Swedenborg was.

Having finished the "Arcana Cœlestia," Swedenborg's pen yet knew no rest. In 1758 he published in London the five following works:—1. An Account of the Last Judgment and the Destruction of Babylon; showing that all the predictions in the Apocalypse are at this day fulfilled; being a relation of things heard and seen. 2. Concerning Heaven and its wonders, and concerning Hell, being a relation of things heard and seen. 3. On the White Horse mentioned in the Apocalypse. 4. On the Planets in our solar system, and on those in the Heavens; with an acconnt of their inhabitants, and of their spirits and angels. 5. On the New Jerusalem and its Heavenly Doctrines, as revealed from heaven. Let us now examine these works in order.

CHAPTER XII.

The Last Judgment

To the early reader of Swedenborg's writings, few of his declarations appear stranger, at first, than his affirmation that the Last Judgment is past, that it took place in 1757. Yet although startling at first, it is a doctrine which, on closer acquaintance, readily comes within the grasp of reason and common sense; and we discover that all its early strangeness was owing to our having looked at it through the mist of prejudice and preconceived opinion.

The treatise on the Last Judgment, (although, as to size, only a pamphlet,) is a most effective and masterly exposition of the nature of the end of the church, the new heavens, and the new earth of the Apocalypse.

In the first place, it is shown that the day of the Last Judgment does not mean that of the destruction of the world; for neither the visible heaven nor the habitable earth will perish, but both will remain forever. The reason is. that the heaven of angels is formed from the human race, all angels having lived the life of men, and none having been so created; and as the perfection of heaven increases to eternity with the increase of regenerate men from the world, it follows that the earth will never cease to exist, nor men to live and be born upon it. The world is the seminary of heaven. Heaven depends upon the world for its growth, increase, and perfection. Heaven could not exist without worlds.

Heaven being formed from the human race, so likewise is Hell; all devils and satans having at one time been men on this or some other earth. "That is not first which is spiritual, but that which is natural."

These doctrines, it will be seen, militate against what are called orthodox opinions, which teach that angels were created before the world, and that no man can go to heaven or to hell before the time of the Last Judgment; when the souls of men having returned into their bodies, the visible world will be burned up; the sun and moon be quenched in nature's night; and the stars, each surrounded with its own system of worlds, having first fallen upon this speck of a globe, are to be wiped out of existence. These common but crude and unscriptural ideas have afforded the best subjects for scoffing at the Christian religion which the skeptic could desire. For he triumphantly asks, How can so vast a heaven, and so many stars, with sun and moon, be destroyed and dissipated? And how can the stars fall from heaven upon the earth, when they are larger than the earth? How can men's bodies, eaten up by worms, consumed by putrefaction, scattered to all winds, absorbed by vegetation, and again incorporated into other men's systems, be re-collected for their souls? What is this day of Judgment? And has it not been expected for ages in vain? Together with many other such questions, all pertinent, but to which the church can give no rational answer.

And yet ignorance on such subjects cannot be excused; for men might have known from the Word that heaven and hell are from mankind, and that man is raised up and lives immediately after death. Information on these subjects might have been obtained from the Lord's words to the thief upon the cross, "Verily I say unto thee, To-day shalt thou be with me in Paradise;" and from those which he spoke concerning the rich man and Lazarus, that the one went to hell, and spoke with Abraham, and that the other went to heaven; and what the Lord told the Pharisees respecting the resurrection, that "God is not the God of the dead, but of the living." And then we see how inconsistent men are with themselves on these subjects. A worthy church-member, who is a firm believer in the burning up of the world, and the resurrection of the dead at the Last Judgment, comes to his death-bed, and straightway all his doctrine passes into forgetfulness; and he talks of going home to glory in heaven, and being within a few hours of the angels. He dies; and his friends, as orthodox as himself, think of him as happy in heaven; and yet they profess to believe in the resurrection of his corrupt and diseased body. What strange inconsistency is this! But it is one of the marks of error, that it is always inconsistent with itself.

The leading fact in Swedenborg's doctrine of the Last Judgment, is, that it takes place in the spiritual world, where all men congregate after death. A judgment takes place in the world of spirits whenever a church comes to its end; that is, when its charity, and consequently its faith is dead, and all things that remain are mere empty forms of life. A judgment took place at the end of the Jewish church. For proof of this, we need only turn to the Gospel of *John*, (xii. 31,) where Jesus said: "*Now* is the judgment of this world: *now* shall the prince of this world be cast out." We all know there was at that time no visible judgment in the natural world. Everything went on as before; yet, we learn from the Lord's own lips, that a judgment was effected.

It is a great mistake, and one which even the best of men labor under, to suppose that the soul of man exists alone, and independent of any influences but those that are external to him, and of which he is conscious. We would ask, Who ever saw a grain of matter independent of the law of gravitation,—that cause which binds it to kindred matter with a bond as indestructible as its own existence? It is the same with men's souls. No man lives independent of spiritual association. Place a man in the middle of some distant and desolate island; yet he is not alone. Around his soul are the spirits of those who have left the world before him, who love as he loves, and think as he thinks. The minds of men and spirits are most closely and intimately conjoined; for in the universe of mind, as in the universe of matter, there is no such thing as isolation and independency. And what can be more philosophical than such a doctrine? The laws of matter represent the laws of spirit; in every particular there exists a perfect correspondence. As matter is everywhere bound to matter, and compacted in firm communion, so likewise are the minds of men to be regarded as a universe of atoms, bound together by loves and affections. In meditating on this subject, we must remember that spirit knows nothing of material space.

The church had been declining from the days of the Apostles. Men had forsaken the pure spirit of the gospel, and had sought to hide their evils of life by doctrines and creeds formed from their own darkened understandings. The popedom had arisen; and in the black night of the dark ages, had established its fearful assumptions, and blasphemously invoked the name of the Highest to sanctify its crimes. The Reformation, the last flicker of an expiring candle, had indeed established free thought, but it failed in its highest aims; and in the erroneous doctrine of justification by faith alone, had deadened the consciences of men, and extinguished all aspirations after spiritual life. Last and worst of all, Atheism reared its horrid front, and openly manifested itself; yet what of it was open and confessed, was as nothing to what lay concealed even under the vestments of the church. Toward the middle of the last century, Christendom had reached its lowest point of degradation; and any one who is anxious to test this affirmation of Swedenborg's, need only turn to the history and literature of that period, and observe the selfishness, the negation and ridicule of everything pure and spiritual, the gross ignorance, the licentiousness and intemperance, and in fact the reduction of humanity to its lowest and most bestial condition. He will then understand the cry of the good, at that time, in the world of spirits, "How long, O Lord, holy and true, dost thou not judge and avenge our blood on them that dwell on the earth?"

It is to be noted that from the time of the Lord's advent, when he effected the Judgment upon the Jewish church, there had been pouring into the world of spirits, in countless myriads, the souls of those who were full of evils and falsities, and who, collecting around terrestrial humanity, lay as thick clouds between it and heaven. Forming themselves into societies by spiritual affinities, the reformed churches were in the middle; the Romanists around them; the Mahommedans in a still outer ring; and the various Gentile nations constituted a vast circumference; while beyond all, lay the appearance of a sea as a boundary. Of the states of those associations, we have a most graphic picture in Swedenborg's treatise; and no where else out of the Apocalypse, do we find a more thorough exposure of the internal atheism of the priests of Rome, their blasphemies and subtlety. But the time of the end had come; the world groaned to be delivered; and the eyes of Swedenborg were favored to behold the process of the great redemption.

The vast concourse of these spirits, formed into societies, is what is meant in the Revelation by the first heaven and the first earth which passed away. The manner in which these societies were dissolved, Swedenborg describes as follows:—"Visitation was made by angels, and admonition given, and the good were singled out and separated by the heavenly ministers, agreeable to the Lord's words, 'He shall send his angels, and they shall gather together the elect from the four winds, from one end of heaven to the other;' and again, 'All nations shall be gathered together before the Son of Man; and he shall separate them one from another, as a shepherd divideth the sheep from the goats, and he shall set the sheep on the right hand, and the goats on the left.'" Then followed destruction. There were great earthquakes, and a vehement wind, which swept all before it. Then gulfs yawned, and seas appeared, into which the wicked threw themselves, and were drawn to their place in hell. "Then," says Swedenborg, "I saw angelic spirits in great numbers rising from below, and received into heaven. They were the sheep who had been kept and guarded by the Lord, and who are understood in the Word by the bodies of saints which arose from their sepulchres and went into the holy city; and by the souls of those slain for the testimony of Jesus, and who were watching; and by those who were of the first resurrection.

"After this, there was joy in heaven, and light in the world of spirits, such as was not before; and the interposing clouds between heaven and mankind being removed, a similar light also then arose on men in the world, giving them new enlightenment."

Such was the Last Judgment. Its centenary draws nigh; and how fruitful in good to mankind has been that century which is now drawing to a close! It is unnecessary to repeat the hackneyed phrases which tell of the progress of the world during the last hundred years. Every newspaper speaks of it. Everybody with open eyes observes it. It has become the universal opinion that the world is moving onwards and upwards; yet how few understand *why* the world is so moving. Men have yet to learn that effects can no more take place without adequate causes in the universe of mind than in the universe of matter. Nowhere out of Swedenborg can we find a description of those spiritual causes which are changing society and revolutionizing the whole world. We, who live in the dawn of the new era, can form, even in our highest states, but a faint conception of its coming glory. Yet we see in the wonderful movements of our age, in its growing benevolence, in its increasing intelligence and thoughtfulness, and in the prodigious advances that are making in every department of science and art, so many indubitable signs that the former things have passed away, and that the Lord is making all things new.

Every one knows that in the Scripture, the second coming of the Lord is described as simultaneous with the Last Judgment. We will hereafter endeavor to prove that the Lord has indeed come, and will describe the manner of his coming.

The reception of the doctrine of the Last Judgment is somewhat difficult, because the comprehension of it demands the understanding of many principles and spiritual laws unknown to the world at large, yet most worthy of any amount of labor requisite to master them. The remembrance of this fact will serve as an apology for any appearance of unfounded assumption in the outline of the doctrine we have given.

CHAPTER XIII.

Heaven and Hell.

THE treatise on Heaven and Hell is among the most charming of Swedenborg's writings. Its subjects possess a universal attraction; for, what believer in the immortality of man has not, at times, longed to penetrate the awful mysteries of the unseen world? And there is nothing unreasonable in the desire. True it is, that, until Swedenborg came, any but the most general knowledge of the nature of the future life had been withdrawn from mankind since the days of primeval innocence; yet not from anything hurtful in the knowledge itself, but simply because the sublime facts of the future state transcended the apprehension of men immersed in worldly loves and cares, and denying and ridiculing every idea which was not an object of sensual perception. For this reason the Lord said to his disciples: "I have yet many things to say unto you, but ye can not bear them now." (*John* xvi. 12.) We frequently see this inability to "bear" things spiritual and divine, manifested in our own experience. We offer Swedenborg's treatise, for perusal, to some man of science, full of self-confidence, with the laws and facts of the universe at his finger's ends; or to some deeply-read theologian. The title page is read,—"Heaven and its Wonders, the World of Spirits, and Hell; being a relation of things heard and seen." It is enough. "What nonsense! What foolishness! The lunatic! What could *he* know of heaven or hell? How could he get there? The impostor! None but a fool could write such a book!" And so on. The title page settles the whole question. Now what can be said in reply to these railers, of whom the world is full? How can one argue with, and combat, such inveterate prejudice? Yet these people are professing Christians. They profess to believe there is a heaven and a hell. But, does not their condemnation of Swedenborg betray a lurking infidelity in their hearts? If they really possessed a living faith in the existence of heaven and hell, it could not appear to them so utterly preposterous that some account of their nature might in these times have been revealed, through the abounding mercy of the Lord.

But the world now contains many who are willing to receive, and able to understand, the truths of the future life. The Lord, who never allows his children to lack any good thing, has, in due season, given them, through Swedenborg, this precious and delightful volume. Let us briefly enumerate its important statements.

The spiritual world divides itself into three great regions, —Heaven, the World of Spirits, and Hell.

Heaven is formed of all who have loved the Lord on earth by living a life in accordance with his laws. The laws of spiritual life are known, more or less perfectly, in all nations, even among the heathen. The lowest of the Gentiles have some faint rays of the light of spiritual truth; and if they live in obedience thereto, regeneration, and consequently, heaven, is attainable by them. Yet heaven has its degrees of bliss. Good persons of every variety of character pass into it. But the promiscuous association of these different kinds of character would not be orderly, and could not be blissful. By the law of spiritual gravitation, (from which the law of natural gravitation is but a derivation, and of which it is a type and image,) all who possess similar affections and intelligence are drawn together, and co-ordinated in the most blissful harmony. The infinite variety of heaven thus arranges itself, in general, into two kingdoms; specifically into three heavens; and in particular, into innumerable societies. The two kingdoms are respectively called celestial and spiritual. The angels forming the celestial kingdom are characterized by their exceeding love of the Lord and of goodness; and the angels who form the spiritual kingdom are distinguished by their exceeding love of their neighbor and of truth. The celestial angels are immensely wiser than the spiritual, and their blessedness is ineffable. Specifically there are three heavens, perfectly distinct, called the first heaven, the second or middle heaven, and the third or highest heaven; or they may be called external, internal, and inmost; or natural, spiritual, and celestial. Of these three heavens the highest or third, together with the internal of the first or lowest heaven, forms the celestial kingdom; and the middle or second, together with the external of the first or lowest heaven, forms the spiritual kingdom. These three heavens and two kingdoms, arising out of the varieties of the human mind, are not arbitrary distinctions. The external, first, or natural heaven, is formed of those who, from a principle of obedience and duty, live in accordance with the Divine will. The second, spiritual, or middle heaven, is formed of such as love truth, delight in things intellectual, and at the same time are in disinterested love to the neighbor. The inmost, third, or celestial heaven, is formed of those who, full of love to the Lord, are in innocence. These celestial angels, gifted with the highest wisdom and peace, yet full of humility, indefinitely exceed all beneath them in beauty and wisdom. The existence and order of the three heavens was represented by the courts of the Jewish temple. The celebrated Oberlin, a diligent reader of Swedenborg, had a plan of the courts of the temple hung upon the walls of his church, by which he taught his hearers, that, according to their humility, piety, fidelity, and love of being useful to each other, would be their elevation in the Lord's kingdom, either to the first, second, or third heaven. We think that no one, in whom reign the heavenly principles of "love" to the Lord and the neighbor; "joy" in duty under all circumstances; "peace" in every change of state; "long-suffering" under all provocations; "gentleness" of behaviour; "goodness" of disposition, ever manifesting itself in good actions; "faith" or truth, believed, loved, and thence trusted in; "meekness" in doing and in suffering; "temperance" both in external and internal delights, Gal. v. 22, would be an unwilling inhabitant of such a heaven as Swedenborg describes. Is not this at least presumptive evidence that he has spoken truly?

The three heavens are further subdivided into innumerable societies, some smaller, and some larger; some consisting of myriads of angels, and some of hundreds. Their association into societies, is a result of similarity of character, which similarity is imaged in their faces; and a general likeness of countenance is observed among the angels who form one society. All who are in similar love know each other, just as men in the world know their kindred, relations, and friends; and thus, as it were, spontaneously associated, they feel at home and in freedom, and thence in the full delight of their life. From this it also follows that angels who differ much are far apart; and few depart out of their own society into another, because to go out from their own society is like going out of themselves, or out of their own life, and passing into another which is not so agreeable. Nevertheless all the societies of heaven are bound together in one perfect form, which is strictly human.

All angels are in the human form, and are just such men and women as they were on earth, except that they have rejected the material body. That we should have to write and enforce such truisms—for such they must appear to a mind really rational,—is owing to the strange and ridiculous fancies that are commonly entertained on this subject. We often hear the departed talked of as shades, and thought of as minds without forms, or mere thinking principles composed of some sort of ethereal vapor; and when artists draw them, we see perhaps an exquisitely beautiful human form, but disfigured with large feathery wings, which, having no adequate muscles, would have no power of motion. None of these vague, shadowy, and erroneous ideas do we find in the Bible. The angels seen by Abraham, Lot, Manoah, the prophets, and the Lord's disciples, were all seen as men, and talked with as men. Our author writes thus explicitly on this subject. "The angelic form is in every respect human; angels have faces, eyes, ears, breasts, arms, hands, and feet; they see, hear, and converse with each other; and, in a word, no external attribute of man is wanting, except the natural body."

And now comes a doctrine which on a first view may appear very mystical, and yet when pondered over, and understood, commends itself to our belief by a thousand irresistible evidences drawn from analogy, and confirmed by right reason. It is, that every society of heaven is in the human form; and that the universal heaven, viewed collectively, is also in the human form; and is called by Swedenborg the Grand or Greatest [Maximus] Man. Wilkinson well expresses this sublime truth. "Heaven," he says, "is supremely human—nay more, it is one man. As the members of the body make one person, so before God, all good men make one humanity: every society of the angels is a heavenly man in a lesser form, and every angel in a least. The reason is, that God himself, (the Lord Jesus Christ,) is a Divine Man, and He shapes His heaven into His own image and likeness, even as He made Adam. The oneness of heaven comes from God's unity: its manhood from His humanity. Heaven has, therefore, all the members, organs, and viscera of a man; its angel inhabitants, every one, are in some province of the Grand Man. Indefinite myriads of us go to a fibre of its humanity. Some are in the province of the brain; some in that of the lungs; some in that of the heart; some in that of the belly; some are in the legs and arms; and all, wherever humanized, that is to say, located in humanity, perform spiritually the offices of that part of the body whereto they correspond. They all work together, however spaced apparently, just as the parts of a single man. Their space is but their palpable liberty, and they touch the human atoms, more closely, by offices which unite them in God, than the contiguous fibres of our flesh." Every society of heaven also increases in number daily, and as it increases, it becomes more perfect; and from its perfection the universal heaven becomes more perfect, because heaven is composed of societies. Since increasing numbers make heaven more perfect, it is evident how much *they* are deceived who believe that heaven will be closed when it becomes full. On the contrary, heaven will never be closed, for the greater its fullness, the greater its perfection; and therefore the angels desire nothing more earnestly than to receive new comers.

This part of our subject would require considerable expansion to make it intelligible to minds that have never meditated on these high themes, and whose theological education has perverted all perception of the truth on these matters. The subject is enticing, but our limits command restraint.

It was a remark of a profane wit and epicure that "as to heaven, he had no great longing, as he could not see what great pleasure there could be in sitting on a cloud and singing psalms to eternity." We have in this expression a thought which we know to be common to many minds, but respect for the externals of religion forbids its expression. The general belief respecting the nature of life in heaven, is so vague, and contains so much of clouds and psalm-singing, that it is not to be wondered at that some free and daring spirits should openly avow their preference for the more substantial realities of this life. And is it not a pity that the divine glories and delights of the heavenly life should become so vailed in mystery as to lose their attraction, and cease to be desirable? With the exception of the church's ignorance of the humanity, unity, and divinity of its Saviour and Lord, no surer evidence could be adduced of its consummation, than its inability to answer the simplest child's questions as to the nature of life in heaven. Let us be thankful that man's utmost wants, in this respect, are satisfied in the writings of that New Church which the Lord is now raising up, and of which Swedenborg was the divinely-appointed herald.

The sun of heaven is the Lord. The light of heaven is the divine truth, and its heat the divine love; both proceeding from the Lord as a sun. The sun of this world is not seen in heaven. Nature commences from the sun of this world, and everything which is produced from it, and subsists by it, is called natural; but the spiritual world in which heaven is, is above nature, and entirely distinct from it, although it is ever to be remembered that nature is a derivation from spirit, and communicates with spirit by correspondences. We shall have more to say on this conjunction yet perfect separation, between nature and spirit, when we come to speak of the doctrine of degrees.

The sun of heaven, or the divine sphere of glory surrounding the Lord, the "light which no man can approach unto," 1 Tim. vi. 6, appears variously to the angels of heaven according to their states of love and intelligence. To the angels of the third heaven, the sun appears fiery and flaming; to the angels of the second heaven, white and brilliant; while to those of the first heaven its light is more subdued and vailed with clouds, yet at intervals bursting forth and pouring his glorious radiance upon them. Although the Lord is thus seen by the angels as a sun above them, yet at times He appears in their midst, in an angelic form, and with a resplendent countenance. What tongue can describe the rapt adoration and ineffable joy which must thrill angelic bosoms on these occasions!

Heaven has its times and its seasons, but they are not like those of earth. In heaven there is no winter and no night. The times and seasons of heaven are consequences of the variations of the states of angelic minds. While to all appearance they are objective as on earth, they are in reality strictly subjective. The external changes of light and heat correspond to the internal changes of love and wisdom in the angelic mind. Now as the angels are sometimes in a state of intense love, and sometimes in a state of love not so intense, morning, noon, evening, and twilight, exist in heaven as the external emblems of these changes. Without such changes life would lose its zest. Eternal uniformity would be eternal dullness.

Since angels are men, and live together in society like men on earth, therefore they have garments, houses, and other things similar to those which exist on earth, but of course infinitely more beautiful and perfect. The garments of the angels correspond to their intelligence. The garments of some glitter as with flame, and those of others are resplendent as with light; others are of various colors, and some white and opaque. The angels of the inmost heaven are naked because they are in innocence, and nakedness corresponds to innocence. It is because garments represent states of wisdom that they are so much spoken of in the Word, in relation to the church and good men. Thus in

Isaiah liii. 1, "Awake, put on strength, O Zion; put on thy *beautiful garments*, O Jerusalem." And in Ezekiel xv. 10, the Lord says of his church: "I girded thee about with fine linen, and covered thee with silk." And in the Apocalypse iii. 4, 5, it is said: "They who have not defiled their *garments*, shall walk with Me in *white*, for they are worthy. He that overcometh, the same shall be clothed in *white raiment*." What a depth of meaning appears in these passages when we remember the spiritual signification of garments!

"The garments of the angels," writes Swedenborg, "do not merely appear to be garments, but they really are garments; for they not only see them, but feel them, and have different ones, which they take off and put on, laying aside those which are not in use, and resuming them when they come into use again. That they are clothed with a variety of garments, I have witnessed a thousand times; and when I inquired whence they obtained them, they told me 'from the Lord,' and that they receive them as gifts, and that they are sometimes clothed without knowing how. They also said that their garments are changed according to the changes of their state."

Since there are societies in heaven, and the angels live as men, it follows that they have habitations, various, like all else in heaven, according to the degree of love and wisdom in which they are principled. No words are like Swedenborg's own on this subject. "Whenever I have conversed with the angels mouth to mouth, I have been present with them in their habitations, which are exactly like the habitations on earth called houses, but more beautiful. They contain chambers, parlors [conclavia], and bed-chambers, in great numbers; courts also, and around them gardens, shrubberies, and fields. Where the angels are consociated their habitations are contiguous, or near to each other, and arranged in the form of a city, with streets, ways, and squares, exactly like the cities on our earth.

"I have seen palaces in heaven, magnificent beyond description. Their upper parts were refulgent as if they were pure gold, and their lower parts as if they were precious stones: some were more splendid than others, and the splendor without was equaled by the magnificence within. The apartments were ornamented with decorations which neither language nor science can adequately describe. On the south were paradises, in which all things were similarly resplendent; for in some places the leaves of the trees were like silver, and the fruits like gold, while the colors of the flowers which were arranged in beds, appeared like rainbows; at the boundaries appeared other palaces, which terminated the view. Such is the architecture of heaven that one might say it is the very art itself; nor is this to be wondered at, because the art itself is from heaven. The angels said that such things, and innumerable others still more perfect, are presented before their eyes by the Lord, but that nevertheless they delight their minds more than their eyes, because in everything they see correspondences of things divine.

"The angels who constitute the Lord's celestial kingdom, dwell for the most part in elevated places, or mountains; those who form the spiritual kingdom, on hills; but those who are in the lowest parts of heaven, in places which appear as rocks. There are also angels who do not live consociated, but separate. These dwell in the midst of heaven, and are the best of the angels.

"The houses in which the angels dwell, are not constructed by hand, like houses in the world, but are given them freely by the Lord, according to their reception of good and truth. All things whatsoever which the angels possess, they hold as gifts from the Lord; and they are supplied with everything they need."

We thus learn that in heaven there are not external, physical, or mental occupations to support bodily wants, as in this world.

It was said above that the angels have not wings, as is commonly supposed. Their power of progression far exceeds anything that wings could supply. They have no idea of space, such as we have in the world. All who are of like disposition spontaneously associate together in the spiritual world. It thus follows that those are near each other who are in a similar state, and distant who are in a dissimilar state; and that what appears to be space in heaven is merely an external appearance, representative of internal differences of mind. From this cause alone the heavens are distinct from each other, and each society of heaven, and every individual in each society. Hence also the hells are altogether separated from the heavens.

From the same cause, any one in the spiritual world appears to be present if another intensely desires his presence; for from that desire he sees him in thought, and puts himself in his state. Again one person is removed from another in proportion as he holds him in aversion; for all aversion is from contrariety of the affections and disagreement of the thoughts; therefore many who appear together in one place in the spiritual world, so long as they agree, separate as soon as they disagree.

Further: when any one goes from one place to another, whether it be in his own city, in the courts, or the gardens, or to others out of his own city, he arrives sooner when he has a strong desire to be there, and later when his desire is less strong; the way itself being lengthened or shortened according to his desire of arrival. Hence again it is evident that distances, and consequently spaces, exist with the angels altogether according to the state of their minds.

These principles settle that often asked question, "Shall we know each other in the future life?" We shall, if we are in the same state as to love and truth; but if in different states, we shall not, but shall be separate; and, moreover, we shall have no desire for acquaintance. The only friendships in heaven are those formed on the ground of similarity of character. If this similarity does not exist,—with the exception perhaps of a short meeting in the world of spirits—death is an everlasting, though in such case not a mournful, farewell.

There are governments in heaven, various according to the varied classes of mind which compose the heavenly societies. The government of mutual love is the only government which exists in heaven. Governors in heaven are distinguished by love and wisdom more than others, and by willing well to all from love; and knowing, from their superior wisdom, how to realize the good they purpose. They do not domineer, and command imperiously, but minister and serve: not making themselves greater than others, but less; for they put their own good last, and the good of their society first: nevertheless they enjoy honor and glory; for they dwell in the midst of their society, in a more elevated situation than others, and inhabit magnificent palaces; but they accept glory and honor, not for the sake of themselves, but for the sake of obedience; for all in heaven know that they enjoy honor and glory from the Lord, and that, therefore they ought to be obeyed. These are the things which are meant by the Lord's words to his disciples: "Whosoever will be chief among you, let him be your servant; even as the Son of Man came not to be ministered unto, but to minister." Matthew xx. 27, 28. "He that is greatest among you, let him be as the younger: and he that is chief, as he that doth serve." Luke xxii. 26. A similar government prevails also in every house in heaven; for in every house there is a master, and there are servants, the master loving the servants, and the servants loving the master, so that they serve each other from love. The master teaches the servants how they ought to live, and directs what they ought to do, while the servants obey, and perform their duties.

Divine worship performed in heaven, is much the same in externals, as on earth. In the heavens, as on earth, there are doctrines, preachings, and temples. As the angels have houses and palaces, so also they have temples in which preaching is performed. Such things exist in heaven because the angels are continually perfecting in wisdom and love. But real divine worship in the heavens does not consist, any more than on earth, in frequenting temples, and hearing sermons, but in a life of love and usefulness; sermons and prayers being only means whereby the mind is enlightened to perform its various duties. "To work is to pray," is a heavenly precept which we should all do well to engrave upon our hearts.

The sermons of heaven are fraught with such wisdom that nothing of the kind in the world can be compared with them. They are all drawn from the Word. The same Bible that we read here, the angels read in heaven; but to them it is a very different book from what it is to us Where we read and think of earthly and material things, they read and think of spiritual and divine things. To them its spiritual and celestial senses are as open as the natural sense is to us. From the Word they derive their highest wisdom; and through continual converse with it, they grow wiser and wiser day by day. The Word is the wisdom of the Lord, and eternity can not exhaust it.

All infants go to heaven, whether born within the church or out of it; whether of pious parents or wicked ones. When infants die, they are still infants in the other life. They are not angels, but become angels. Every one, on his decease, is in a similar state of life to that in which he was in the world; an infant in the state of infancy, a boy in a state of boyhood, and a youth, a man, or an old man, in the state of youth, of manhood, or of age; but the state of every one is afterwards changed. As soon as infants are raised from the dead, which takes place immediately after decease, they are carried up into heaven, and delivered to the care of angels of the female sex, who in the life of the body loved infants tenderly, and at the same time loved God. By these good angels, they are educated and brought up until they attain a suitable age, when they are transferred to other teachers. They grow up and become young men and women; are instructed in wisdom, and trained in the duties of the heavenly life: and when their character is fully developed, they become settled in some society, either of the celestial or spiritual kingdom, in agreement with their inherited genius or disposition. What a delightful faith is this! Do not its beauty and rationality prove its truthfulness?

Many persons imagine that infants are forever infants in heaven, and that there is indeed something infantile about all angels. This idea probably arises from the pictures which are frequently seen, in which angels are drawn as infants. But this is a great mistake. Children in heaven grow up into young men and women, and the aged return to the freshness of early manhood. They who are in heaven are continually advancing to the spring-time of life, and the more thousands of years they live, the more delightful and happy is the spring to which they attain; and this progression goes on to eternity. Good women who have died old and worn out with age, after a succession of years come more and more into the flower of youth, and into a beauty which exceeds all the conceptions of beauty which can be formed from what the eye has seen. In a word, *to grow old in heaven is to grow young*. It is worthy of note, that the human form of every man after death, is beautiful in proportion as his love and practice of divine truths is interior. The angels of the inmost heaven are consequently the most beautiful, because their love of truth is the deepest, and their lives are the most perfect. "I have seen," says Swedenborg, "the faces of angels of the third heaven, which were so beautiful, that no painter, with the utmost power of art, could depict even a thousandth part of their light and life; but the faces of the angels of the lowest heaven may, in some measure, be adequately depicted."

It is believed by many in the world that heaven is a place of idleness, full of refined sensual delights, of pleasant sights and harmonious sounds; in short, some such place as a laborious tradesman, struggling for a fortune, fancies he shall enjoy when his gains shall have enabled him to "*retire.*" But this is a great mistake. Man's nature remains the same in heaven as on earth; and who has not felt that his happiest moments are not those of mere pleasure and idleness, but those in which he was rendering himself most eminently useful? Happiness is as little consonant with idleness in heaven as on earth. Jesus himself said: "My Father worketh hitherto, and I work." John v. 17. The angels are employed. All the delights of heaven are conjoined with uses, and are inherent in them. In proportion to an angel's usefulness, is his bliss. Some spirits, we read, conceived the opinion that heavenly happiness consisted in a life of ease, and in being served by others; but they were told that happiness by no means consists in mere rest from employment, because every one would then desire to take away the happiness of others to promote his own; and since all would have the same desire, none would be happy; that such a life would not be active but indolent, and that indolence makes life torpid; and that without activity there can be no happiness, and that *cessation from employment is only for the sake of recreation*, that a man *may return*, with new vigor, to the *activity* of his life. They who entertained the idea that heavenly joy consists in a life of indolence, and sucking in eternal delight without employment, were allowed some experience of such a life; and they perceived that it is most sorrowful, and that all joy being destroyed, they would after a time loathe and nauseate it.

Some spirits who believed that heavenly joy consists solely in praising and celebrating God, were instructed that to praise and celebrate God is not properly an active life; and that God has no need of praise and celebration. The Lord's will is that all should perform uses; and the angels testify that in the performance of good works is the highest freedom, conjoined with ineffable delights.

From all this it follows that heaven is full of employments, in comparison with which those of the world are few. There are societies whose occupation consists in taking care of infants; other societies, whose employment is to instruct and educate them as they grow up; others which in like manner instruct and educate the young; others which instruct the simply good from the Christian world, and lead them in the ways of heaven; others which perform the same office to Gentile nations; others which defend novitiate spirits, or those who are newly arrived from the world, from the infestations of evil spirits; some also are attendant on those who are preparing in the world of spirits for heaven; and some are present with those who are in hell, to restrain them from tormenting each other beyond limit: there are also others who attend those who are being raised from the dead. In general, angels of every society are sent to men, that they may guard them, and withdraw them from evil affections and consequent evil thoughts, and inspire them with good affections, so far as they are willing to receive them. All these employments are performed by the Lord through their instrumentality; and hence it is that by *angels* in the Word, in its internal sense, are not meant *angels*, but something of the Lord; and for the same reason, *angels* in the Word are called *gods*.

These employments of the angels are their general employments, but every one has his own particular duty; for every general use is composed of innumerable others, which are called mediate, ministering, and subservient uses. But in heaven there are so many offices that it is impossible to enumerate them on account of their multitude. All angels feel delight in their employment derived from the love of use, and none from the love of self or of gain; nor is any one influenced by the love of gain for the sake of his maintenance, because all the necessaries of life are freely given them; their habitations, their clothes, their food.

It is De Quincey, we think, who accuses Swedenborg of sensualizing heaven, and reducing its sublime glories to the common order of things in this world. The assertion could only have been made through want of personal acquaintance with the writings of Swedenborg. No one can use the words, Isaiah lxiv. 4, quoted by the Apostle, 1 Cor. ii. 9: "Eye hath not seen, nor ear heard, neither have entered into the heart of man, the things which God hath prepared for them that love him," with more fervor and truth than the New Church preacher. Everywhere we are told by Swedenborg, that the joys and delights of heaven transcend the highest power of language to express; everywhere we are told that our highest ideas formed from natural things, fall indefinitely short of the common realities of the heavenly life. Yet we also learn that the common humanities and pleasures of this life are not lost in the next, and that as men and women we carry with us to our eternal home every faculty of thought and affection which we possess here. In this most rational doctrine there is gain every way. In thinking of heaven we know we can never overrate its bliss, think as we will; and yet with this idea is associated nothing of dreamy vagueness. We feel that as we live well we are but walking onwards to a pleasant home, in which all that is truest and best in this life will go with us. What stronger incentive can a man have to a pure and religious life than this divine faith. Entertaining it, with what feeling may he, at the close of life, utter the poets's words,—

> "Draw near, sweet death;
> Come raise me into life!"

The condition of admission into heaven is the possession of a soul whose existence is a continual fulfillment of those two commandments on which the Lord says, "hang all the law and the prophets"—love to God, and love to man. To enter heaven, we must habitually place self last, and our neighbor first; and unless we can do this, we can never know eternal bliss. Now we are born into this world selfish; and hence it is truly said we are hereditarily depraved. It is the Divine will to take all to heaven. To do this, it is necessary that we should be divested of our corrupt hereditary nature; as the Lord said to Nicodemus: "Verily, verily, I say unto thee, except a man be born again, he cannot see the kingdom of God." This regeneration of mind, this change from a supreme love of self, to a supreme love of God and our neighbor, is, of necessity, a gradual work. It is not accomplished in a day, nor in a month, nor in a year. Like all Divine works, it proceeds gradually, step by step; "first the blade, then the ear, after that the full corn in the ear." The regeneration of man is a Divine work, and as the Divine end in the creation of man was the formation of heaven out of the human race, the Lord's providence is unceasingly exerted to draw man out of evil, by all means consonant with the maintenance of the inalienable freedom of his will. It thus follows that the Lord, in all his dealings with man, has respect solely to his eternal state, and amid all the apparent accidents and vicissitudes of life, he is present, bending them and making them all conduce to man's everlasting peace. Life in this world, its cares, trials, pleasures, comforts, friendships, sympathies, and affections, form the divinely-appointed regenerative process; and those who will only believe this great truth, and submit to the Divine leading, will encounter nothing in life but what is good for them; and existence here, however bitter and painful at times, will resolve itself into a series of lessons devised by infinite wisdom to uproot all latent and known evils, transforming the patient sufferer into a true child of God. The Lord permits one man to be rich, powerful, and famous, and another to be afflicted with disease and perplexed with poverty; one to have a settled and calm peace of mind, while another is tried and tormented with doubts and anxieties; nor for any ultimate purpose on earth, but solely as a means of spiritual regeneration,—as a means of making man happy in the eternal life to come. All man's states are under the minute guardianship of the Lord; and each day comes round with its circle of pleasant and unpleasant occurrences, often, apparently, the result of accident and chance, but in truth all provided of the Divine Providence for the eradication of evil, and the growth and nurture of goodness. There is no trial encountered, no circumstance met, or cross endured, but has its eternal issue; and man's conduct in relation to it is looked upon by the Lord with a love and interest infinitely transcending our highest conception. All has been foreseen; and these daily recurring tasks are appointed by that wisdom which guides the stars in their courses, and by that love which requires eternity to satisfy the ardor with which it would bless.

With what dignity does such a faith clothe existence! What earnestness and celestial patience must it infuse into life!

From all that has now been said, it will be very evident that heaven is not a gift of immediate Divine mercy, to be obtained by a verbal confession of faith at the hour of death. If man could be saved by immediate mercy, all would be saved; even the inhabitants of hell, and hell itself would not exist; because the Lord is Mercy itself, Love itself, and Good itself, and wills the salvation of all, and the damnation of no one. But man's spirit is substantial; and if formed to evil, to change it would be equivalent to annihilation. "The angels declare that it were easier to change a bat into a dove, or an owl into a bird of paradise, than to change an infernal spirit into an angel of heaven." "Ample experience," writes Swedenborg, "enables me to testify that it is impossible to implant the life of heaven in those who have led an opposite life in the world. There were some who believed that they should easily receive divine truths after death, when they heard them from the angels; and that they would believe them then, amend their lives, and be received into heaven; and the experiment was made on great numbers of them, in order that they might be convincrd that repentance is not possible after death. Some understood the truths they heard, and seemed to receive them; but as soon as they returned to the life of their love, they rejected them, and even argued against them. Some rejected them instantly, from entire unwillingness to hear them; but others were desirous that *the life of the love they had contracted in the world, might be taken away from them; and that angelic life, the life of heaven, might be infused in its place.* This was permitted; but when the life of their love was taken away, they lay as if dead, and deprived of all their faculties. From this it was manifest that no one's life can possibly be changed after death, that evil life can not be changed into good life, nor the life of an infernal into that of an angel; because every spirit is from head to foot of the same quality as his love, and therefore of the same quality as his life; and consequently to transmute his life into its opposite is to destroy him altogether." All this goes to confirm the Lord's declaration before quoted, "Except a man be born again, he can not see the kingdom of God." On no other terms can heavenly bliss be gained.

We now come to speak of the World of Spirits, which Swedenborg thus defines: "The world of spirits is neither heaven nor hell, but an intermediate place or state between both, into which man enters immediately after death; and then after a certain period, the duration of which is determined by the quality of his life in the world, he is either elevated into heaven, or cast into hell.

"The spirits in the world of spirits are immensely numerous, because that world is the general assembly of all immediately after their resurrection, and all are examined there and prepared for their final abode; but the length of their sojourn in that world is not in all cases the same. Some only enter it, and are immediately taken up into heaven, or cast down into hell; some remain there a few weeks, and others several years, but none (since the Last Judgment,) more than thirty years."

A belief in the existence of an intermediate state has been entertained in all times and churches, except among Protestants, who, in their anxiety to divest themselves of every remnant of Popery, rejected the doctrine entirely, through aversion to the follies of Purgatory. A return to the truth is however slowly taking place; not a few Protestant divines having expressed their faith in the existence of Hades, or the intermediate state alluded to in the literal sense of Scripture. But the world of spirits is not to be thought of as a revived idea of Purgatory. The soul of no man is changed in the world of spirits. "As the tree falls so it lies." The discipline of this life is perfected at death, and its opportunities never return. The world of spirits is a place where the externals of man are brought into correspondence with his internals; for no one, either in heaven or in hell, is allowed to have a divided mind, understanding one thing and willing another. What any one wills, he must understand, and what he understands he must will; therefore he who wills good in heaven, must understand truth; and he who wills evil in hell, must understand falsities. On this account also, falses are removed from the good in the world of spirits, and there are given them truths which agree and harmonize with their good; but truths are removed from the evil, and they take to themselves falses which agree and harmonize with their evil. Let us explain this subject further.

We suppose the generality of our readers will admit that countless thousands of good men and women among the Mahommedans, Chinese, Hindoos, and all the heathen nations, who live according to the measure of their light, are saved and taken to heaven. But it is very evident that they can not go to heaven carrying with them false notions on religious subjects, and knowing nothing of that good Lord into whose kingdom they are about to pass. They must be instructed. They must have errors removed from their minds, and truths implanted in their stead. Time is required to effect these changes, and the world of spirits is the school in which the process is accomplished. Instruction in truth is readily received by the simply good; and after being enlightened and purified from falsity, they are led to their eternal homes among the blessed—to those of a disposition and order of mind like themselves.

Then, again, among Christians, there are many who die with slight failings pertaining to them, with infirmities of temper, with bad habits of one kind and another; yet who are really sound-hearted and good men. Their lot can not be hell; yet with these flaws in their character, their presence in heaven could not be pleasant, because their state of mind is at variance with the perfect order and peace of heaven. Such, then, remain in the world of spirits, passing through trials, and temptations, and sufferings, until they reject all that is disorderly and impure. The processes by which this removal of external evils is accomplished, are frequently extremely painful, and extend over many years. Their removal might with less difficulty have been accomplished in the present life. The Lord warns us of this in these words: "Agree with thine adversary quickly, while thou art in the way with him; lest at any time the adversary deliver thee to the judge, and the judge deliver thee to the officer, and thou be cast into prison. Verily I say unto thee, Thou shalt by no means come out thence till thou hast paid the uttermost farthing." Matthew v. 25, 26. Our adversary is the truth. Truth is ever an adversary to the evil. Elijah the prophet represented the Divine Truth. When he approached the wicked Ahab, Ahab cried: "Hast thou found me, O mine enemy?" "In the way with him" is in the present life; and the "prison" is the world of spirits, often so called in the Word, out of which we shall not be delivered until entirely divested of selfish affections, and false principles of thought. How practical, thus viewed, becomes our Lord's advice! But without a knowledge of the world of spirits, and the spiritual sense of Scripture, it is quite mystical and unintelligible.

There are many in the Christian world who have confirmed their minds in false ideas on many religious doctrines. With such erroneous ideas they can not enter heaven, where truth alone prevails. They therefore remain in the world of spirits until, through instruction, they see and reject the false persuasions they had contracted on earth. In some cases, where false doctrine has been deeply reasoned upon, and ground, as it were, into the mind, the process of its removal and rejection is attended with deep and prolonged suffering.

As the good reject all false ideas in the world of spirits, so the evil cast off all true ones. It may be asked, Why? Why should bad be made worse? Bad is not made worse. It is for the peace of the evil themselves that they should be divested of all truth. The presence of truth with the wicked only adds to their torment by the continual protest it makes against their sin. It is also well that the evil lose all truth, for the sake of the good, whom they might trouble and disturb through the power that truth would afford them to assume an angelic appearance; to become wolves in sheep's clothing; or as Paul states it, "Satan transforming himself into an angel of light." Hypocrites, who have used truth to subserve their own selfish ends, remain longer than others in the world of spirits, and endure much suffering ere they allow their means of subtlety and mischief to depart from them. The process of divesting the evil of the truths they possess, is described by the Lord in these words: "Take heed, therefore, how ye hear: for whosoever hath, to him shall be given; and whosoever hath not, from him shall be taken even that which he seemeth to have." Luke viii. 18. What is heard is truth. The good alone have truth, for their goodness loves truth, and cherishes it. Truth thus loved, multiplies; therefore it is said, "more shall be given." The bad may have truth in their memory, may use it for selfish purposes, and talk much about it; nevertheless it is not theirs. Their internal evil hates it. "Every one that doeth evil hateth the light;" and in the future life the truth which he seemed to have, is taken from him. How just, and at the same time how merciful, is this judgment!

Hell is the congregation of all evil spirits. As there are many heavens, so likewise there are many hells. As the inhabitants of heaven are arranged from similarity of goodness and truth, so the inhabitants of hell are arranged from similarity of evil and falsity. The hells are arranged so distinctly according to the differences of evil, that nothing more orderly and distinct can be conceived. The Lord, speaking through David, says: Psalm lxxxvi. 13: "Thou hast delivered my soul from the *lowest hell.*" Thus from Scripture we derive a direct proof, if proof were wanted, of the gradations of evil. There are several other texts to the same effect.

The scenery of hell, like that of heaven, is in perfect correspondence with the states of those there. It is an outbirth from the minds of its inhabitants; and as *they* are deformed and full of every pollution, so their scenery is full of horrors and things abominable. "In hell there is no sun, but the inhabitants roam in darkness corresponding to themselves, for they are darkness: their light is artificial, as of coal fires, meteors, ignes fatui, and the lights of night. They inhabit scenery of which they are the souls, as bogs, fens, tangled forests, caverns, dreary deserts, charred and ruined cities. In the milder hells, there appear, as it were, rude cottages, which are in some cases contiguous, and resemble the streets and lanes of a city. Within the houses infernal spirits are engaged in continual quarrels, enmities, blows, and violences, while the streets and lanes are full of robberies and depredations. The inhabitants are at continual war, hating and tormenting one another, and the cruelties they practice are indescribable." "It is impossible to give a description of the horrible forms of the spirits of hell. No two are alike, although there is a general likeness in those who are in the same evil. They are forms of contempt of others, of menace against those who do not pay them respect, of hatreds of various kinds, and of revenge; and in these forms, outrage and cruelty are transparent from within; but when others commend, venerate, and worship them, their faces are drawn up, and have an appearance of gladness arising from delight. Some of their faces are direful and void of life, like corpses; some are black, and others fiery, like torches; others are disfigured by pimples, warts, and ulcers; and frequently no face appears, but instead of a face something hairy and bony, and sometimes nothing but teeth. Their bodies are monstrous, and their speech is the speech of anger, of hatred, of revenge; for every one speaks from his own false, and the tone of his voice is from his own evil. In a word they are all images of their own hell."

"And does Swedenborg relate such horrors?" some may ask. For facts, we answer, Swedenborg is not to blame. Like the Israelites of old, we would fain have our prophets "speak unto us smooth things." Let us rid ourselves of all morbid delicacy, and seek to know the truth. We should all do well to peruse with patience those pages wherein our author narrates the horrors of hell, so that we may see, shun, and detest the evils which make hell. It is well that every man should know whither his lust, his pride, his avarice, or anger, is leading him. If he shudder, it is for his eternal good.

The universal hell, like heaven, is as one man,—not of beauty, as heaven, but a hideous monster. In its collective capacity, it is the Devil and Satan; the Devil is the name of its evil, and Satan is the name of its falsity. There is no individual evil spirit ruling hell, and bearing either of those names. An enlightened view of Scripture confirms this doctrine in every point, and rids us of the innumerable absurdities which the commonly received theory in regard to the Devil involves. There is no spirit in hell who was not once a man on earth. There is no spirit in hell who was ever an angel in heaven. The Lord himself rules the hells, and by all means possible restrains their violence and mitigates their suffering.

Some people believe that God turns away his face from man, rejects him, and casts him into hell, and that he is angry with him on account of his evils; and others go still further, and affirm that God punishes man, and brings evil upon him. They also confirm this opinion from the literal sense of the Word, in which expressions occur that appear to sustain it. But these opinions are formed through ignorance of the real sense of these passages, and from a blind neglect of others, the literal sense of which teaches that God is goodness and mercy itself, and that fury is not in him. Isaiah xxvii. 4. True doctrine declares that the Lord never turns away his face from man, never rejects him, never casts any one into hell, and is never angry. The Lord is continually withdrawing man from evil and leading him to goed; but man's freedom is never taken away. If man *will love* evil and *will do* perversely, the Lord does not prevent. That man should go to hell is at variance with the Divine design; but to infringe man's freedom would be to destroy his life and take from him all that is human, reducing him to the level of a machine or a brute. Those who are in hell, cast themselves down thither, and keep themselves where they are. "This is," as Wilkinson says, "the last dogma of free will,—that of a finite being perpetuating for ever his own evil, standing fast to selfishness without end, excluding Omnipotence in all its dispensations, and making the 'will not' into an everlasting 'cannot,' to maintain itself out of heaven, and contrary to heaven."

This is a very brief abstract of the leading ideas in Swedenborg's wondrous treatise on Heaven and Hell. We are well aware how far short it falls of doing full justice to the work. Let us hope that what has been said may induce some to make a personal acquaintance with it; and then they will understand the difficulties we labor under in condensing within a few pages its multitudinous facts and closely linked logic.

It remains only to add, that the treatise on Heaven and Hell has been translated into English, French, and German. The English editions have been many, and in some cases large. The latest may be accepted as a sign of the times, being in the form of an eighteen-penny volume, a second edition of which has been called for. We lay no claim to the gift of prophecy, but we feel certain that the time is coming when Swedenborg's "Heaven and Hell" will be the most popular and extensively read of religious books.

CHAPTER XIV.

The White Horse—The Earths in the Universe—The New Jerusalem and its Heavenly Doctrine.

1. THE treatise on the White Horse mentioned in the Apocalypse, forms a tract of about twenty pages. It is an exposition of the spiritual sense of Revelation xix. 11–16. It is shown that by the heavens being opened, the White Horse, and its rider, are represented the Lord and his Word, and the quality of those to whom the internal truth of the Word is revealed. The particulars of the text are all gone into and expounded, and copious references made to the Arcana Cœlestia for fuller details. It is to be noted that voluminous as are Swedenborg's theological works, that they form one harmonious whole bound together in the unity of truth, and mutually confirming each other. Literature, we believe, contains no example of so great a mass of writing permeated with such a consistent spirit, and so little affected by the author's humors and fluctuations of mood. So far does this uniform spirit extend, that, had it been possible, we might imagine his many volumes had been struck out of thought in one short day, instead of being written continuously through a course of nearly thirty years.

In this small treatise we have a list of the books in our Bible which form the true *Word of God.* They are, in the Old Testament, the five books of Moses; the book of Joshua; the book of Judges; the two books of Samuel; the two books of Kings; the Psalms of David; the Prophets, Isaiah, Jeremiah, the Lamentations, Ezekiel, Daniel, Hosea, Joel, Amos, Obadiah, Jonah, Micah, Nahum, Habakkuk, Zephaniah, Haggai, Zechariah, Malachi; and, in the New Testament, the four Evangelists, Matthew, Mark, Luke, and John: and the Revelation. The rest have not the internal sense, and are not to be regarded as a part of the inspired Word. We shall have to speak of the plenary inspiration of the Word, when we come to Swedenborg's treatise on the Sacred Scripture, and show how broad is the line of distinction between the Word of God and the writings of men. It requires but a slight acquaintance with the doctrine of correspondences, to perceive that this distinction between the books contained within the covers of the authorized version of the Bible is not arbitrary; that it is a distinction as marked and visible as that between God and man, or nature and art. Apart, however, from the doctrine of correspondences, the distinction may be sustained by the authority of the Jews, and the indirect testimony of many of the Fathers of the Christian Church, coupled with numerous natural reasons founded on a critical examination of style, etc.

"The book of Job," says Swedenborg, "was a book of the Ancient Church," and therefore, with the exception of the first chapters of Genesis, is the oldest portion of the Bible. It has a kind of internal sense, but not like that of the Word.

The exclusion of the Epistles from the Books of the Word, is perhaps, to a new reader, the most startling of Swedenborg's announcements. For this exclusion and its reasons, we will simply quote his own words. Writing to Dr. Beyer, he says: "With regard to the writings of St. Paul, and the other Apostles, I have not given them a place in my 'Arcana Cœlestia,' because they are dogmatic writings merely, and are not written in the style of the Word, as are those of the Prophets, of David, of the Evangelists, and of the Revelation of St. John. The style of the Word consists throughout in correspondences, and thence effects immediate communication with heaven; but the style of these dogmatic writings is quite different, having, indeed, communication with heaven, but only mediately or indirectly. The reason why the Apostles wrote in this style, was, that the First Christian Church was then to begin through them; consequently, the same style as is used in the Word would not have been proper for such doctrinal tenets, which required plain and simple language, suited to the capacities of all readers. Nevertheless, the writings of the Apostles are very good books for the Church, inasmuch as they insist on the doctrine of charity, and faith from charity, as strongly as the Lord himself has done in the Gospels, and the Revelation of St. John, as will appear evidently to any one who studies these writings with attention."

2. The treatise on the "Earths in the Universe" is formed from several of those portions of the "Arcana Cœlestia," occurring between the chapters, expository of the spiritual sense of Genesis and Exodus. It forms a pamphlet of about fifty pages.

Many and prolonged have been the discussions as to whether other planets are, like our own, the abodes of human beings. Great as has been the progress of astronomical science, the learned are yet far from being unanimous on the question, as is evident from the recent controversy between Prof. Whewell and Sir David Brewster. Swedenborg does not entertain us with prolix reasonings as to whether or not the earths of the universe are inhabited. That was a question far too trivial for his masculine understanding. He saw that these vast spaces were not formed by the Lord, except for the highest end, the creation of a heaven of intelligent human beings, capable of satisfying the infinite desires of Divine Love. The earths of the universe are peopled even as our own globe, or are in course of preparation for it. Any other view than this is unworthy of acceptance, and dishonorable to the highest truths of reason and revelation.

Swedenborg was permitted to see, and hold converse with, the inhabitants of other earths; and most interesting are his relations concerning them. Wilkinson aptly remarks that the work now under consideration "may be characterized as a Report on the Religion of the Universe." Swedenborg tells us that the dwellers in these distant spheres think of the Lord and worship him. He describes the quality of their love and wisdom, and how they conduct themselves toward each other. It is a pleasant thought that the people of this world are the worst of humanity, the most sensual, and the least abounding in true intelligence and spirituality. In other words there is sin, and its consequent suffering, arising from the same cause as with us; but it is not so deep nor so wide spread. The fact of the Divine Incarnation is likewise known in other worlds, and is regarded as the great truth of faith.

Swedenborg affirms that the moon is inhabited. We know that even those scientific men who hold to the doctrine of a plurality of worlds, do not believe in the habitability of the moon; because, say they, it lacks alike water and atmosphere. To say that it has no atmosphere is very unphilosophical. The atmosphere may not be of the same density as that of our earth; but that it should have no sphere or aura around it, we cannot for a moment believe. Swedenborg tells us that the Lunarians are dwarfs, like boys of seven years old, with robust bodies and pleasant countenances. They do not speak from their lungs, on account of the attenuated nature of their atmosphere, but from a quantity of air collected in the abdomen.

It is but just to state that Swedenborg speaks of Saturn as the outermost planet of the solar system, he not being permitted to anticipate Herschel or Neptune. An opponent might make merry over this, and say: "Don't you see that Swedenborg was but a dreamer? How could he know aught of the inhabitants of other earths when he did not even know that beyond Saturn rolled two immense worlds?" We reply, that it would have been disorderly for him to have become possessed of such knowledge by spiritual means. "But how so?" Because it would have compelled belief in the spiritual doctrines he taught, without due thought and examination, as soon as science had established the existence of these orbs; because miracles and prophecy are not permitted in these times, for they force and destroy man's freedom. How easy it would be for the Lord to witness to the truth of His Word by supernatural signs in the natural world! Yet he does not, although belief in his Word, and life according to it, is essential to man's highest happiness. Belief so induced would be worthless, because compelled. It may be said that this is mere special pleading; but it is not so. The laws laid down in a later work of Swedenborg's, on the "Divine Providence," fortify, in a most rational manner, the truth as we have endeavoured to set it forth. It is also to be remarked that natural truth must be discovered by its appropriate means,—natural investigation. It was necessary that Swedenborg should be skilled in all natural science previous to his illumination, so that he might possess a basis for many spiritual facts which could neither have been expressed nor made intelligible without at the same time giving their correspondence in nature. It would have been altogether contrary to the Divine order to have taken Swedenborg in his early youth and ignorance, and, making him a seer, have communicated natural truth to him in a supernatural manner.

3. "The New Jerusalem and its Heavenly Doctrine" is a brief exposition of the leading truths of the New Church.

After each of its chapters follow references, (in some cases more extensive than the chapter itself,) to the "Arcana Cœlestia." These references, so numerous in Swedenborg's writings, do not form a dry and unreadable index, but may be looked on as a series of precepts pertaining to moral and spiritual life. Were we gathering a volume of gems of thought, we should find an abundance to suit our purposes in these references.

This work has been printed as a cheap pamphlet. We know of no other work which could more appropriately be placed in the hands of a stranger desiring to know, without much reading, the nature of those doctrines which Swedenborg was commissioned to reveal to the world.

CHAPTER XV.

Anecdotes.

THE trite observation that the lives of literary men are devoid of those incidents which make up a stirring and lively biography, applies with great truth to the career of Swedenborg. His quiet and unostentatious life afforded but few materials for anecdotes; hence we have but faint traces of his outward course. While writing the works we have just noticed, from 1747 to 1758, the principal portion of his time must have been passed in London. Few men in those days were capable of sympathy or communion with the elevated and spiritualized mind of Swedenborg. Yet though living as it were alone, he could not have been melancholy or desolate. Under the care and guidance of the Lord, favored with the company and converse of angels, and enjoying the consciousness of fulfilling high and holy duties, he had every reason to be the cheerful and contented man that contemporary testimony represents him. His evenings he used often to spend with his printer, Mr. Hart, of Poppin's court, Fleet street. Mrs. Lewis, his publisher's wife, knew him, and "thought him a good and sensible man, but too apt to spiritualize things." Beyond a few particulars such as these, we know nothing of his private life.

On the 19th of July, 1759, we find Swedenborg at Gottenburg. Here occurred the following circumstance, of which Immanuel Kant, the celebrated transcendentalist, is the narrator.

"On Saturday, at 4 o'clock, P. M.," says Kant, "when Swedenborg arrived at Gottenburg from England, Mr. William Castel invited him to his house, together with a party of fifteen persons. About 6 o'clock, Swedenborg went out, and after a short interval returned to the company, quite pale and alarmed. He stated that a dangerous fire had just broken out in Stockholm, at Sundermalm, (distant three hundred miles from Gottenburg,) and that it was spreading very fast. He was restless, and went out often. He said that the house of one of his friends, whom he named, was already in ashes, and that his own was in danger. At 8 o'clock, after he had been out again, he joyfully exclaimed: 'Thank God! the fire is extinguished the third door from my house.' This news occasioned great commotion among the company. It was announced to the governor the same evening. The next morning, Swedenborg was sent for by the governor, who questioned him concerning the disaster. Swedenborg described the fire precisely, how it had begun, in what manner it had ceased, and how long it had continued. On the same day the news was spread through the city; and as the governor had thought it worthy of attention, the consternation was considerably increased, as many were in trouble on account of their friends and property, which might have been involved in the disaster. On Monday evening, a messenger arrived at Gottenburg, who was despatched during the time of the fire. In the letters brought by him, the fire was described precisely in the manner stated by Swedenborg. On Tuesday morning, a royal courier arrived at the governor's with the melancholy intelligence of the fire, of the loss it had occasioned, and of the houses damaged and ruined, not in the least differing from that which Swedenborg had given the moment it had ceased: the fire had been extinguished at 8 o'clock.

"What," continues Kant, "can be brought forward against

the authenticity of this occurrence? My friend who wrote this to me, has not only examined the circumstances of this extraordinary case at Stockholm, but also, about two months ago, at Gottenburg, where he is acquainted with the most respectable houses, and where he could obtain the most authentic and complete information, as the greatest part of the inhabitants, who are still alive, were witnesses to the memorable occurrence."

This narrative is taken from a letter written by Kant, in 1768, to Charlotte de Knobloch, a lady of quality. Kant, it may be remarked, was no adherent of Swedenborg's. Two years before writing this letter, he had attacked him in a small work entitled, "Dreams of the Great Seer Illustrated by Dreams of Metaphysics." Received from such a source, we can entertain no doubt as to the truth of the story.

At home, in Stockholm, Swedenborg did not fail to excite much curiosity and attention, and his conduct and deportment were carefully watched. It was observed that he seldom went to church, or received the sacrament. This was owing partly to the contrariety of the Lutheran doctrine to his own views, and partly, Robsahm says, to the disease of the stone, which troubled him. In 1760, two bishops, his relations, remonstrated with him in a friendly manner upon his remissness. He answered, that, religious observances were not so necessary for him as for others, as he was associated with angels. They then represented that his example would be valuable, by which argument he suffered himself to be persuaded. A few days previously to receiving the sacrament, he asked his old domestics to whom he should resort for the purpose, for "he was not much acquainted with the different preachers." The elder chaplain was mentioned. Swedenborg objected that "he was a passionate man and a fiery zealot, and that he had heard him thundering from the pulpit with little satisfaction." The assistant chaplain was then proposed, who was not so popular with the congregation. Swedenborg said, "I prefer him to the other, for I hear that he speaks what he thinks, and by this means has lost the good-will of his people, as generally happens in this world." Accordingly he took the sacrament from this curate.

"In general," says Robsahm, "Swedenborg would not enter into dispute on matters of religion. If he was necessitated to defend himself, he did it with mildness and in a few words; but if any one would not be convinced, and became warm in argument, he retired, saying, 'Read my writings attentively and without prejudice; they will answer you in my stead, and will afford you reason to change your ideas and opinions on such things.'

"He used, at first, freely to speak of his visions and spiritual explications of the Scriptures; but as this displeased the clergy, who proclaimed him a heretic and madman, he resolved to be less communicative of his knowledge in company, or, at least, more cautious, lest the censorious should have room to blame what they could not comprehend like himself. I once," says Robsahm, "addressed the rector of the parish where he lived, an old and respected clergyman, asking him what he thought of Swedenborg's visions and explanations of the Bible. The venerable man answered: 'God alone can judge of this; but I can not think him to be such a person as many do; I have myself conversed with him, and in company where we have been together, and I have found him to be a good and a holy man.'

"It was remarkable that Swedenborg never endeavored to persuade any person to receive his opinions. He was in nowise led by that self-love which is observable in those who publish new opinions concerning church doctrines; neither did he seek to make many proselytes, not even communicating his thoughts and sentiments, except to those whom he thought virtuous, disposed to hear them with moderation, capable of comprehending them, and lovers of truth.

"It is a very singular circumstance," continues Robsahm, "that all who have read the writings of Swedenborg, with a desire to refute them, have finished the attempt by adhering to his sentiments." This assertion must be received, however, with qualification.

Though busied with the composition of his works, and immersed in spiritual contemplations, Swedenborg was not forgetful of the world and of his duties to his country. In 1761 he took part in the Swedish Diet or Parliament. Three of his memorials or addresses to the Diet, are preserved. In the first of these he congratulates the House upon its meetings, and counsels the redress of all grievances which cause disaffection. In the second he advocates an alliance with France instead of England from prudential motives, at the same time strongly protesting against the evil of despotic governments, and the danger to liberty in the extension of the Roman Catholic faith. The third memorial is on the subject of finance. Count Hopken, the Swedish prime minister at that time, leaves on record that "the most solid memorials, and the best penned, at the Diet of 1761, on matters of finance, were presented by Swedenborg; in one of which he refuted a large work in 4to on the same subject, quoted the corresponding passages of it, and all in less than one sheet." He was likewise a member of the secret committee of the Diet, an office to which only the most sage and virtuous were elected. Consider, reader, for a moment, the dignity, the wisdom, and the abounding common sense which must have permeated the whole being of Swedenborg, to enable him to live down the obloquy attached to the name of a "ghost-seer," and be received with high favor and acceptance by men of the world, sceptical and sensual!

Soon afterwards Swedenborg left Stockholm; and we find him in July, 1762, at Amsterdam. Jung Stilling received from a friend the following interesting anecdote respecting him at this time. "I was in Amsterdam," says he, "in 1762, in a company in which Swedenborg was present, on the very day that Peter III., Emperor of Russia, died. In the midst of our conversation his countenance changed, and it was evident that his soul was no longer there, and that something extraordinary was passing in him. As soon as he came to himself again, he was asked what had happened to him. He would not at first communicate it; but at length, after having been repeatedly pressed, he said: 'This very hour, the Emperor Peter III. has died in his prison,' mentioning at the same time the manner of his death. 'Gentlemen will please to note down the day, that they may be able to compare it with the intelligence of his death in the newspapers.' The newspapers subsequently announced the Emperor's death as having taken place on that day."

CHAPTER XVI.

Doctrines of the Lord—The Sacred Scripture, Faith, and Life.

In 1763, Swedenborg published, at Amsterdam, the following works:—1. The Doctrine of the New Jerusalem respecting the Lord; 2. The Sacred Scripture; 3. Faith; 4. Life; 5. Continuation respecting the Last Judgment and the Destruction of Babylon; and 6. Angelic Wisdom concerning the Divine Love and the Divine Wisdom. We will now speak of these works seriatim.

1. The Doctrine of the New Jerusalem concerning the Lord, is a small treatise: but within its limits is concentrated so much light and rationality, that we might say the question it deals with was finally settled, did we not too well know the perversity and pertinacity of theological error, in closing the mind against the perception of truth, though it were manifested with angelic wisdom.

The great truth in the treatise is the Supreme Divinity of the Lord Jesus Christ. This truth is brought forth from the collation of nearly every passage of Scripture which, in the literal sense, bears upon the subject. It is shown, by an invincible logic, that there is but one God; and that, in the Bible itself, the doctrine of three persons in the Godhead is not to be found. It is then shown that God the Lord, in the fullness of time, came to earth, and put on human nature, or became incarnate. The object sought to be effected by the incarnation, was the salvation of man. From the days of Adam, mankind had been treading a downward path.

Through wickedness, all true faith and spirituality had perished. Hell had drawn near to men, even to the possession of their bodies, as we read in the Gospels. Isaiah describes the state of mankind thus: "Hell hath enlarged herself, and opened her mouth without measure." Humanity was thus hastening to destruction, and final extinction. But the Lord Jehovah interposed. Clothing himself with an arm of flesh, he met the powers of hell on their own ground; and rendering himself accessible to their attacks, in a series of the most direful temptation-combats, He reduced Hell to order, and redeemed mankind forever from the absolute dominion of devils. But this was not all. The human nature that the Lord had assumed, full of hereditary corruption, was taken from the race of Jewish kings, the most depraved and perverted to be found on earth. He purified, glorified, and made it divine, ascending with it to heaven. The new influences flowing through the medium of this Divine Humanity, are called the Holy Spirit. Of the truth of this we have the most convincing proof in John vii. 39, where it is said, "the Holy Ghost was *not yet, because* Jesus was not yet glorified."

From this it is very evident that the Trinity is not, as commonly taught, a Trinity of persons, but of principles. In ourselves we see a finite image of this Divine and Infinite Trinity. The soul of man may be taken as the representative of Jehovah; his body represents the Divine Humanity, or Jesus Christ; and his action or influence on others corresponds to the Holy Spirit. Regarded in this light, that most mystical and incomprehensible dogma of three Persons, and yet one God, is annihilated, and we come into the enjoyment of a faith at once scriptural, intelligible, and rational. It is impossible for us here to go into the details of this doctrine, or give even an outline of its proofs. To an earnest seeker after truth we can conceive no pleasure exceeding an acquaintance with this treatise on the Lord. If, especially, he has vexed and worn himself in reading the profitless controversies and lucubrations of learned divines on the Trinity, his fretted and heated mind will experience a spiritual relief similar to the natural one which results when patience has become exhausted in vain endeavors to unfasten a lock, and a skilled mechanic draws near, takes the work out of our hands, and with dexterity and ease accomplishes the task in a moment. Swedenborg lays his hand on the tangled mass of mysticism and perverted Scripture, and straightway the Gordian knot is untied. The simplicity of explanation fills us with amazement, and we wonder that it was never done before.

2. The Doctrine of the New Jerusalem respecting the Sacred Scripture, next demands our attention. The primary truth of this treatise is, that the Sacred Scripture, or the Word, is Divine Truth itself, thus the Lord himself. Let us see how this can be.

We are too apt to abstract books from their authors, and to regard them as matters impersonal,—as type and paper merely. Now this is a childish error, and a proof of the loose and external way in which we are accustomed to think. When I speak, or write, I manifest spiritual influences; and the force of these influences is proportionate to my earnestness, and their effect is proportionate to the state of reception of my hearers. Words are thus perceived to be the representatives of spiritual forces. The action of spirit on spirit is inappreciable by the senses; but could we look behind the vail of nature when a crowd or a congregation is swayed hither and thither by the speech of one man, we should see that the influence exerted was as real and actual as muscular force. From this we learn that words are not mere sounds, but are the sheaths or cases of spiritual life, and on this ground we at once see the force of the Lord's declaration, "The words that I speak unto you, they are spirit, and they are life." John vi. 63.

When we think of the Lord's words, we must conjoin with the thought an idea of the Divine Nature and Attributes. The Lord's speech being the manifestation of His life, must partake of its every quality, thus of infinity and of independence of time, and consequently of adaptation to every possible condition of mind, for infinity includes all. Bearing these facts in mind, we can easily perceive how true it is that the Word is the Lord Himself.

But while the Word in its inmost is the Lord, and is thus infinite, yet as apprehended by man, who is finite, it necessarily wears a finite aspect. It is plain that as man's ideas become sensualized and bound down to matter, his view of the Divine Truth, or Word, must involve many illusions; true, certainly, in relation to him, but very far removed from the absolute Divine Truth. Now the literal sense of the Word, as we read it in our Bibles, is the presentation, if we may so phrase it, of the aspect of the Lord to the natural man, whose senses constitute his court of appeal. The Jews, to whom the Word in its literal sense was delivered, were just such men.

Above this natural state of mind, there are two marked grades of intelligence—the spiritual and celestial. To these, the Lord's words bear a far wider meaning, and are more fully instinct with the glory of the Divine Wisdom, and the warmth of the Divine Love.

It is thus said that the Word of God has three senses—the natural, the spiritual, and the celestial. We attribute these senses to the Word: more correctly we should charge them to the universal human mind, whose capacity of reception they express. To no two men, or angels, does the Lord,—or in fact anything,—bear precisely the same appearance, or suggest the same meaning.

These three grades, separated by discrete degrees, make up the universe of humanity; and the enlightened eye of the true philosopher may trace in every object of external creation an image and representation of them. But space forbids further explanation on this head; our author's reasoning is, moreover, so closely linked as to admit of no curtailment. Suffice to say, that after demonstrating the existence of an internal sense in the Scripture, he proceeds to show the many uses of the literal sense, and, at the same time, the manifold abuses to which it is liable, when the laws by which it is written are not understood.

Accepting the sublime philosophy of this treatise, we find in it a perfect refuge from the attacks of the sceptic, and discover a thousand reasons for one we had before, for loving God's Holy Book, trusting in its wisdom, and committing our lives to its guidance.

3. The Doctrine of Faith of the New Jerusalem, may be best understood by a few extracts from the treatise itself. Swedenborg writes: "The idea attached to the term faith at the present day is this, that it consists in thinking a thing to be so, because it is taught by the church, and because it does not fall within the scope of the understanding. For it is usual with those who inculcate it, to say, 'You must believe, and not doubt.' If you answer: 'I do not comprehend it,' it is replied: 'That is the very circumstance which makes a doctrine an object of faith.' Thus the faith of the present day is a faith in what is not known, and may be called a blind faith: and as being the dictate of one person abiding in the mind of another, it is a historical faith. But this is not spiritual faith.

"Genuine faith is an acknowledgment that a thing is so, because it is true. For he who is in genuine faith thinks and speaks to this effect:—'This is true; and therefore I believe it.' For faith is the assurance with which we e nbrace that which is true; and that which is true is the proper object of faith. A person of this character, also, if he does not comprehend a sentiment, and see its truth, will say: 'I do not know whether this is true or not; therefore I do not yet believe it. How can I believe what I do not comprehend? Perhaps it may be false.'

"But the common language is, that nobody can comprehend things of a spiritual or theological nature, because they transcend our natural faculties. Spiritual truths, however, are as capable of being comprehended as natural truths. The reason that spiritual things admit of being comprehenedd, is, because man, as to his understanding, is capable of being elevated into the light of heaven, in which light no other objects appear than such as are spiritual.

"Hence now it is that those who are in the spiritual affection of truth, enjoy an internal acknowledgment of it. As the angels are in that affection, they utterly reject the tenet that the understanding ought to be kept in subjection to faith: for they say, 'How can you believe a thing, when you do not see whether it is true or not?' And should any one affirm that what he advances must nevertheless be believed, they reply: 'Do you think yourself a God, that I am to believe you? or that I am mad, that I should believe an assertion in which I do not see any truth? If I must believe it, cause me to see it.' The dogmatizer is thus constrained to retire. Indeed, the wisdom of the angels consists solely in this, that they see and comprehend what they think.

"There is a spiritual idea of which few have any knowledge, which enters by influx into the minds of those who are in the affection of truth, and dictates interiorly whether the thing which they are hearing or reading is true or not. In this idea are those who read the Word in illumination from the Lord. To be in illumination is to be in perception.

Those who are in this illumination are said to be taught of Jehovah, and of them it is said in Jeremiah: 'Behold, the days come that I will make a new covenant:—this shall be the covenant,—I will put my law in their inward parts, and write it in their hearts; and they shall teach no more every man his neighbor, and every man his brother, saying, Know ye the Lord; for they shall all know me.' xxxi. 31, 33, 34.

"From these considerations it is plain that faith and truth are one. This also is the reason that the ancients, who were more accustomed to think of truth from affection than the moderns, instead of faith used the word truth: and for the same reason, in the Hebrew language, truth and faith are expressed by one and the same word, amuna, or amen.

"If any one thinks with himself, or says to another, 'Who can have that internal acknowledgment of truth which is faith? I can not.' I will tell him how he may. Shun evils as sins, and apply to the Lord; then you will have as much as you desire."

Such then is the New Church doctrine of faith. Faith is the perception and acknowledgment of truth from a right understanding of it. True faith is something that grows. It is not the gift of a moment. It is attained by leading a good life, and through obedience to the truth so far as we know it. In the course of time we find that a pure life is clearing our spiritual vision, and extending its range. Spiritual truths which we had laid up in our memories, and perhaps fancied that we had believed, are brought forth, are seen in new and striking light, are elevated into the understanding, and are in reality believed. Thus a living faith is attained. This doctrine finds a Divine seal in these words of the Lord: "If any man will do his will, he shall know of the doctrine, whether it be of God." John vii. 17.

The remainder of this little treatise is taken up with an

exposure of the fallacies involved in the common doctrines of faith prevailing in the Protestant and Roman Catholic churches. Faith separated from charity, is proved to have no existence, because evil can by no possibility love truth. Spiritual and Divine Truth may, it is true, be reasoned upon, defended, and expounded, by wicked men, for the promotion of their own selfish ends; but internally they are in deep hatred and denial of them, and in the other life their detestation of them causes them to cast them forth even from the memory. Thus the wicked have no faith and no truth.

4. The treatise on the Doctrine of Life is a brief and compendious exposition of the nature of that life which leads to heaven and happiness. In the first place, it asserts that all religion has relation to life, and that the life of religion is to do good; agreeable to the Lord's saying: "He that hath my commandments and keepeth them, he it is that loveth me." John xiii. 17. It is then shown that no one can do good, which is really good, from himself, as is taught in John, where we read: "A man can receive nothing, except it be given him from heaven," iii. 27; and again: "He that abideth in me, and I in him, the same bringeth forth much fruit; for without me ye can do nothing;"—"He that abideth in me, and I in him, the same bringeth forth much fruit," signifies that all good is from the Lord; fruit signifies good: "without me ye can do nothing," signifies that no one can do good from himself.

Now, it may be asked, "Why can a man not do good of himself?" For this simple reason, that, as there is no goodness out of the Lord, if man does good, his power and disposition to do it must, in all certainty, be derived from the Lord alone. Man, in his highest state, is but a medium for the manifestation of the Divine Life or Goodness. Yet while only a medium, he must act in freedom, as of himself.

The appearance is that the good he does is self-originated, and born of his own will; and this appearance can never be removed, because on it depends his freedom of action. Man must subdue all tendencies to spiritual pride arising therefrom, by habitual reference to the truth that the Lord is all in all; and that if he has done good, or been useful, he has been indebted for the motive as well as for the wisdom, to the Divine Mercy alone; as Paul said to the Philippians: "For it is God which worketh in you *both to will and to do* of his good pleasure." ii. 15. While thus saved by the Divine Mercy, through a good life, and brought into spiritual health by obedience to divine laws, man has no reason whatever to boast, or to take credit to himself for his bliss and salvation. The advocates of justification and salvation by faith alone, charge spiritual pride and merit, as a necessity, upon all who believe that heaven and its happiness are attained through the regenerative influence of a good life; but this accusation falls to the ground when it is acknowledged that the power to lead a good life is the continual gift and inspiration of God. If man would only think truly, he would see that humility is the acknowledgment of the grand primal truth of existence, that nothing we have, or can do that is good, is of ourselves, but solely of the Lord; and that just as we are left to ourselves and our own wisdom, we do evil, and perpetrate folly and mischief. Salvation through a good life, when thus rightly stated and understood, is seen to involve nothing of merit, but only the strongest reasons for gratitude, humility, and worship.

CHAPTER XVII.

The Divine Love and Divine Wisdom—The Continuation of the Last Judgment.

THE treatise on the Divine Love and Wisdom, is a book which, when mastered, affords a key to the whole philosophy of the New Church, and to a rational understanding of all the writings of Swedenborg. When we say this, it will be easily understood that it is not a book to be read in a few hours, or hastily glanced over. Every page is pregnant with thought, and many of its peragraphs might be expanded into volumes. It is a book which, full of thought on the deepest subjects, demands an exercise of like thought on the part of its reader; and if he has patience, and a simple love of truth for its own sake, happy will he be when he has made himself familiar with the divine thoughts which, like stars, gem every page of this matchless treatise.

The book is divided into five Parts. The First Part sets forth, in the simplest language, the doctrine of the Divine Nature. The Lord's essence is shown to be Infinite Love, and its manifestation to be Infinite Wisdom. It is proved that the Divine Love is the only life in the universe, and that in God "all things live, move, and have their being." The Lord is also proved to be very and essential Man, yet above and independent of all space and time, filling all spaces of the universe without space, and all time without time; and being in the greatest and the least things evermore the same. These statements may appear inconsequential, but in our limited space, we can not explain more fully. We could not give the proofs satisfactorily, without quoting the volume itself. Argument is so linked to argument, that they hardly admit of separation.

The Second Part of the work treats of the sun of heaven, and the sun of our world. It is shown that from the Lord flows a Divine Sphere, which appears in the spiritual world as a sun. From its heat, angels and man have their love, and from its light their wisdom, thus their life. This sun is not God, but it is the first proceeding from the Divine Love and the Divine Wisdom of God-Man. By means of this sun the Lord created the universe and all things in it. The sun of the natural world is pure fire, and therefore dead; and since nature derives its origin from that sun, it also is dead. Without two suns, the one living and the other dead, there could be no creation. The end of creation is, that all things may return to the Creator, and conjunction may exist in its ultimates.

Part Third declares that in the spiritual world there are atmospheres, waters and earths, as in the natural world; but that the former are spiritual, whereas the latter are natural. We are then introduced to the doctrine of degrees—a doctrine which must be studied and understood, before any one can with justice speak of Swedenborg; for it is a doctrine which lies at the basis of that peerless spiritual philosophy of which he was the promulgator. All that we can do here in the way of exposition, is to quote the heads of his articles which express the truth far more lucidly than we could do.

"There are three degrees of Love and wisdom, and thence degrees of heat and light, and degrees of atmosphere. Degrees are of two kinds, degrees of altitude and degrees of latitude. The degrees of altitude are homogeneous, and one derived from the other in a series, like end, cause, and effect. The first degree is in all the subsequent degrees.

All perfections increase and ascend with degrees, and according to degrees. In successive order the first degree constitutes the highest, and the third the lowest; but in simulaneous order, the first degree constitutes the inmost, and the third the outmost. The ultimate degree is the complex, continent, and basis, of the prior degrees. The degrees of altitude in their ultimate, are in their fullness and power. There are degrees of both kinds in the greatest and least of all created things. There are three infinite and uncreated degrees of altitude in the Lord, and three finite and created degrees in man. These three degrees of altitude are in every man from his birth, and may be opened successively, and as they are opened, a man is in the Lord, and the Lord in him. Spiritual light flows into man by three degrees, but not spiritual heat, except so far as he avoids evils as sins, and looks to the Lord. If the superior or spiritual degree is not opened in a man, he becomes natural and sensual. The natural degree of the human mind, considered in itself, is continuous, but by correspondence with the two superior degrees, while it is elevated, it appears as if it were discrete.

"The natural mind, being the tegument and continent of the higher degrees of the human mind, is a re-agent; and if the superior degrees are not opened, it acts against them, but if they are opened, it acts with them. The abuse of the faculties which are proper to man, called rationality and liberty, is the origin of evil. A bad man may enjoy these two faculties as well as a good man; but a bad man abuses them to confirm evils and falses, while a good man uses them to confirm goods and truths. Evils and falses, when confirmed, remain; and become parts of a man's love and life. The things which become parts of a man's love and thence of his life, are communicated hereditarily to his offspring.

"All these evils and consequent falses, both hereditary and

acquired, reside in the natural mind. Evils and falses are entirely opposed to goods and truths; because evils and falses are diabolical and infernal, and goods and truths are divine and heavenly. The natural mind, which is in evils and falses, is a form and image of hell, and descends by three degrees. These three degrees of the natural mind, which is an image and form of hell, are opposed to the three degrees of the spiritual mind, which is a form and image of heaven: thus the natural mind which is a hell, is in complete opposition to the spiritual mind which is a heaven. All things of the three degrees of the natural mind, are included in works, which are performed by acts of the body."

Part Fourth teaches that the Lord from eternity, who is Jehovah, created the universe and all things therein from Himself, and not from nothing; this would not have been possible if the Lord were not a Divine Man; He from himself producing the sun of the spiritual world, and by it creating all things. In the substances and matters of which earths consist, there is nothing of the Divine in itself; but still they are from the Divine in itself. All created things in the created universe, viewed from uses, represent man in an image; this testifies that God is Man. All things created by the Lord are uses; and they are uses in the order, degree, and respect, in which they have relation to man, and by man to the Lord their Creator. Evil uses were not created by the Lord, but originated together with hell, after man's fall. The visible things in the created universe testify that nature has produced nothing, and does produce nothing; but that the Divine has produced and does produce all things from Himself, and through the spiritual world.

Part Fifth is devoted to a description of man's spiritual nature. It is shown that "the Lord has formed and created in man two receptacles and habitations for Himself, called the will and the understanding; the will for His Divine Love, and the understanding for His Divine Wisdom. The will and understanding are in the brains, in the whole and every part thereof, and thence in the body, in the whole and every part thereof. There is a correspondence of the will with the heart, and of the understanding with the lungs; and all things that can be known of the will and understanding, or of love and wisdom, consequently all that can be known of man's soul, may be known from the correspondence of the heart with the will, and of the understanding with the lungs."

There are many volumes in the world whose thinly spun thought, spread over page after page, it would be easy to condense into one brief paragraph; but the treatise on the Divine Love and Wisdom is not such a work. It is one of those rare books which suggest and expand thought, but can bear no abridgment or compression. We have well studied it, but do not expect to finish it during our life on earth. Time was, when, immersed in man made systems of faith, and wont to walk abroad in the green fields and woods, by the sea-side, and on the mountains—we found it difficult, nay we should rather say impossible, to see the God we read of in our books, and thought of in our chamber, to be the same kind Father to whom those wide and beauteous scenes owed their existence. Justification by faith—Jerusalem—the Jews—ephod and teraphim—the Temple, and the sacrifice—seemed to have no connection with the landscape, the wind, the falling rain, the flowing river, and the broad and limitless ocean. We knew it should not be so. If the Bible were God's book, it must have some closer affinity with his great work of nature. We knew that one Lord was over all, and that this disunity should by no means exist. Much mental pain and travail were our portion. The easy soothsayings of Atheism beguiled us. We "wandered in the wilderness in a solitary way, and found no city (doctrine) to dwell in." We longed for the rest of Zion. We sighed not in vain. The divine philosophy of this precious book was revealed to us, and we knew the blessing of a faith which finds a confirmation in every item and phase of creation, and makes the Bible and nature evermore at one, each confirming and illustrating the other. It gave to life new aims and aspects. It brought a mental peace we had never hoped to enjoy, and we went on our journey of life rejoicing.

"The Continuation of the Last Judgment," is a small pamphlet forming a supplement to the treatise on the Last Judgment, with which it is now generally published. It contains a very interesting account of the Last Judgment upon the Reformed. By the Reformed, upon whom the Last Judgment was effected, Swedenborg means those who professed a belief in God, read the Word, heard sermons, partook of the sacrament of the Supper, yet lived in all manner of evils. Living like Christians in externals, and outwardly in unity with heaven, while inwardly united with hell, they were permitted after death to form societies, and to live as in the world; and by arts unknown in the world, to cause splendid appearances, and by this means to persuade themselves and others that they were in heaven. From this outward appearance, therefore, they called their societies heavens. The heavens and the lands in which they dwelt, are understood by the "former heaven, and the former earth, which passed away." Rev. xxi. 7.

At the time of the Last Judgment, the hypocrisy of these spirits was revealed in the light of heaven, and the simple good with whom they had associated, separated themselves with horror from them. No longer able to simulate Christian lives, they rushed with delight into evils and crimes of every description, openly appeared as devils, and found for themselves the hells corresponding to their loves. At the same time all the splendid appearances they had made for themselves vanished away; their palaces were turned into vile huts; their gardens into stagnant pools; their temples into piles of rubbish; and the hills on which they dwelt, into heaps of gravel, in correspondence with their depraved dispositions and lusts.

"After the Judgment was effected," writes Swedenborg, "there was joy in heaven, and also light in the world of spirits, such as was not before. A similar light also then arose on men in the world, giving them new enlightenment. I then saw angelic spirits, in great numbers, rising from below, and elevated into heaven. They were the sheep there reserved, and guarded by the Lord for ages back, lest they should come into the malignant sphere of the dragonists, and their charity be suffocated. These are they who are understood in the Word by those who went forth from the sepulchers; also by the souls of those slain for the testimony of Jesus, who were watching; and by those who are of the first resurrection."

After this follows a description of many things seen in the spiritual world. He writes: "There are lands in the spiritual world, just as in the natural world: there are hills and mountains, plains and valleys, also fountains and rivers, lakes and seas; there are paradises, and gardens and groves, and woods, and palaces, and houses; there are writings, and books, functions, [*functiones,*] and employments; there are precious stones, gold and silver; in short, there are all the things, in general and in particular, which exist in the natural world; but in the heavens all these things are infinitely more perfect."

He then describes "the noble English nation" in the spiritual world; the more excellent of whom are in the centre of all Christians, because they have interior intellectual light. This light they derive from the liberty they enjoy of thinking, and thence of speaking and writing. The Dutch are then described, and then the Papists, and the Popish saints. The Mohammedans, the Africans, and the Gentiles follow; and finally the Jews, the Quakers, and the Moravians. The description of all these people, as they appear beyond the grave, has an interest of a most absorbing kind; and the light thrown by Swedenborg on their internal character, serves to show cause for much that happens in the external world, otherwise difficult of explanation.

CHAPTER XVIII.

Angelic Wisdom Concerning the Divine Providence.

STILL living in Amsterdam, Swedenborg published, in 1764, his work entitled "Angelic Wisdom Concerning the Divine Providence." Its purpose is to

> "assert eternal Providence,
> And justify the ways of God to man."

In the first place, it is shown that the Divine Providence is the government of the Love and the Wisdom of the Lord. This Providence has for its sole end the formation of a heaven from the human race, and thus has respect only to what is infinite and eternal. In the Divine sight, things temporal and natural are of no importance except so far as they contribute to man's salvation.

Although the Lord thus wills and works for man's eternal happiness, yet, after all, heaven can only be attained through man's coöperation. The Lord ever performs his share of the work, but man too often fails to do his. Weeping over Jerusalem, the Lord exclaimed: "O Jerusalem, Jerusalem, thou that killest the prophets, and stonest them that are sent unto thee, how often would I have gathered thy children together, even as a hen gathereth her chickens under her wings, *and ye would not!*" Matthew xxiii. 37. How powerfully and tenderly is here expressed the Divine willingness to save, and how pointedly and decisively is man's misery attributed to his own obstinacy. As the Lord Jesus is another place says: "Ye *will not* come to me that ye might have life." John v. 40.

In all the operations of the Divine Providence, human freedom is respected. The Lord forces no man to do what is good, or believe what is true. He drives none to heaven. It is of the Divine Providence that whatsoever a man hears, sees, thinks, speaks, and does, should appear altogether as his own. Without this appearance, men would have no reception of Divine Truth, no determination to do good, no appropriation of love and wisdom or of charity and faith, and thence no conjunction with the Lord; consequently no reformation and regeneration, and thereby salvation. Without this appearance, it is evident there could be no repentance and no faith; and man would not be man, but void of rational life like a beast. It is plain, then, that in order that man may be saved, he must be induced to live a good life by means which in nowise trench upon this appearance of free and independent life. Regeneration is effected by man's removing evils from his external life, *as of himself;* yet, knowing that all good and truth is from the Lord, he acknowledges, as a consequence, that all power to remove these evils is derived from the Lord alone.

Intensely as the Lord desires that man should shun evils and lead a holy life in obedience to his commandments, yet He only seeks to win man to peace and heaven by means which do not infringe upon his freedom. It is a law of His Divine Providence, that man should not be forced by external means to think and will, and so to believe and love the things which are of religion. It has been asked by atheists, "If there be a God, why does he not write so on the sun, and so save men from unbelief?" Swedenborg answers this question most satisfactorily, by showing that miracles, signs, visions, conversations with the dead, threats, and punishments, are totally ineffective to produce that state of love and spiritual life which make true happiness and heaven; because these force, and destroy the rationality and liberty which constitute the inmost life of humanity, and by the exercise of which, man can alone be delivered from evil.

Let us read Swedenborg's testimony on miracles. He writes: "That such is the nature of miracles, may plainly appear from those wrought before the Jewish and Israelitish people. Although they saw so many miracles in Egypt, afterwards at the Red Sea, others in the Desert, and especially upon Mount Sinai, when the law was promulgated, yet, in the space of a month, when Moses tarried upon that mountain, they made themselves a golden calf, and acknowledged it for Jehovah who brought them out of the land of Egypt. The same also may appear from the miracles wrought afterwards in the land of Canaan, notwithstanding which the people so often departed from the worship that was commanded; and from the miracles which the Lord wrought before them when he was in the world, notwithstanding which they crucified him. The reason why miracles were wrought among the Jews and Israelites was, because they were altogether external men, and were introduced into the land of Canaan merely that they might represent a church and its internal principles by the external things of worship; and a wicked man may be representative, as well as a good man. The external things of worship among them were rituals, all which signified spiritual and celestial things. Even Aaron, although he made the golden calf, and conducted the worship of it, could, nevertheless, represent the Lord and his work of salvation. And as they could not, by the internal principles of worship, be led to represent these things, therefore they were led, yea forced and compelled, to do it by miracles. The reason why they could not be brought to such representation by the internal principles of worship was, because they did not acknowledge the Lord, although the whole Word, which was among them, treats of Him only; and he who does not acknowledge the Lord, can not receive any internal worship. But after the Lord manifested himself, and was received and acknowledged in the churches as the eternal God, miracles ceased.

"The effect of miracles upon the good, however, is different from what it is upon the wicked. The good do not desire miracles, but they believe the miracles which are recorded in the Word; and if they hear anything of a miracle, they attend no otherwise to it than as a light argument which confirms their faith; for they think from the Word, consequently from the Lord, and not from a miracle. It is otherwise with the wicked: they indeed may be driven and forced into faith, and even into worship and piety, but only for a short time; for their evils being shut in, the inclinations thereto, and the delights thence derived, continually act against the external of their worship and piety; and in order that these evils may escape from confinement and break out, they think about the miracle, and at length call it a delusion, or an artifice, or an operation of nature, and so return into their evils; and he who returns into his evils after worship, profanes the truths and goods of worship, and the lot of profaners after death is the worst of all. Besides, if miracles were to be wrought before those who do not believe in consequence of the miracles recorded in the Word, they must be continually performed, and constantly presented to their view. From these considerations, the reason may appear why miracles are not performed at this day."

It is thus seen that the Lord will not force a man to lead a good life; because, in forcing him, his humanity would be destroyed, and all that makes life worthy and manly would be lost, seeing that the exercise of rationality and liberty would be annihilated.

It is a law of the Divine Providence, that a man should be led and taught from the Lord out of heaven by the Word, and by doctrine and preaching from the Word, and this in all appearance as from himself. The Lord, as we have before seen, is the Word; and when man reads the Word, he brings his thought into contact with the Divine Wisdom, and when he obeys its teachings he is in very truth led by the Lord. Yet we all see that this teaching and leading of the Lord is effected without any violation of man's freedom, for he is led and taught in externals to all appearance as of himself.

It is a law of the Divine Providence that a man should not perceive and feel anything of the operation of the Divine Providence, but yet should know and acknowledge it. If a man perceived and felt the operation of the Divine Providence, he would not act from liberty according to reason, nor would anything appear to him as his own. It would also be the same if he foreknew events. "The reason why it is not granted man to foreknow events, is, that he may be able to act from liberty according to reason; also, that there is nothing that a man revolves in his reason which is not from a desire that it may come into effect by thought. If, therefore, he knew the effect or event from divine prediction, reason would become quiescent, and with reason love; for love, with reason, terminates in the effect, and from that begins anew. It is the very delight of reason, that from love in the thought it may see the effect,—not in the effect, but before it, or not in the present, but in the future. Hence a man has what is called Hope, which in reason increases and decreases, as it sees or expects the event. This delight is fulfilled in the event, but afterwards is obliterated with the thought concerning the event; and it would be the same with an event foreknown." The whole zest of life would be dissipated coulu man foreknow the future.

While the operation of the Divine Providence is thus veiled from man's eyes, and it appears to him that he is alone in the world, and that on his small prudence hangs all things,—if he would be wise he must not be led by appearances, but rising above them, acknowledge the truth "that self-derived prudence is nothing, and *only appears as if it were something*, [and ought so to appear;] but that the Divine Providence in things most singular is universal." And because our life and intelligence are momentarily derived from the Lord, it follows as a necessary consequence, that all which we do that is orderly and effective, is done by the Lord, through our yielding ourselves to Him as His instruments.

It is often urged as a reason against believing in an overruling and universal Divine Providence, that the world is full of evil and wickedness; and if there be an omnipotent God, he would surely never suffer such things to exist. Swedenborg enters very fully into this question. The reasons why Adam was permitted to fall, and Cain to slay Abel; Solomon to establish idolatrous worship, and many kings after him to profane the holy things of the church; the Jews to crucify the Lord; why impiety is allowed to exist, and the impious and profligate to be promoted to riches and honors, while the worshipers of God and the doers of righteousness remain in contempt and poverty; why wars are permitted, men slaughtered, the property of the innocent destroyed, and victories go with force and not with justice; why the earth is permitted to remain covered with idolatries, and the Christian religion to occupy so small a place, and even there to be deeply corrupted and devastated with heresies,—are stated at length and most satisfactorily. It is made plain, that, were the Lord to interfere and prevent such evils by force, it would defeat the end for which He created man, namely, salvation and eternal life in heaven.

Now as man can only be regenerated and enter heaven through the free exercise of his understanding and free choice of his will, any external interference of the Divine Providence with outward circumstances would suspend the action of man's faculties; would, in short, dehumanise the race, and leave only animals to be dealt with. It is not of the Lord's will, indeed, that evil should exist; and His Providence is unceasingly exerted to modify and mitigate it, alike in its origin and in its effect; but, since to prevent its manifestation would be to take from man all that makes him man, its permission is a necessity.

It was said that the Providence of the Lord is unceasingly exerted to modify and mitigate evil, alike in its origin and in its effects. Swedenborg very beautifully and amply illustrates this truth, and shows that the Divine Providence is equally with the wicked and the good. The wicked man, of his own free choice, continually plunges himself more and more deeply into evil; because as he wills and does evil, he introduces himself more and more deeply into infernal societies. But the Lord, by a thousand invisible means, continually withdraws him from evil; and where a cure or complete prevention is impossible, mitigates his fearful fate by providing circumstances and situations in life which serve to lead the evil into less hurtful developments. The operation of the Divine Providence in saving man begins at his birth, and continues to the end of his life. The Lord sees what a man is, and what he desires to be, consequently what he will be; therefore the Lord foresees his state after death, and provides for it from his birth to the end of his life; with the wicked He provides by permitting and continually withdrawing them from evils; with the good He provides by leading them to good. Thus the Divine Providence is continually in the effort to save men; but more cannot be saved than desire to be saved. Those who acknowledge God and are led by Him, desire to be saved; and those who do not acknowledge God, but guide themselves, do not desire to be saved: for the latter do not think of eternal life and salvation, but the former do. This the Lord sees; but still He leads them according to the laws of His Divine Providence, against which He cannot act, for to act against them would be to act against Himself. Now, as the Lord foresees the states of all after death, and knows the places of those who are not willing to be saved, He, as far as is consistent with human freedom, labors to soften man's evil; and if He cannot lead him to heaven, still preserves him from sinking to the lowest hell.

From this it follows that every man may be reformed, that there is no such thing as predestination, and that it is a man's own fault if he is not saved. All are created for heaven, and none for hell; and if man sink into perdition, he does so through his own obstinacy, and through the deliberate choice of a life of evil. As saith the Apostle: "The Lord is long-suffering to usward, *not willing that any should perish*, but that all should come to repentance." 2 Peter iii. 9. And the Lord himself says: "Fear not, little flock; it is your *Father's good pleasure to give you the kingdom.*" Luke xii. 32.

Such, in brief, are a few of the principles in the treatise on the Divine Providence. Nothing but a perusal of the work can give an adequate idea of its multiplicity of details, from the laws which regulate the affairs of kingdoms, to those which govern games of chance; and all expounded with a lucidity of thought, which finds few parallels in works on such recondite themes. No book in the whole circle of literature more satisfactorily disposes of the objections against religion, current among secularists and worldlings. The inward temptations and doubts of the devout heart, and the weariness, cares, and fret of life, are shown in its pages to be all permitted by that Divine Love which suffers not a sparrow to fall unheeded; and the minutest incidents of life are seen to be forever encircled by that Omniscience, which knows how most effectually to guard us from evil and draw us into the holy courts of heaven.

Any view which we take of the Divine Providence that does not recognize this life as a beginning, a progress, and not a consummation, is necessarily erroneous. Life here is but a discipline, an apprenticeship. It is a school wherein we are scholars, learning such lessons as will fit us for uses in a higher and eternal sphere. Were life consummated by what men call death, we might have reason to complain that the comforts and pleasures of existence were so unequally distributed; and the natural man might exclaim with the Psalmist: "I was envious at the foolish, when I saw the prosperity of the wicked. They are not in trouble as other men; neither are they plagued like other men. Their eyes stand out with fatness: they have more than heart could wish. Behold, these are the ungodly who prosper in the world; they increase in riches." But when we look at the matter from higher grounds, and in the light of the Divine wisdom, or as the Psalmist did when he said: "I went into the sanctuary of God; then understood I their end: how are they brought into desolation as in a moment! they are utterly consumed with terrors:"—"The evil doers shall be cut off; but those that wait upon the Lord, they shall inherit the earth: for yet a little while, and the wicked shall not be; yea thou shalt diligently consider his place, and it shall not be: for the Lord loveth judgment, and forsaketh not his saints;"—then we obtain a right view of the matter, and find an all-sufficient reason for being patient and not fretting ourselves. Hard though our lot in life may seem, let us remember that

"The vain and fleeting things of earth,
(Though counted vain, alas! by few,)
In his esteem are nothing worth,
Who keeps eternal ends in view."

Or, as Cowper says:

"The path of sorrow and that path alone,
Leads to the land where sorrow is unknown.
No traveler ever reached that blest abode
Who found not thorns and briers in his road."

CHAPTER XIX.

Life in Amsterdam—Character of the Dutch—Meets Dr. Beyer—Republishes his "New Method of Finding the Longitudes"—The Apocalypse Explained.

It is very trying to the biographer of Swedenborg that he can find so little to narrate of his outward life. Of his life in Amsterdam we have no particulars whatever, No Boswell was there to note down his sayings, describe his doings, his company, and conduct. But had even a Boswell been there, we fear he would have found but little to note. Quiet days in his study, calm reserve toward all around, musing, solitary rambles in the streets, would supply but few incidents for the pen of the biographer. We must be content to know that, from out his quiet study in Amsterdam, proceeded books destined to be centers of spiritual light to the church and to the world.

Swedenborg liked the Dutch, and with good reason, for he was favored to know them in that land where the secrets of all hearts are unvailed. He reports that the Dutch, above all other people, are under the influence of the *spiritual* love of trade, valuing it for its uses, and regarding money only as a means to these uses, and not, like the Jews, as the final end. They are, moreover, inflexible in their obedience to the truth, when known; and in many other respects are an estimable people.

It is probable that Swedenborg returned home toward the end of 1764; for, in the first half of the next year, we find him in Stockholm. Soon, however, he set out upon new travels; and in 1765, while at Gottenburg, waiting for a vessel to England, he accidentally (as men say) met with Dr. Beyer, Professor of Greek, and a member of the Consistory of Gottenburg. Having heard that Swedenborg was mad, he was surprised to hear him talk sensibly, and manifest no symptom of his suspected infirmity. He therefore invited Swedenborg to dine with him the following day, in company with Dr. Rosen. After dinner, Dr. Beyer expressed a desire to hear from himself a full account of his doctrines; upon which Swedenborg, animated by the request, spoke so clearly, and in so wonderful a manner, that the Doctor and his friend were quite astonished. They gave him no interruption; but when he ceased, Dr. Beyer requested Swedenborg to meet him the next day at Mr. Wenngren's and to bring with him a paper, containing the substance of his conversation, in order that he might consider it more attentively. Swedenborg came the day following, according to promise; and, taking the paper out of his pocket, in the presence of the other two gentlemen, he trembled, and appeared much affected, the tears flowing down his cheeks. Presenting the paper to Dr. Beyer, "Sir," said he, "from this day the Lord has introduced you into the society of angels, and you are now surrounded by them." They were all greatly affected. He then took his leave, and the next day embarked for England.

Dr. Beyer sent immediately for Swedenborg's writings, and soon became deeply engrossed in their study. In order to arrange their subjects more distinctly in his mind, he set about compiling an Index to them; which as he prepared it, he sent, sheet by sheet, to Amsterdam to be printed. He was thirteen years in compiling the work, and on the day he sent off the last sheet corrected, he sickened, took to his bed, and in a few days departed to the spiritual world.

The result of Dr. Beyer's study of Swedenborg's writings,

was a firm belief in their doctrines, and an open and enlightened advocacy of them, declaring in the public Consistory his full assent to them. As might naturally be expected, he suffered much obloquy and persecution for his adherence to the truth; but he was consoled in having the firm friendship of Swedenborg, and in being favored with receiving from him many letters, sympathizing with him in his trials, and answering many of his questions on doctrinal and psychological matters.

Swedenborg did not make a long stay in England; but after a few weeks, or perhaps months, proceeded to Holland, spending the winter of 1765–66 at Amsterdam. There, in the spring of 1766, he republished (it is supposed by the solicitation of friends,) his youthful work on a "New Method of Finding the Longitudes." "This method," as he informed the Swedish Archbishop, Menander, "of calculating the ephemerides by pairs of stars, several persons in foreign countries were then employing, who had experienced great advantage by the observations made according to it for a series of years."

From the time of the completion of the Arcana Cœlestia, in 1756, Swedenborg had been gradually composing an extensive work on the Apocalypse. The exposition was continued as far as the tenth verse of the nineteenth chapter, filling four large quarto volumes. He then laid the work aside—thinking, probably, that it was too voluminous and elaborate—and commenced anew, but on a considerably reduced scale. The former Exposition, a clearly written manuscript, ready for the printer, after sustaining a narrow escape from burning, (the house of a gentleman who had it for perusal having caught fire,) was published in the original Latin, in four quarto volumes, in 1790, eighteen years after the author's death. It was translated into English and printed in six octavos, under the title of the Apocalypse

Explained, in 1815. It is a most valuable work, and one that could not well be spared from the Swedenborg Library. Within its pages are several distinct treatises on very important subjects, which, if extracted, would form complete and excellent books of themselves. The exposition of the spiritual sense of the text is very copiously illustrated by parallel passages from other parts of the Word; and thus it must ever be a most useful work to the New Church preacher, as affording him a ready key to the internal sense of the Scriptures.

The shorter exposition Swedenborg himself published at Amsterdam, in 1766, under the title of the Apocalypse Revealed. As was his custom, he distributed copies of the work widely, sending it to the universities and superior clergy, and to many eminent persons in England, Holland, Germany, France, and Sweden.

We will now make a few notes on some of the most remarkable features of Swedenborg's exposition of that strange and mysterious book, the Apocalypse.

CHAPTER XX.

The Apocalypse Revealed.

EVERY one who is acquainted with theological literature, knows that innumerable volumes of speculation have been written in attempted explanation of the Apocalypse. He is aware that expositors have differed about it from the earliest times; that Protestants have found Catholicism the subject of all its denunciations, and that Catholics have discovered that Paganism and Protestant heresy were in reality the matters alluded to; that sceptics have proved that it refers to none of these creeds, but is a worthless astrological treatise; and that many good Christians, vexed and wearied with this endless contest of opinion, have wished the book expunged from the canon of Scripture, as altogether incomprehensible, and a mere breeder of strife. And still the controversy goes on. The press swarms with volumes and pamphlets, all professing to have found the key to the mystery, informing the world of the future destiny of Europe, of the result of its wars and battles, the precise month of the fall of the Papacy, and the time of the descent of the New Jerusalem, the Second Advent, and the restoration of the Jews to Canaan, and, so far as the political arrangement of the kingdoms of the earth is concerned, almost superseding the necessity of newspapers to the credulous believer. Wise men generally now turn a deaf ear to these soothsayings, convinced by long and repeated experience of their utter futility, and thinking shrewdly enough that had the

Divine Providence intended that man should know the future, the foreknowledge would have been communicated intelligibly and not through the medium of mysteries interpreted by men more conspicious for temerity than for any endowment of wisdom or common sense above their fellows. "It is a part of this prophecy," as Sir Isaac Newton remarks, —and the same principle is applicable to all prophecies,— "that it should not be understood before the last age of the world; and therefore it makes for the credit of the prophecy that it is not yet [about 1710] understood. The folly of interpreters has been, to foretell times and things by this prophecy, as if God designed to make them prophets. By this rashness, they have not only exposed themselves, but brought the prophecy also into contempt. The design of God was much otherwise. He gave this, and other prophecies of the Old Testament, not to gratify men's curiosity by enabling them to foreknow things, but that, after they were fulfilled, they might be interpreted by the events; and his own Providence, not the interpreters, be then manifested thereby to the world. For the event of things, predicted many ages before, will then be a convincing argument that the world is governed by Providence. For, as the few and obscure prophecies concerning Christ's first coming, were for setting up the Christian religion, *which all nations have since corrupted;* so the many and clear prophecies concerning the things to be done at Christ's second coming, are not only for predicting but also for effecting a recovery and re-establishment of the long-lost truth, and setting up a kingdom wherein dwells righteousness. The event will prove the Apocalypse; and this prophecy, thus proved and understood, will open the old prophets; and all together will make known the true religion, and establish it."

With no claim to superior understanding or acuteness did Swedenborg present his exposition of this mysterious book to the world. He humbly declares that the mysteries of the Apocalypse are totally beyond the power of human intellect to unravel, and that whatever of truth is to be found in his work, owed its existence to the immediate illustration of his mind by the Lord. We shall presently show what powerful reason there was for this protestation on his part.

The Apocalypse, we are taught, is a portion of the Divine Word. It was dictated directly by the Lord,—John, in Patmos, being simply an amanuensis.

The Apocalypse is a prophetic book, descriptive of the decline and consummation of the Christian Church, and the establishment of the new and spiritual dispensation signified by "the New Jerusalem descending from God out of heaven." Being a prophetic book, it would have been at variance with the laws of the Divine Providence for man to have understood its prophecies until after the events it described were past; for, as we have seen, a knowledge of the future would take from man all freedom of action, all inclination to labor, and the whole hope and pleasure of life. Therefore it was that the Apocalypse remained a sealed book until the Christian Church had reached its consummation, and the Last Judgment was effected, in 1757, when the Lord graciously opened the eyes of Swedenborg and manifested to him, in clear light, the deep mysteries of this prophecy.

Wilkinson, in his admirable Biography, well says: "A volume, unless it were a reprint, would not give an analysis of the Apocalypse Revealed. When we say that the commentary takes the text word by word, and translates it into spirit, we still convey but a slender idea of what is done. Our own first impressions on reading the work will not soon be forgotten. Following the writer through the long breadths and flights of this vast empyrean, we were momently in anxious fear that to sustain a context of such was impossible. Each fresh chapter seemed like a space that mortal wing must not attempt; and yet the fear was groundless, for our guide sailed onward with a tranquil motion as if he knew the stars. History and common sense, panting and grasping science, philosophy in its better part, above all, the confidence in a Divine support and a supernal mission, appeared to be covertly and unexpectedly present, to annihilate difficulties, and pave the skyey way of this humble voyager. And when we had again alighted from that perusal which strained every faculty to the utmost, it was as though we had been there before, so entire was the impression of self-evidence that was left upon the mind. Genesis and the Revelation were closely at one in this marvellous Apocalypse—thenceforth the most open of the Bible pages: the two ends of the Scripture called to each other; an arch of Divine light spanned the river of the Word, and the original Eden blossomed anew in the midst of the street of the holy city."

The Rev. O. P. Hiller, in his Memoir of Swedenborg, writes: "In the Apocalypse Revealed, the mysterions book is taken up and examined chapter by chapter, verse by verse, word by word, in the same manner as was done with the books of Genesis and Exodus in the Arcana Cœlestia; and the interior meaning, the spiritual sense, of every part, set forth in such a manner as to present a clear, connected, and rational meaning throughout the whole book, from the first chapter to the last. And what is especially to be remarked, the spiritual sense of this book, the last of the New Testament, is shown to be founded on the same principles, and discovered by the same rules of interpretation, as the spiritual sense of the books of Genesis and Exodus, the first of the Old Testament, written, as they were, by other hands, and more than fifteen hundred years before; a strong proof, certainly, that however varied the human instruments there was One Divine Author of the whole. Thus, with any particular word, for instance, occurring in the book of Genesis, and declared to have a certain spiritual signification,—when that word occurs in the book of Revelation, it is shown to have the same signification; and this holds good in all cases. And, moreover, while all these various signfications, taken together, make in the book of Genesis a complete spiritual sense, so in the book of Revelation they make their own complete spiritual sense. Now it will be readily seen, that such a coincidence would be altogether unaccountable, nay, impossible, unless there really existed such a spiritual sense in the Word of God: and it is, indeed, this uniform spiritual sense, full of high and heavenly truth, that raises the holy volume infinitely above all other works of history or morals; and the existence of such a sense is the strongest proof of the Divine character of those writings which we call the Sacred Scriptures. And truly, had Swedenborg done only this, he would have deserved the gratitude of all who seriously revere the Word of God, for thus bringing a new and most powerful argument from internal evidence, in favor of the inspiration and divinity of the sacred volume."

Well, then, might Swedenborg disclaim the authorship of the ideas in the Apocalypse Revealed, and ask: "What man can draw such things from himself?" Those who tell us that Swedenborg was self-deceived, must either know very little of what they speak about, or must be quite as ignorant of the capacity of the human mind and its powers of invention. For ourselves, we could as readily believe that Swedenborg created the world, as we could believe that the spiritual sense of the Apocalypse, and of the whole Word, was a fiction of his brain. Were the spiritual sense of the Word such a fiction, then it must be said that there lived a man in the last century, with an intellect and creative faculty, compared with which those of all the philosophers and poets of past and present time combined, were as nothing. We leave revilers of Swedenborg to make their choice; either to admit the existence of the spiritual sense of the Word; or, denying its existence, and pronouncing Swedenborg's discovery either a delusion or an imposture, to admit that Swedenborg was a man wholy unique—a genius infinitely surpassing any which the world has ever known, and endowed with a power of invention which the mind of a nation incarnate in one man could never hope to rival.

But it will never come to such a pass. Any one who will take the trouble candidly to examine the subject, will become convinced of the spiritual sense of the Word, and of the truth of Swedenborg's revelations regarding it. The denial and mockery of them can only coexist with an ignorance, more or less profound, of their nature; or, worse still, from a hatred of the truth, grounded in the life and love of evil. The spiritual sense of the Word is no invention. It is a discovery,—accomplished by Divine means, however,—just as the finding of Australia was a discovery; and we shall believe in its existence if we become *practically* acquainted with it through reverent thought and study; even as we should know Australia best, did we go there.

It may be said: "Well, suppose the spiritual sense of the Apocalypse does describe the fall of the Christian Church, and the inauguration of the New Church; and typifies the doctrine of justification by faith alone by the Dragon; and the Romanists and their lust of dominion and atrocious deeds by Babylon and the great Harlot sitting upon many waters; what then? It is true such descriptions must ever have a certain interest, but not sufficient to render them subjects of universal study in all ages. and worthily forming a part of that Divine Book which is read by angels in heaven, as well as by men on earth." The objection is a sound one so far as it goes, but it is made in ignorance of a great but very simple truth, namely, that all that is true of a church is true of an individual. The trust in mere truth in the intellect, and the lust of power and glory,—the former signified by the Dragon, and the latter by Babylon,—are evils which exist in all minds to a greater or less degree; and the Divine description of their nature and awful consequences may be thought of apart from any idea of Geneva or Rome. The Apocalypse being a divine work, has infinite applications, and will be read to eternity in spheres where the names of Romanist and Protestant are unknown; and in societies of glorified spirits, compared with whose number and influence this world is insignificant.

CHAPTER XXI.

Travels—Habits—Anecdotes.

In April, 1766, Swedenborg again visited England in order to observe the effect of his writings upon the English people. Of this visit we have no account, except in reference to its conclusion, in September of the same year, when he returned to Stockholm. Mr. Springer, the Swedish Consul in London, an old friend of Swedenborg's, has left the following interesting record of some incidents connected with his return.

"Swedenborg was about to depart for Sweden, and desired me to procure him a good captain, which I did. I made the agreement with a person named Dixon. Swedenborg's effects were carried on board the vessel, and as his apartments were at some distance from the port, we took, for that night, a chamber at an inn near it, because the captain of the vessel was to come and fetch him in the morning. Swedenborg went to bed; and I went to sit in another room, with the master of the house, with whom I was conversing. We both heard a remarkable noise, and could not apprehend what it could be, and therefore drew near to a door, where there was a little window that looked into the chamber where Swedenborg lay. We saw him with his arms raised toward heaven, and his body appeared to tremble. He spoke much for the space of half an hour, but we could understand nothing of what he said, except that when he let his hands fall down, we heard him say with a loud voice,

'My God!' But we could not hear what he said more. He remained afterwards very quietly in his bed. I entered into his chamber with the master of the house, and asked him if he was ill. 'No,' said he; 'but I have had a long discourse with some of the heavenly friends, and am at this time in a great perspiration.' And as his effects were embarked on board the vessel, he asked the master of the house to let him have a shirt; he then went again to bed, and slept till morning.

"When the captain of the vessel came to fetch Swedenborg, I took my leave of him, and wished him a happy voyage. I then asked the captain if he was provided with good and necessary provisions. He answered me, that he had as much as was needful for the voyage. On this, Swedenborg said: 'My friend, we shall not need a great quantity: for this day week we shall, by the aid of God, enter the port of Stockholm at two o'clock.' It happened exactly as he foretold, as Dixon informed me; saying, that a violent gale accelerated the voyage, that the wind was favorable at every turn of the vessel, and that he never in all his life had so prosperous a voyage."

Arriving at Stockholm on the 8th of September, Swedenborg resided in the Sudermalm, the southern suburb of the city. Robsahm tells us: "His house was built and arranged after his own taste; the apartments were rather small, but suitable for himself. Although he was a man of most profound learning, no other books were seen in his study than the Hebrew and Greek Bible, together with his own indexes to his works, whereby he saved himself the trouble, when referring to different passages, of going through all he had before written.

"Adjoining the house was a rather large garden, in the midst of which he had a summer-house, or pavilion. There were four doors to the apartment, which formed a square, and was occasionally turned, in an instant, into an octagon, by means of four other doors that belonged to it. One of these doors shut with a secret lock, which being opened, there appeared a glass door placed opposite a fine green hedge, where a bird was seen in a cage. This new spectacle produced an agreeable surprise of a second garden to the person who opened the door, which Swedenborg used to say was more agreeable than the first. At the entrance of the garden there was a parterre, well covered with flowers, which he was very fond of. He derived no other advantage from the garden, for he gave the whole produce of it to the gardener who waited on him; so also that of a very excellent green-house, in which he took much pleasure.

"The gardener and his wife were the only servants he had; of the latter he never desired other service than that of making his bed, and of bringing water into his apartment. He generally made his own coffee on the fire in his study, and took much of it, well sweetened. When at home, his dinner consisted of a small loaf put into boiled milk, and at that time he neither drank wine nor any spirituous liquor, nor did he take any supper. Though he was very sparing in his eating and drinking, yet he would sometimes, when in company, take a glass of wine, but was always in one equal temper of mind, and cheerful.

"He had a fire constantly kept up in his study, from autumn, throughout the winter, until spring; but his bed-room, contrary to the usual custom in Sweden, was always cold; and according as the cold was more or less severe, he made use of three, or four, blankets. When he awoke, he went into his study, where there were always live coals, on which he laid wood, with birch-bark, having a number of small bundles ready for use, and to make a quick fire before he sat down to write.

"In his parlor was a table of black marble, on which, one

would have supposed, at first sight, that a hand of cards had been carelessly thrown, the imitation being so perfect. He made a present of this table to the Royal College of Mines, who preserve it with great care. This room was neat and genteel, but furnished in a plain style.

"His wardrobe was simple, yet suitable to the season. He wore in winter a fur gown; and when at home, in summer, a morning robe.

"He spoke very distinctly. When he began to talk in company, every one was silent, as well from the pleasure they had in hearing his discourse, as from a sense of his well known great erudition, which he did not show but on occasions in which he found himself compelled to prove his assertions, or the little weight of the arguments of some with whom he conversed. Besides the learned languages, in which he was well versed, he understood the French, English, Dutch, German, and Italian."

We are thankful indeed for these details, trifling though they are. They evince the quiet practical character of Swedenborg, and the strong common sense which guarded him from all extravagance and eccentricity.

From the gardener's wife, Robsahm received the following statement:—"Entering one day, after dinner, into Swedenborg's chamber, I saw his eyes like unto a most bright flame. I drew back, saying, 'In the name of goodness, Sir, what has happened extraordinary to you? for you have a very peculiar appearance.' 'What kind of look have I?' answered he. I then told him what struck me. 'Well, well,' replied he, which was his favorite expression, 'don't be frightened, the Lord has so disposed my eyes, that by them spirits may see what is in our world.'" In a short time this appearance passed away, as he said it would. "I know," said she to Robsahm, "when he has conversed with heavenly spirits, for there is a pleasure and calm satisfaction in his countenance, which charm those who see it; but after he has conversed with evil spirits, he has a sorrowful look."

Concerning his temptations, they said that their master, in the night, often spoke aloud, when evil spirits were with him, which they could easily hear, their room being adjoining. When asked what caused his disturbance in the night, he answered that it had been permitted the evil spirits to blaspheme, and that he had spoken against them zealously. It happened often that, weeping bitterly, he cried with a loud voice, and prayed to the Lord that he might not be forsaken in his temptation, when they assailed him. His words were, 'Lord help me! Lord, my God, do not forsake me!' Those who saw him in these states, supposed he was sick; but when delivered from them, he returned thanks to God, and said to those who were troubled for him, 'God be eternally praised! Comfort yourselves, my friends, all has passed away; and be assured that nothing happens to me but what the Lord permits, who never lays a burden on us more weighty than we are able to bear.'"

Once it was remarkable that after such a state he went to bed, and did not rise for several days and nights. This gave his domestics much uneasiness, and they consulted together, and supposed he was dead. They intended to break open the door, or to call their neighbors. At last the gardener went to the window, and discovered, to his great joy, that his master was alive, and turning in his bed. The next day he rang the bell. The woman went in, and related her own and her husband's uneasiness for him. He told her with a cheerful countenance, that he had been very well, and had wanted nothing.

The following anecdote, narrated to Robsahm by the gardener's wife, places Swedenborg's moral courage in a strong light, and shows the use of judicious plain speaking. Bishop Halenius, the successor of Swedenborg's father, paying Swedenborg a visit one day, the conversation turned on the nature of common sermons. Swedenborg said to the bishop, "You insert things that are false in yours;" on this, the bishop told the gardener, who was present, to retire, but Swedenborg commanded him to stay. The conversation went on, and both turned over the Hebrew and Greek Bibles, to show the texts that were agreeable to their assertions. At length the interview ended, by some observations intended as reproaches to the bishop on his avarice and various unjust actions; "You have already prepared yourself a place in hell," said Swedenborg: "but," added he, "I predict that some months hence you will be attacked with a grievous illness, during which time the Lord will seek to convert you. If you then open your heart to his holy inspirations, your conversion will take place. When this happens, write to me for my theological works, and I will send them to you." Some months after, an officer from the province and bishopric of Skara visited Swedenborg. On being asked how bishop Halenius was, he replied: "He has been very ill, but at present he is quite recovered, and has become altogether another person, being now a practicer of what is good, full of probity, and returns sometimes three or four-fold of the property which he had before unjustly taken into his possession." From that time to the hour of his death, he was one of the greatest supporters of the doctrine of the New Church of the Lord, and declared openly, that the theological writings of Swedenborg were the most precious treasures given for the welfare of mankind. What a blessed result was this of the few severe but really kind words of Swedenborg, spoken in season!

In Stockholm, Swedenborg was very accessible, and visitors sought his advice for all purposes. Widows went to him to inquire about the state of their husbands in the other world; and others fancying him a wizard, beset him with questions about lost and stolen property. Notwithstanding the number and frequency of these visits, from people of all ranks, he would never receive any particular ones, and more especially those of females, without one of his domestics being present. He also required his visitors to speak in the language of the country, saying, "I will have witnesses of my discourse and conduct, that all pretensions to malicious assertions and scandal may be taken away." He had probably suffered from the tongues of busybodies: it would have been strange if he had not; and it was prudent for him to take this effectual plan to cut away the foundation of all idle and malicious gossip.

Nicholas Collin, a young clergyman, at this time visited Swedenborg, and thus pleasantly narrates his interview. "In 1765, I went to reside at Stockholm, where I continued for nearly three years. During that time, Swedenborg was a great object of public attention in the metropolis, and his extraordinary character was a frequent topic of discussion. He resided at his house in the southern suburbs, which was in a pleasant situation, neat and convenient, with a spacious garden and other appendages. There he received company. Not seldom he also appeared in company, and mixed in private society; sufficient opportunities were therefore given to observe him. I collected much information from several respectable persons who had conversed with him; which was the more easy, as I lived the whole time as a private tutor in the family of Dr. Celsius, a gentleman of distinguished talents, who afterwards became bishop of Scania. He, and many of the eminent persons that frequented his house, knew Swedenborg well.

"In the summer of 1766, I waited on him at his house. Introducing myself with an apology for the freedom I took, I assured him that it was not in the least from youthful presumption. I was then twenty, but had a strong desire to converse with a character so celebrated. He received me very kindly. It being early in the afternoon, delicate coffee, without eatables, was served, agreeable to the Swedish custom; he was also, like pensive men in general, fond of this beverage. We conversed for nearly three hours; principally on the nature of human souls, and their states in the invisible world; discussing the principal theories of psychology by various authors. He asserted positively, as he often does in his works, that he had intercourse with spirits of deceased persons. I presumed, therefore, to request of him, as a great favor, to procure me an interview with my brother, who had departed this life a few months before, a young clergyman, and esteemed for his devotion, erudition, and virtue. He answered, that God, having for good and wise purposes separated the world of spirits from ours, a communication is never granted without cogent reasons; and asked what my motives were. I confessed that I had none besides gratifying brotherly affection, and an ardent wish to explore scenes so sublime and interesting to a serious mind. He replied, that my motives were good, but not sufficient; but that if any important spiritual or temporal concern of mine had been the case, he would then have solicited permission from those angels who regulate these matters. He showed me his garden. It had an agreeable building, a wing of which was a kind of temple, to which he often retired for contemplation; its dim religious light rendering it suitable for such a purpose.

"We parted with mutual satisfaction; and he presented by me, to the said Dr. Celsius, an elegant copy of his Apocalypsis Revelata, then lately printed in Amsterdam."

Swedenborg was of a very mild temper, upright, just, and incapable of perverting the truth. Robsahm, one day, asked him if a certain preacher, lately deceased, and greatly esteemed in Stockholm for his flowery sermons, had a place in heaven. "No," said Swedenborg, "he went directly into the abyss; for he left his devotion in the pulpit: he was not pious, but a hypocrite; proud and greatly vain of the gifts he had received from nature, and the goods of fortune he was continually seeking to acquire. Truly," continued he, "false appearances will stand us in no stead hereafter; they are all separated from man at his decease; the mask then falls from him; and it is then made manifest to all, whether he is inwardly good or evil."

The exact month of Swedenborg's next foreign travel is uncertain; but just before he undertook it, Robsahm met him in his carriage, and asked him how he could venture to take a voyage to London, at the age of eighty, and expressed a fear lest he should not see him again. "Be not uneasy, my friend," said he, "if you live, we shall see one another again, for I have yet another voyage of this kind to make."

At Elsinore, on these voyages, he frequently visited M. Rahling, the Swedish Consul, and during this transit, he made the acquaintance of General Tuxen, at the Consul's table. The General asked him how a man might be certain whether he was on the road to salvation or not. Swedenborg answered, "That is very easy. A man need only examine himself and his thoughts by the Ten Commandments; as, for instance, whether he loves and fears God; whether he is happy in seeing the welfare of others, and does not envy them; whether on having received a great injury from others, which may have excited him to anger and to meditate revenge, he afterwards changes his sentiments, because God has said that vengeance is His, and so on; then he may rest assured that he is on the road to heaven: but when he discovers himself actuated by contrary sentiments, he may know that he is on the road to hell."

This led Tuxen to think of himself, as well as others; and he asked Swedenborg whether he had seen King Frederick V.

of Denmark, deceased in 1766, adding that though some human frailty attached to him, yet he had certain hopes that he was happy. Swedenborg said, "Yes, I have seen him, and he is well off; and not only he, but all the kings of the house of Oldenburg, who are associated together. This is not the happy case with our Swedish kings." Swedenborg then told him that he had seen no one so splendidly ministered to in the world of spirits as the Empress Elizabeth of Russia, who died in 1762. As Tuxen expressed astonishment at this, Swedenborg continued: "I can also tell you the reason, which few would surmise. With all her faults, she had a good heart, and a certain consideration in her negligence. This induced her to put off signing many papers that were from time to time presented to her, and which at last so accumulated that she could not examine them, but was obliged to sign as many as possible on the representation of her ministers; after which she would retire to her closet, fall on her knees, and beg God's forgiveness, if she, against her will, had signed anything that was wrong."

At the conclusion of this interesting interview, Swedenborg went on board his vessel, leaving a firm friend and future disciple in General Tuxen. Some years after, Tuxen wrote: "I thank our Lord, the God of heaven, that I have been acquainted with this great man and his writings. I esteem this as the greatest blessing I ever experienced in this life, and hope I shall profit by it in working out my salvation."

Swedenborg's stay in London at this time must have been brief; for on the 28th of November, 1768, we meet him again in Amsterdam, whither he had gone to print another important work, "Conjugial Love, and its chaste Delights; also Adulterous Love and its insane Pleasures." This book he published with his name, as written "by Emanuel

Swedenborg, a Swede." This is the first of his theological works to which he affixed his name. His reason for giving it in this instance, is said to have been, that no other person might be censured for writing on this delicate subject. We wil now examine the contents of this wondrous book.

CHAPTER XXII.

Conjugial Love.

A WISE man might well suspect the soundness of any system of morals which did not take into careful consideration the conjugial relation. Marriage—the most important event in life, the relation which occupies the whole thought of one sex, and the most serious regards of the other, the institution around which all that is highest and holiest in life groups itself, family, home, all that human hearts hold dear—must ever hold a prominent place in a true code of moral and spiritual laws. How then could the subject be omitted from the heavenly writings of the New Jerusalem? or how could its apostle forget or pass it by.

Swedenborg, in his treatise on Conjugial Love, first speaks of marriages in heaven. He shows that a man lives a man after death, and that a woman lives a woman; and since it was ordained from creation that the woman should be for the man, and the man for the woman, and thus that each should be the other's,—and since that love is innate in both, it follows that there are marriages in heaven as well as on earth.

Marriage in the heavens is the conjunction of two into one mind. The mind of man consists of two parts, the understanding and the will. When these two parts act in unity, they are called one mind. The understanding is predominant in man, and the will in woman; but in the marriage of minds there is no predominance, for the will of the wife becomes also the will of the husband, and the understanding of the husband is also that of the wife; because each loves to will and to think as the other wills and thinks, and thus they will and think mutually and reciprocally. Hence their conjunction; so that in heaven, two married partners are not called two, but one angel. When this conjunction of minds descends into the inferior principles which are of the body, it is perceived and felt as love, and that love is conjugial love.

To this doctrine of marriage in heaven will arise an objection from the Lord's words to the Sadducees, when they asked Him whose wife, in the resurrection, a woman should be, who had been married in succession to seven brethren. The Lord replied: "The children of this world marry, and are given in marriage; but they which shall be accounted worthy to obtain that world and the resurrection from the dead, neither marry nor are given in marriage."—Luke xx. 34, 35. To understand this reply, we must bear in mind the nature of the question. A woman had been married, quite in accordance with worldly usage, to seven husbands. Of course, nothing of this kind takes place in heaven; for, as the Lord says, there "neither can they die any more." After that fashion indeed there is no marrying or giving in marriage in heaven. In truth, marriages, such as they are in heaven, could never have been comprehended by the gross and carnal-minded Jews; and had the Lord entered into detail, He would have been as grossly misapprehended by them as when He said, "Destroy this temple, and in three days I will raise it up." And they said: "Forty and six years was this temple in building, and wilt thou rear it up in three days?" not knowing that he "spake of the temple of his body." John ii. 19—21. Now Swedenborg very plainly shows that Christians think as naturally of marriage as the Jews did of the temple, if they suppose that the true marriage of minds does not take place in heaven, or that it was any but the carnal and sensual connections of earth that the Lord declared had no place in eternity. In the spiritual sense of the Lord's words, by the marriage that does not take place in heaven, is meant the spiritual marriage, or union of goodness and truth in the mind; in other words, regeneration: this must be accomplished in this life, or not at all. When the spiritual sense of the Word is understood, this interpretation becomes manifest as the only true and rational mode of understanding the text; and all the rest of Scripture goes to confirm it.

Moreover it is true that there is no marriage in heaven in the exact sense of the word. Partners are born into this world, and by life in it are disciplined for each other. Separate, they are but parts of one whole; and in each there is a continual longing for unition. Seen by the eye of Omniscience, they are ever married; they are one, however divided they may be by space or circumstances. Their meeting in heaven and recognition of each other is only the external completion of what had before in essentials been effected. And in this sense it may be said that there are no marriages in heaven; for all are married, in reality, before they reach heaven.

Marriages on earth, Swedenborg teaches, are at this day entered upon so generally from merely worldly and sensual motives, and with so little regard for similarity of mind, that, save in few cases, they are not maintained and perpetuated in the other life. Married partners commonly meet after death; but as their internal differences of mind are manifested, they separate; for no married partners can be received into heaven, except such as have been interiorly united, or are capable of being so united into one; which is understood by the Lord's words: "They are no longer two, but one flesh." Such as are thus separated—possibly both very good people—meet, in due time, congenial partners, whose souls incline to union with their own, so that they no longer wish to be two lives, but one.

The meeting of young partners in heaven is thus charmingly described:—"The divine providence of the Lord extends to everything, even to the minutest particulars concerning marriages, because all the delights of heaven spring from the delights of conjugial love, as sweet waters from the fountain head. On this account it is provided that conjugial pairs be born, and these pairs are continually educated to their several marriages under the Lord's auspices, neither the boy nor the girl knowing anything of the matter; and after a stated time, when both of them become marriageable, they meet in some place as by chance, and see each other, and in this case they instantly know, as by a kind of instinct, that they are pairs; and by a kind of inward dictate, think within themselves—the youth that she is mine, and the virgin that he is mine; and when this thought has existed some time in the mind of each, they accost each other from a deliberate purpose, and betroth themselves. It is said as by chance, by instinct, and by dictate, and the meaning is by Divine Providence: since, while the Divine Providence is unknown, it has such an appearance; for the Lord opens internal similitudes, that they may see each other."

We are now led by Swedenborg, and introduced to a knowledge of the nature of conjugial love, and shown in what consists its essential blessedness. He shows that this love originates in the marriage of goodness and truth. Every one who has experienced anything of regeneration, knows that there is no bliss so intense, no joy so extatic, as that arising from well-doing, and snbmission to the will of the Lord. When right is done because it is right, when truth in the understanding is carried into action, then good is inseminated in the will by the Lord, and conjoining itself to truth in the understanding, the soul overflows with the sweetest peace, and the most interior delight. The conjunction of goodness and truth is the heavenly marriage, to which the Lord compares the kingdom of heaven; and He says that it is not here, nor there, but within us. Under the symbols of marriage and love, the regeneration of the soul is continually described in the Word; and the meeting of Jacob and Rachel at the well, when "Jacob kissed Rachel," and for very joy, "lifted up his voice and wept," beautifully typifies the meeting of goodness and truth, and the gladness resulting from their approaching union.

It was said that in man the understanding predominates, and in woman the will. In the mind of each, then, it is evident, there never can be a perfect marriage, seeing that individual minds are in themselves imperfect, the balance of the will and intellect being in no case equal. The mental perfection or *wholeness* of man then necessitates marriage. Truth loves good, and good loves truth; and so the will and the understanding ever long for conjunction. It is plain, then, that in man there must always be an unsatisfied desire, if he remain by himself; and so, also, to even a greater degree, with the woman. This insatiable desire for conjunction of soul, can not well appear in its strength in this life for many reasons; nor can it receive here its full satisfaction, as it will in eternity.

True conjugial love can exist only between two; and in polygamists and adulterers it is utterly destroyed. Again, it can only exist with the regenerate, with those who love the Lord and their neighbor, and delight in keeping the divine commandments. In proportion as married partners so live, they become more and more closely and interiorly conjoined; and their minds flowing into one, their peace, joy, and bliss are ineffably increased. With the wicked there is no conjugial love. Their life, being internally evil, conceals the deepest hatred; and the apparent affection which they may display in the world, arises either from sensual love, or worldly expediency. Be it well noted by all, that marriage can yield real happiness only to the religious—to those who love God and honor His laws.

It is impossible for us to give, even by way of catalogue, a view of the details into which the treatise on Conjugial Love enters. It is so richly studded with great principles, that no condensation is possible. It is thus with all of Swedenborg's books; so that an exhaustive review is impossible. He never treats his readers to long moralizings that can be condensed into one paragraph; but all his writings are crowded with thought, so that one is prompted not to condensation, but to expansion. This excuse, which we have had to present on previous occasions, must form our apology for the following extracts, selected as illustrations of some of the leading truths in this treatise.

The Delights of Conjugial Love.—"As conjugial love is the foundation love of all good loves, and as it is inscribed on all the parts and principles of man, even to the most particular, it follows that its delights exceed the delights of all other loves, and also that it gives delight to the other loves, according to its presence and conjunction with them; for it expands the inmost principles of the mind, and at the same time the inmost principles of the body, as the most delightful current of its fountain flows through and opens them. The reason why all delights, from first to last, are collated into this love, is on account of the superior excellence of its use, which is the propagation of the human race, and thence of the angelic heaven; and as this use was the chief end of creation, it follows that all the beatitudes, satisfactions, delights, pleasantnesses, and pleasures, which the Lord the

Creator could possibly confer upon man, are collated into this love."—n. 68.

Love truly Conjugial is essential Chastity.—"The reasons are, 1. Because it is from the Lord, and corresponds to the marriage of the Lord and the church. 2. Because it descends from the marriage of good and truth. 3. Because it is spiritual, in proportion as the church exists with man. 4. Because it is the foundation love, and head of all celestial and spiritual loves. 5. Because it is the orderly seminary of the human race, and thereby of the angelic heaven. 6. Because on this account it also exists with the angels of heaven, and gives birth with them to spiritual offspring, which are love and wisdom. 7. And because its uses are thus more excellent than the other uses of creation. From these considerations, it follows that love truly conjugial, viewed from its origin and its essence, is pure and holy, so that it may be called purity and holiness, consequently, essential chastity."—n. 143.

Conjugial Love in Ancient Times.—"I have been informed by the angels, that those who lived in the most ancient times, live at this day in the heavens, in separate houses, families, and nations, as they lived on earth, *and that scarce any one of a house is wanting;* and that the reason is, because they were principled in love truly conjugial; and that hence their children inherited inclinations to the conjugial principles of good and truth, and were easily initiated into it more and more interiorly by education received from their parents, and afterwards as from themselves, when they became capable of judging for themselves, were introduced into it by the Lord."—n. 205.

Marriage elevates Humanity to its Highest Form.—"The most perfect and noble human form results from the conjunction of two forms, by marriage, so as to become one form; thus from two fleshes becoming one flesh according to creation. In such a case the man's mind is elevated into superior light, and the wife's into superior heat."—n. 201.

The Children of Good Parents.—"Children born of parents who are principled in love truly conjugial, derive from their parents the conjugial principle of good and truth, by virtue whereof they have an inclination and faculty, if sons, to perceive the things appertaining to wisdom, and if daughters, to love those things which wisdom teaches. Hence a superior suitableness and facility to grow wise, is inherited by those who are born from such a marriage, and also to imbibe the things relating to the church and heaven."—n. 202–4.

The capacity of women to perform the duties of men, and men those of women, is thus spoken of.

"The wife can not enter into the duties proper to the man, nor on the other hand the man into the duties proper to the wife, because they differ like wisdom and the love thereof, or like understanding and the will thereof. In the duties proper to the man, the primary agent is the understanding, thought, and wisdom; whereas in the duties proper to the wife, the primary agent is will, affection, and love; and the wife from the latter principles performs her duties, and the man from the former performs his; wherefore their duties, from the nature of them, are diverse, but still conjunctive in a successive series. It is believed by many that women can perform the duties of men, if they were initiated therein like boys, at an early age. They may indeed be initiated into the exercise of such duties, but not into the judgment, on which the rectitude interiorly depends; wherefore those women who have been initiated into the duties of men, are bound, in matters of judgment, to consult men, and then, if they are left to their own disposal, they select from the counsels of men what favors their own particular love. It is also supposed by some, that women are equally capable with men of elevating the intellectual vision, and into the same sphere of life, and of viewing things in the same altitude; and they have been led into this opinion by the writings of certain learned authoresses; but these writings, when examined in the spiritual world, in the presence of the authoresses, were found to be the productions, not of judgment and wisdom, but of ingenuity and wit; and what proceeds from these two latter principles, on account of the elegance and neatness of style in which it is written, has the appearance of sublimity and erudition; yet only in the eyes of those who call all ingenuity by the name of wisdom. In like manner, men can not enter into the duties of women, and perform them aright, because they are not in the affections of women, which are altogether distinct from the affections of men. As the affections and perceptions of the male and female sex are thus distinct by creation, and consequently by nature, therefore, among the statutes given to the sons of Israel, this was also ordained: 'A woman shall not put on the garment of a man, neither shall a man put on the garment of a woman; because this is an abomination.' Deut. xxii. 5. The reason is, because all in the spiritual world are clothed according to their affections; and the affections of the woman and the man can not be united, except as subsisting between two, and in no case as subsisting in one."—n. 175.

The latter portion of the treatise on Conjugial Love is devoted to the melancholy subject of the disorders of the married life, to coldnesses and quarrels, separations and divorces; and finally to adulteries, fornications, and all the abuses of the sexual relations. Of this it would be out of place to speak here, except to remark, that it follows, as a consequence of the fact that conjugial love makes man's highest bliss and purest heaven, that its violations and abuses must needs lead to the bitterest misery and deepest hell. This portion of the treatise has subjected Swedenborg to some gross calumny, which, if sincere, could only have arisen from a very superficial acquaintance with the principles of its author. And yet it is hardly possible for a man to write on such subjects, without provoking the censure of the sickly virtuous and the hypocritically pure. Religious people too generally treat the dire sexual evils which infest and corrupt society with silence and aversion; passing them by as the priest and the Levite did the wounded traveler. When the spirit of Jesus more fully actuates the church, and the love of the neighbor prompts to heal the world's evils by all efficient means, then, we have no doubt, Swedenborg on Scortatory Love will be taken into council.

We have used the term "conjugial," after Swedenborg, who generally uses the Latin adjective *conjugialis,* in preference to *conjugalis,* perhaps because softer in sound.

Interspersed between the various chapters of the treatise, are memorable relations of scenes which the author beheld in the spiritual world, and conversations which he had with spirits and angels on the subject of conjugial love. Many of these possess the most fascinating interest, and convey at the same time the most profound and beautiful truths. One interview which he had with two angels of the third heaven is so beautiful that we present it at length.

"One morning I was looking upwards into heaven, and I saw over me three expanses, one above another. I wondered at first what all this meant; and presently there was heard from heaven a voice as of a trumpet, saying, 'We have perceived, and now see, that thou art meditating concerning conjugial love. We are aware that no one on earth at present knows what true conjugial love is in its origin and essence. Yet it is of importance that it should be known. With us in the heavens, especially in the third heaven, our heavenly delights are principally derived from conjugial love; wherefore in consequence of leave granted us, we will send down to thee a conjugial pair for thy inspection and observation:' and lo! instantly there appeared a chariot descending from the third or highest heaven; in which there was seen one angel; but as it approached there were seen therein two. The chariot, at a distance, glittered before my eyes like a diamond, and to it were harnessed young horses white as snow; and those who sat in the chariot held in their hands two turtle doves. * * * When they came nearer, lo! it was a husband and his wife; and they said, 'We are a conjugial pair; we have lived blessed in heaven from the first age of the world, which is called by you the golden age, and during that time in the same perpetual flower of youth in which thou seest us at this day. I viewed each attentively, because I perceived that they represented conjugial love in its life and its adorning; in its life in their faces, and in its adorning in their raiment. * * * The husband appeared of a middle age between manhood and youth; from his eyes darted forth sparkling light derived from the wisdom of love; by virtue of which light his face was radiant from its inmost ground; and in consequence of such radiance, the skin had a kind of refulgence in the outermost surface, whereby his whole face was one resplendent comeliness. He was dressed in an upper robe which reached down to his feet, and underneath it was a vesture of hyacinthine blue, girded about with a golden girdle, upon which were three precious stones, two sapphires on the sides, and a carbuncle in the middle; his stockings were of bright shining linen, with threads of silver interwoven; and his shoes were of velvet: such was the representative form of conjugial love with the husband. But with the wife it was this; her face was seen by me, and it was not seen; it was seen as essential beauty, and it was not seen because this beauty was inexpressible; for in her face there was a splendor of flaming light, such as the angels of the third heaven enjoy, and this light made my sight dim; so that I was lost in astonishment: she, observing this, addressed me, saying, 'What dost thou see?' I replied, 'I see nothing but conjugial love and the form thereof; but I see, and I do not see.' Hereupon she turned herself obliquely from her husband; and then I was enabled to view her attentively. Her eyes were bright and sparkling from the light of her own heaven, which light, as was said, is of a flaming quality, which it derives from the love of wisdom; for in that heaven wives love their husbands from their wisdom and in their wisdom: and husbands love their wives from that love of wisdom and in it, as directed towards themselves; and thus they are united. This was the origin of her beauty; which was such that it would be impossible for any painter to imitate and exhibit it in its form, for he has no colors bright and vivid enough to express its lustre; nor is it in the power of his art to depict such beauty. Her hair was adjusted in becoming order so as to correspond with her beauty; and in it were inserted diadems of flowers: she had a necklace of carbuncles, from which hung a rosary of chrysolites; and she had bracelets of pearl: her upper robe was scarlet, and underneath it was a stomacher of purple, fastened in front with clasps of rubies. But what surprised me was, that the colors varied according to her aspect in regard to her husband, and also according thereto were sometimes more glittering, and sometimes less; in mutual aspect more, and in oblique aspect less. When I had made these observations, they again discoursed with me; and when the husband spoke, he spoke at the same time as from his wife; and when the wife spoke, she spoke at the same time as from her husband; such was the union of their minds from whence speech flows; and on this occasion I also heard the sound or tone of voice of conjugial love; inwardly it was simultaneous, and it likewise proceeded from the delights of a state of innocence and peace. At length they said, 'We are recalled; we must depart:' and instantly they appeared again conveyed in a chariot as before. The way by which they were conveyed was a paved way through flowering shrubberies, from the beds of which rose olive and orange trees laden with fruit. When they approached their own heaven they were met by several virgins, who welcomed and introduced them."

CHAPTER XXIII

Attacked by Dr. Ekebom—Visits France—Letter to Hartley, and Hartley's Opinion of Swedenborg.

IN the spring of 1769, Swedenborg published at Amsterdam, A Brief Exposition of the Doctrine of the New Church, "in which work," he says, writing to Dr. Beyer, "are fully shown the errors of the existing doctrines of justification by faith alone, and of the imputation of the righteousness or merits of Jesus Christ." He sent the little book to all the clergy throughout Holland, and to the most eminent in Germany; but, on second thought, sent only one copy to Sweden, to Dr. Beyer, requesting him to keep it to himself, for true divinity in Sweden was in a wintry state.

Swedenborg's long preservation from attack and controversy, at this time came to an end. On the 22d of March, 1769, Dr. Ekebom, Dean of the Theological faculty of Gottenburg, laid before the Consistory there a series of objections against Swedenborg's theological writings, laden with untruth, and full of personal invective. The Dean branded his doctrine "as in the highest degree heretical, and, on points the most tender to every Christian, Socinian." He stated, further, that he "*did not know Assessor Swedenborg's religious system, and should take no pains to come at the knowledge of it.*" As for Swedenborg's chief works, he "*did not possess them, and had neither read nor seen them.*" Swedenborg's written reply, transmitted from Holland, was mild and effectual. He cited his writings themselves, and proved that, according to Scripture, the Apostolic Creed, and whatever was not self-contradictory in the orthodoxy of the churches, his doctrine was anything but heretical. But the self-acknowledged ignorance and prejudice of the Dean were not to be removed by anything he might say. "Was not this," to quote Swedenborg's own words, "to be blind in the forehead, and to have eyes behind, and even those covered with a film? To see and decide upon writings in such a fashion, can any secular or ecclesiastical judge regard as otherwise than criminal?"

About the end of May, or the beginning of June, Swedenborg left Amsterdam for Paris, "with a design which," in writing to Dr. Beyer, he says, "must not be made public beforehand." We hardly understand the remark, except that he anticipated some difficulty with regard to the object of his journey,—the publication of another little work, entitled, "The Intercourse Between the Soul and the Body," in the French capital.

On his arrival in Paris, Swedenborg submitted his tract to M. Chevreuil, Censor Royal, who, having read it, informed him that a tacit permission to publish would be granted, on condition, as was customary in the case of doubtful books, that the title should say, "printed at London," or "at Amsterdam." This, Swedenborg's nice sense of truth and honor could not submit to, and he abandoned his intention of publishing it in Paris. His enemies in Gottenburg then circulated a report that he had been ordered to quit Paris, which he, in a letter to Dr. Beyer, pronounced a direct falsehood, and appealed for the truth of the case to the Swedish Ambassador to France.

"Rumor also," writes Wilkinson, "has been busy with Swedenborg upon this journey. The French 'Universal Biography' connects him with an artist,—Elie,—who, it is alleged, supplied him with money, and furthered his presumed designs. Indeed, he has been accused of a league with the *illuminés*, and with a certain politico-theological freemasonry, centuries old, but always invisible, which was to overturn society, and foster revolutions all over the world. We can only say that our researches have not elicited these particulars, and that every authentic document shows that Swedenborg stood always upon his own basis, accepted money from no one, and was just what he appeared—a theological missionary, and nothing more."

The short visit to Paris was terminated by his departure for London, where, unfettered by censors, he published his little book—"The Intercourse Between the Soul and the Body."

One of Swedenborg's warmest and most intelligent English friends, was the Rev. Thomas Hartley, A. M., rector of Winwick, Northamptonshire,—himself an author, and assistant translator of the first English edition of "Heaven and Hell." At this time he wrote to Swedenborg, fearing that he might be in want of money, and offering to supply his needs; also requesting an account of his past life and connections, as a means of refuting calumnies. In his reply, Swedenborg satisfied him on these points. He says to Mr. Hartley: "I take pleasure in the friendship you express for me in your letter, and return you sincere thanks for the same: but as to the praises you bestow upon me, I only receive them as tokens of your love of the truths contained in my writings, and so refer them to the Lord and Saviour, from whom is all truth, because he is the Truth. John xiv. 6.

"I live on terms of familiarity and friendship with all the bishops of my country, who are ten in number; as also with the sixteen senators, and the rest of the nobility; for they know that I am in fellowship with angels. The King and Queen also, and the three princes, their sons, show me much favor. I was once invited by the King and Queen to dine at their table,—an honor which is, in general, granted only to the nobility of the highest rank; and likewise, since, with the hereditary Prince. They all wished for my return home,—so far am I from being in any danger of persecution in my own country, as you seem to apprehend, and so kindly wish to provide against; and should anything of the kind befall me elsewhere, it can not hurt me. But I regard all that I have mentioned as matters of little moment; for, what far exceeds them, I have been called to a holy office by the Lord himself, who most graciously manifested himself in person to me, his servant, in the year 1743; when he opened my sight to the view of the spiritual world, and granted me the privilege of conversing with spirits and angels, which I enjoy to this day. I am a Fellow, by invitation, of the Royal Academy of Sciences at Stockholm: but I have never sought admission into any other Literary Society, as I belong to an angelic society, wherein things relating to heaven and the soul are the only subjects of discourse and entertainment; whereas the things which occupy the attention of our Literary Societies are such as relate to the world and the body. As for the world's wealth, I have what is sufficient, and more I neither seek nor wish for. Your letter has drawn the mention of these things from me, with the view, as you suggest, that any ill-grounded prejudices may be removed. Farewell! and from my heart I wish you all felicity in this world and in the next; which I make no doubt of your attaining, if you look and pray to our Lord.—E. Swedenborg." Dated, London, 1769.

Mr. Hartley, in 1781, when far advanced in years, thus gives his opinion of Swedenborg:—

"The great Swedenborg was a man of uncommon humility. He was of a catholic spirit, and loved all good men of every church, making at the same time all candid allowance for the innocence of involuntary error. However self-denying in his own person, as to gratifications and indulgences, even within the bounds of moderation, yet nothing severe, nothing of the precisian, appeared in him; but on the contrary, an inward serenity and complacency of mind were manifest in the sweetness of his looks and outward demeanor. It may reasonably be supposed that I have weighed the character of our illustrious author in the scale of my best judgment, from the personal knowledge I had of him, from the best information I could procure respecting him, and from a diligent perusal of his writings; and according thereto, I have found him to be the sound divine, the good man, the deep philosopher, the universal scholar, and the polite gentleman; and I further believe, that he had a high degree of illumination from the spirit of God, was commissioned by Him as an extraordinary messenger to the world, and had communication with angels and the spiritual world far beyond any since the time of the Apostles. As such, I offer his character to the world, solemnly declaring, that, to the best of my knowledge, I am not herein led by any partiality or private views whatever, being now dead to every worldly interest, and accounting myself as unworthy of any higher character than that of a penitent sinner."

Two others of Swedenborg's English friends were Dr. Messiter and Dr. Hampé, who had been preceptor to George I. From a letter of Dr. Messiter's, we extract the following remarks on Swedenborg's character:—

"I have had the honor of being frequently admitted to Swedenborg's company, when in London, and to converse with him on various points of learning, and I will venture to affirm that there are no parts of mathematical, philosophical, or medical knowledge, nay, I believe I might justly say, of human literature, to which he is in the least a stranger; yet so totally insensible is he of his own merit, that I am confident he does not know that he has any; and as he himself somewhere says of the angels, he always turns his head away on the slightest encomium."

Swedenborg's stay in England at this time does not seem to have been longer than sufficed for the transaction of his business; for in September, 1769, he sailed for Stockholm, arriving there at the beginning of October. But we must now suspend the narrative of his life to offer a few remarks on his little works,—"A Brief Exposition of the Doctrine of the New Church," and "The Intercourse Between the Soul and the Body."

CHAPTER XXIV.

"Brief Exposition of the Doctrines of the New Church," and "The Intercourse between the Soul and the Body."

"THE Brief Exposition of the Doctrines of the New Church" is an exposition effected by means of comparisons between the doctrines of the New Church and those of Catholics and Protestestants. The work is avowedly only a sketch, and the precursor of a larger book—"The True Christian Religion"—a work of some years, which will shortly demand our attention. The Catholic doctrinals are taken from the records of the Council of Trent; and the Protestant from the Formula Concordiæ, composed by persons attached to the Augsburg Confession. The disagreements between the tenets of the Old and New Churches are considered under twenty-five Articles, the heads of which we will condense and present to the reader.

The Churches which, by the Reformation, separated themselves from the Roman Catholic Church, differ in various points of doctrine; but they all agree in the Articles concerning a Trinity of Persons in the Godhead, original sin from Adam, imputation of the merit of Christ, and justification by faith alone. The Roman Catholics, before the Reformation, held and taught exactly the same things as the Reformed did after it, in respect to these points; only with this difference, that they conjoined faith with charity or good works.

The leading Reformers, Luther, Melancthon, and Calvin,

retained all the tenets concerning a Trinity of Persons in the Godhead, original sin, imputation of the merits of Christ, and justification by faith, just as they were, and had been, among the Roman Catholics; but they separated charity or good works from that faith, and declared at the same time that they were not of a saving efficacy, with a view to be totally severed from the Roman Catholics as to the very essentials of the Church, which are faith and charity. Nevertheless the leading Reformers adjoined good works, and even conjoined them to their faith, but in man as a passive subject; whereas the Roman Catholics conjoin them in man as an active subject; and notwithstanding this, there is actually a conformity between the one and the other as to faith, works, and merit.

The whole system of theology in the Christian World, at this day, is founded on an idea of three Gods, arising from the doctrine of a Trinity of Persons, and when this doctrine is rejected, then all the tenets of the aforesaid theology fall to pieces. The truth of this must be apparent to every one. The Doctrine of a Trinity of Persons in the Divine Being, is the key-stone of Roman Catholic and Protestant theology. If this Doctrine be false, the whole structure totters to its fall.

When the faith in three Gods is rejected, then it is possible to receive the true and saving faith, which is a faith in One God, united with good works.

This faith is in God the Saviour Jesus Christ, and in its simple form is as follows: 1. That there is One God, in whom is a Divine Trinity, and that He is the Lord Jesus Christ. 2. That saving faith is to believe in Him. 3. That evils ought to be shunned, because they are of the devil and from the devil. 4. That good works ought to be done, because they are of God and from God. 5. That they ought to be done by man as of himself, but with a belief that they are from the Lord, operating in him and by him.

The faith of the present day has separated religion from the Church, since religion consists in the acknowledgment of One God, and in the worship of Him from faith grounded in charity; but the faith of the present Church cannot be conjoined with charity, and produce any fruits which are good works, because imputation supplies everything, remits guilt, justifies, sanctifies, regenerates; imparts the life of heaven, and thus salvation; and all this freely, without any works of man. In this case, what is charity, which ought to be united with faith, but something vain and superfluous, and a mere addition and supplement to imputation, and justification, to which, nevertheless, it adds no weight or value?

From this faith results a worship of the mouth and not of the life. Now the Lord accepts the worship of the mouth in proportion as it proceeds from the worship of the life.

The doctrine of the present Church is interwoven with many paradoxes, which are to be embraced by faith. Therefore its tenets gain admission into the memory only, and not at all into the understanding, which is superior to the memory, but merely into confirmations below it. Thus the tenets of the present Church cannot be learned or retained without great difficulty, nor can they be preached or taught without using great care and caution to conceal their nakedness, because sound reason neither discerns nor perceives them.

The doctrine of the faith of the present Church ascribes to God human passions and infirmities; as, that He beheld man from anger, that He required to be reconciled, that He is reconciled through the love He bore towards the Son, and by His intercession; and that He required to be appeased by the sight of His Son's sufferings, and thus to be brought back to mercy; and that He imputes the righteousness of His Son to an unrighteous man who supplicates it from faith alone; and that thus from an enemy He makes him a friend, and from a child of wrath a child of grace:—all which dogmas are the opposite of the truth, and repulsive to every wise man.

The faith of the present Church has produced monstrous births; for instance, instantaneous salvation by an immediate act of mercy; predestination; the notion that God has no respect unto the actions of men, but unto faith alone; that there is no connection between charity and faith; that man in conversion is like a stock; with many more heresies of the same kind; likewise concerning the sacraments of Baptism and the Holy Supper, as to the advantages reasonably to be expected from them, when considered according to the doctrine of justification by faith alone; as also with regard to the person of Christ: and that heresies, from the first ages to the present day, have sprung up from no other source than from the doctrine founded on the idea of three Divine Persons or Gods.

The last state of the present church, when it is at an end, is meant by the consummation of the age, and the coming of the Lord at that period. Matt. xxiv. 3.

The infestation from falses, and thence the consummation of every truth, or the desolation which at this day prevails in the Christian Churches, is meant by the great affliction, such as was not from the beginning of the world, nor ever shall be: Matt. xxiv. 21: and that there would be neither love nor faith, nor the knowledge of good and truth, in the last time of the Christian Church, is understood by these words in the same chapter of Matthew: "After the affliction of those days, the sun shall be darkened, and the moon shall not give her light, and the stars shall fall from heaven, and the powers of the heavens shall be shaken," verse 29.

They who are in the present justifying faith, are meant by the he-goats in Daniel and Matthew; and they who have confirmed themselves therein, are meant in the Apocalypse by the dragon and his two beasts, and by the locusts; and this same faith, when confirmed, is there meant by the great city which is spiritually called Sodom and Egypt, where the two witnesses were slain; as also by the pit of the abyss, whence the locusts issued.

Unless a New Church be established by the Lord, no one can be saved. This is meant by these words: "Unless those days should be shortened, there should no flesh be saved." Matt. xxiv. 22. The reason why no flesh could be saved, unless those days should be shortened, is, because the faith of the present Church is founded on the idea of three Gods, and with this idea no one can enter heaven. Not that all who are believers in the doctrine of a tripersonal God are lost; but that, unless a New Church were provided by the Lord, and spiritual truth revealed, man, wanting truth, could never become regenerate, could never enter heaven, and thus the end of his creation would be defeated. In spite, however, of false doctrine, men are saved by the laying hold, as it were, of the truths leading to a good life, which exist in the most corrupt faiths, and goodness always contains an internal acknowledgment and love of truth, although false doctrine may fill the memory. Yet it is true, nevertheless, that false doctrine perverts, discourages, and in the end destroys all inclinations to live well. For this reason, then, the First Christian Church has come to its end, or has been consummated; and the Lord is raising up a New Church, endowed with truth capable of leading the world in the way of life, and to heaven.

The opening and rejection of the tenets of the faith of the

present Church, and the revelation and reception of the tenets of the faith of the New Church, is meant by these words in the Apocalypse:—"He that sat upon the throne said, Behold I make all things new; and He said unto me, Write; for these words are true and faithful." xxi. 5. The New Church about to be established by the Lord, is the New Jerusalem, treated of in chapters xxi. and xxii., which is there called the Bride and the Wife of the Lamb.

Such, briefly expressed, are the heads or leading ideas of the little work, "A Brief Exposition of the Doctrines of the New Church," a treatise which, as Wilkinson truly remarks, "is unequaled among Swedenborg's works for its destructive logic."

"The Intercourse Between the Soul and the Body," is a small treatise designed to illustrate a subject which has puzzled many minds from time immemorial. Various have been the theories of philosophers on this subject; but few could satisfy the intelligent mind, or explain the varied phenomena of being. Swedenborg, in many of his previous works, had, with greater or less fullness, explained the nature of the soul's union with the body, and this treatise is, to some extent, but a repetition of what he had elsewhere written,—cleared, however, from extraneous matter.

His view of the subject is simple and intelligible, as is all truth. The soul of man is a spiritual substance, of the same form as his body; transfusing all the body's tissues, and wearing the body as a garment, even as the body wears its clothes. The body lives from the soul. In itself, the body is dead and without sensation, as is evident when the man leaves it at death; it then returns to its inorganic elements. As the body is diseased or injured, the soul is more or less deprived of its power of action in the natural world, but the soul itself is uninjured. We see an illustration of this in the use of spectacles. Man's external organ of sight is defective, and he cannot see objects distinctly. Glasses are put before his eyes, and he sees as well as ever. Now it is certain the glasses in themselves do not restore his sight. They merely complete the defective organ, and the eye of the spiritual man uses them as a means to look forth into the material world. Observation and meditation will supply a multitude of confirmations of this doctrine of the spiritual body animating and transfusing the material.

At death the spiritual body lays down the material, and makes its appearance in its higher sphere. Whether it is beautiful or deformed, depends upon the man's conduct on earth. If the soul has loved goodness and truth, it is a beautiful human form, and increases in grace and loveliness to eternity in heaven; if, on the other hand, it has lived in evil and hated truth, it is deformed and hideous, and finds its place in hell, the abode of all that is ugly and abominable.

But from this it is not to be concluded that the soul has life in itself. Like the body, it also is dead, and is only a form receptive of life from the One Only Infinite Life, in whom the whole universe lives, moves, and has its being,—the Lord. The material body is proximately sustained by the light and heat of the material sun. The spiritual body of man is sustained by the light and heat of the spiritual Sun, which is the circumambient sphere of the Divine Love and Wisdom. From this spiritual Sun, our natural sun exists, even as our material bodies live from our spiritual bodies. But all alike exist and subsist from the Lord alone.

Such, in a few words, is the leading idea of this little treatise. For the details, the charming confirmation and the able and simple refutation of the doctrines of Leibnitz and other philosophers, who have treated on the same subject, we can only refer to the book itself. We append the concluding paragraph of the treatise, as a delightful specimen of spiritual analogy:—

"I was once asked, how I, who was previously a philosopher, became a theologian; and I answered, 'In the same manner that fishermen became the disciples and apostles of the Lord: and that I also from my youth had been a spiritual fisherman.' On this, he asked, 'What is a spiritual fisherman?' I replied,—'A fisherman, in the spiritual sense of the Word, signifies a man who investigates and teaches natural truths, and afterwards spiritual truths in a rational manner.' On his inquiring, 'How is this demonstrated?' I said, 'From these passages of the Word: 'And the waters shall fail from the sea, and the rivers shall be wasted and dried up. The fishers also shall mourn, and all they that cast a hook into the brook shall lament.' Isaiah xix. 5, 8. And in another place it is said, respecting the sea, whose waters were healed, 'The fishers shall stand upon it, from Engedi even unto Eneglaim; they shall be present to spread forth nets; their fish shall be according to their kinds, as the fish of the great sea, exceeding many.' Ezekiel xlvii. 10. And in another place, 'Behold I will send for many fishers, saith Jehovah, and they shall fish them.' Jeremiah xvi. 16. Hence it is evident why the Lord chose fishermen for his disciples, and said, 'Follow me, and I will make you fishers of men;' Matthew iv. 18, 19; Mark i. 16, 17; and why he said to Peter after he had caught a multitude of fishes, 'Henceforth thou shalt catch men.' Luke v. 9, 10. I afterwards demonstrated the origin of this signification of fishermen from the Apocalypse Revealed; namely, that since water signifies natural truths, as does also a river, a fish signifies those who are in possession of natural truths; and thence fishermen, those who investigate and teach truth. On hearing this, my interrogator said, 'Now I can understand why the Lord called and chose fishermen to be his disciples; and therefore I do not wonder that he has also chosen you, since, as you have observed, you were from early youth a fisherman in a spiritual sense, that is, an investigator of natural truths; and the reason that you are now become an investigator of spiritual truths, is because they are founded in the former.' To this he added, being a man of reason, that 'the Lord alone knows who is the proper person to apprehend and teach the truths of His New Church, whether one of the primates, or one of their domestic servants. Besides,' he continued, 'what Christian theologian does not study philosophy in the schools, before he is inaugurated a theologian.' At length he said, 'Since you are become a theologian, explain what is your theology.' I answered, 'These are its two principles, *God is one, and there is a conjunction of charity and faith.*' To which he replied, 'Who denies these principles?' I rejoined, 'The theology of the present day, when interiorly examined.' "

CHAPTER XXV.

Persecution.—Letter to the Academy of Sciences.—Leaves Stockholm for the last time.

ON Swedenborg's arrival in Stockholm, he found that the long peace he had enjoyed from external interference and persecution was at an end. The first manifestation of hostility took place in the seizure of some copies of his treatise on Conjugial Love, at Norkjoping, which he had sent from England, intending to present them to his countrymen. The ground of their seizure was, a law prohibiting the introduction of any works into Sweden at variance with the Lutheran faith. The seizure having taken place in the diocese of his nephew Filenius, he naturally turned to him for explanation and redress. Filenius thereon embraced and kissed his uncle, and assured him that he would fulfill all his desires, and procure the restoration of his books. But his actions were the reverse of his words; for he was, in fact, the prompter of the seizure, and secretly did all he could to insure their confiscation. By and by Swedenborg discovered the hypocrisy, and remonstrated with Filenius; whereupon he dropped the mask, and insisted on the books undergoing clerical revision before they could be surrendered. Swedenborg urged that as his treatise was not theological, but chiefly moral, its revisal by the clergy was absurd, and that such censorship would pave the way for a dark age in Sweden. But Filenius was unmoved; and Swedenborg, now fully convinced of his double dealing, likened him, as he well might, to Judas Iscariot, and said that "he who spoke lies, lied also in his life." Having brought some copies of his treatise on Conjugial Love with him to Sweden, he presented them to many of the Senators, the Bishops, and the royal family. He had no fear of the result of free and open criticism. But worse things lay in store. Dean Ekebom, of Gottenburg, was indignant that Doctors Beyer and Rosen should have embraced Swedenborg's views, and the clerical deputies from that town were instructed to complain of Swedenborg and his disciples to the Diet. They found in bishop Filenius, then President of the House of Clergy, a willing instrument to further their designs. They plotted to have Swedenborg put upon his trial, presuming that when questioned he would openly assert his divine commission and powers of spiritual intercourse, and then they would pronounce him insane, and have him committed to a mad-house. Count Hopken revealed to Swedenborg this cunning device of his enemies, and advised him to fly the kingdom. At this news, Swedenborg was much afflicted; and going into his garden, he fell on his knees, and prayed to the Lord to direct him what to do. After this prayer, he received the consolatory answer that *no evil should touch him.* And so it turned out. His inoffensive bearing, his rank and connections, all tended to intimidate his adversaries, and prevent the execution of their designed outrage. Had he been a farmer's or a tradesman's son, instead of being a bishop's, his fate might have been very different.

Bishop Filenius, however, succeeded in gaining the appointment of a committee of the House of Clergy on the Swedenborgian case. Its deliberations were kept secret. Nothing came of it that was unfavorable to Swedenborg. They disregarded the charges of Filenius, and spoke "very handsomely and reasonably of Swedenborg."

Filenius gained one point, however, in the presentation of

a memorial to the king, requesting the attention of the Chancellor of Justice to the troubles at Gottenburg. To this request the king yielded; and the members of the Consistory of Gottenburg were commanded to send in an unequivocal representation of the light in which they regarded Swedenborg's principles. On January 2d, 1770, Dr. Beyer, as one of the members of the Consistory, rose, and gave his bold and honest testimony in favor of Swedenborg and his writings. He said: "Convinced by experience, I must in the first place observe, that no man is competent to give a just and suitable judgment on those writings, who has not read them; or who has read them superficially, or with a determination in his heart to reject them, after having perused, without examination, some detached parts only; neither is he competent, who rejects them as soon as he finds anything that militates against those doctrines which he has long cherished and acknowledged as true, and of which perhaps he is but too blindly enamored; nor is he competent, who is an ardent, yet undiscriminating biblical scholar, who, in explaining the meaning of the Scriptures, confines his ideas to the literal expression or signification only: and, lastly, neither is he competent, who has altogether devoted himself to sensual indulgences, and the love of the world." He then entered into the details of New Church doctrine, and concluded in these words: "In obedience, therefore, to your Majesty's most gracious command, that I should deliver a full and positive declaration respecting the writings of Swedenborg, I do acknowledge it to be my duty to declare, in all humble confidence, that as far as I have proceeded in the study of them, and agreeably to the gift granted to me for investigation and judgment, I have found in them *nothing but what closely coincides with the words of the Lord himself, and that they shine with a light truly divine.*" These were noble and brave words to speak in the midst of enemies.

The debate on his doctrines dragged its slow length along. His enemies, full of spite, were yet full of fear, and seemed to dread the result of an open attack upon Swedenborg. Still the petty persecution continued, until, at last, May 10th, 1770, Swedenborg took up his pen and addressed himself directly to the king. In this letter, he complains that he had met with usage the like of which had been offered to none since the establishment of Christianity in Sweden, and much less since there had existed liberty of conscience. He recapitulated his grievances. He said that he had been attacked, calumniated, and menaced, without the opportunity of defending himself; though truth itself had answered for him. He reminded his Majesty of their former interview. With great simplicity, he says: "I have already informed your Majesty, and beseech you to call it to mind, that the Lord our Saviour manifested himself to me in a sensible personal appearance; that he has commanded me to write what has been already written, and what I have still to write; that He was afterwards graciously pleased to endow me with the privilege of conversing with angels and spirits, and of being in fellowship with them. I have already declared this more than once to your Majesty in the presence of all the royal family, when they were graciously pleased to invite me to their table, with five senators, and several other persons; this was the only subject discoursed of during the repast. Of this I also spoke afterwards to several other senators; and more openly to their Excellencies Count de Tessin, Count Bonde, and Count Hopken, who are still alive, and were satisfied with the truth of it. I have declared the same in England, Holland, Germany, Denmark, and at Paris, to kings, princes, and other particular persons, as well as to those in this kingdom. If the common report is to be believed, the Chancellor has declared that what I have been reciting are untruths, although the very truth. To say that they cannot believe and give credit to such things, therein will I excuse them; for it is not in my power to place others in the same state in which God has placed me, so as to be able to convince tham, by their own eyes and ears of the truth of those deeds and things I publicly have made known. I have no ability to capacitate them to converse with angels and spirits, neither to work miracles to dispose or force their understandings to comprehend what I say. When my writings are read with attention and cool reflection, (in which many things are to be met with, heretofore unknown,) it is easy enough to conclude, that I could not come to such a knowledge but by a real vision, and by conversing with those who are in the spiritual world. This knowledge is given to me from our Saviour, not for any private merit of mine, but for the great concern of all Christians' salvation and happiness; and as such, how can any one venture to assert that it is false? That these things may appear such as many have had no conception of, and which, of consequence, they can not easily credit, has nothing remarkable in it, for scarcely anything is known respecting them." He concluded by throwing himself upon the king's protection, and requesting him to command for himself the opinion of the clergy on the case; also the production of various documents that had been produced at Gottenburg and elsewhere; in order that he, and those maligned together with him, might be heard in their defence, this being their right and privilege. He protested, that the only advice he had given to Doctors Beyer and Rosen, was to address themselves to our Lord and Saviour Jesus Christ, as a means to heavenly good and blessedness; for He only has all power in heaven and on earth. Matthew xxviii. 18. Were this doctrine of the Supreme Divinity of the Lord Jesus Christ taken away, he averred that he would rather live in Tartary than in Christendom.

Had the Consistory declared this doctrine heretical, it must have led to many strange issues. But the Consistory came to no decision, and their report on Swedenborg's writings was never written. A short time before Swedenborg left Stockholm for the last time, the king said to him: "The Consistory has been silent on my letters and your works;" and, putting his hand on Swedenborg's shoulder, he added, "We may conclude that they have found nothing reprehensible in them, and that you have written in conformity to the truth."

Throughout all this affair, Swedenborg remained perfectly calm; and, though a very old man, worked on as industriously as ever. It might seem, from what has been said, that the controversy had terminated entirely in his favor. But it was not so, as he, in the following year, 1771, found out; for then it appeared that his adversaries had succeeded in obtaining a strict prohibition against the importation of his writings into Sweden. It was his intention to send in a formal complaint to the States General, appealing against this prohibition; but it does not appear whether he fulfilled his intention, or not.

Finally, he addressed a letter to the Universities of Upsal, Lund, and Abo, asserting that each of the estates of the kingdom ought to have its own Consistory, and ought not to acknowledge the exclusive authority of that of Gottenburg. He declared that religious matters belong to others as well as the priests. Thus ends our account of this affair. It may be said to be the only thing approaching to persecution that Swedenborg endured; and considering the many heterodox opinions that he broached, we can not but think that he had, on the whole, but little to complain of. Many who have followed him in the propagation of the new theology, have not gone so far, yet have fared worse. The gentleness and simple prudence which, during so many years, shielded him from interference, we can not too highly admire. But, above all, we must be struck with the remarkable providence of the Lord, shown in his protection: the Divine promise was truly kept, that he *should not be harmed.*

His old associates of the Royal Academy of Sciences at Stockholm, received, at this time, his last communication. He wrote them a letter explaining some of the correspondences of Scripture, and their origin. In it, he says: "The science of correspondences was esteemed, by the ancients, the science of sciences, and constituted their wisdom; it would surely be of importance for some one of your society to devote his attention to it. Should it be desired, I am willing to unfold the meaning of the Egyptian hieroglyphics, which are nothing else but corrrespondences; these being discovered and proved from the Word, in the Apocalypse Revealed; and to publish their explications, is a work which no other person could accomplish." We have no record as to how the Academy received this proposal. A copy of this letter was sent to Mr. Hartley, and Swedenborg desired that he and his friends would think over the subject. The letter is now published as an appendix to his treatise on the White Horse.

Swedenborg now prepared to leave Stockholm for another journey. Writing under date of July 23d, 1770, to Dr. Beyer, he says: "As I am going, in a few days, to Amsterdam, I shall take my leave of you in this letter, hoping that our Saviour will support you in good health, preserve you from further violence, and bless your thoughts."

Robsahm tells us that, on the day that Swedenborg departed, he called on him, and "I then asked him," says he, "if we should meet again. He answered me in a tender and touching manner: 'I do not know whether I shall return; but I am assured I shall not die before I have finished the publication of the book entitled the True Christian Religion; and for which only I am now about to depart. But should we not see one another again in this lower world, we shall meet in the presence of the Lord our Heavenly Father, if so be that we observe to do his commandments.' He then took a cheerful leave, and started on his last journey, with the apparent vigor of a man of thirty years of age, although he was then eighty-two. He took ship for Amsterdam, leaving his native land, never again, in the body, to return."

CHAPTER XXVI.

Swedenborg in intercourse with General Tuxen and Paulus ab Indagine—His reply to Dr. Ernesti—Letter to the Landgrave of Hesse Darmstadt.

On the voyage to Amsterdam, the ship that carried Swedenborg being detained, by adverse winds, off Elsinore, General Tuxen, hearing that Swedenborg was in the offing, determined to improve the opportunity; and, taking a boat, went off to see him. Introduced by the captain into the cabin, he found Swedenborg seated in an undress,—his elbows on the table, and his hands supporting his face, which was turned towards the door,—his eyes open and much elevated. The General at once addressed him. At this, he recovered himself, (for he had been in a state of vision,) rose with some confusion, advanced a few steps in visible uncertainty, and then bade him welcome, asking whence he came. Tuxen replied that he had come with an invitation from his wife and himself, to request him to favor them with his company at their house; to which he immediately consented, and dressed himself alertly. The General's wife, who was indisposed, received him in the house, and requested his excuse if in any respect she should fall short of her wishes to entertain him: adding that for thirty years she had been afflicted with a painful disease. Swedenborg politely kissed her hand, and answered, "Let us not speak of this; only acquiesce in the will of God, and it will pass away, and you will return to the same health and beauty as when you were fifteen years old." The lady made some reply, to which he rejoined, "Yes, in a few weeks." From which they concluded him to mean that diseases which have their foundation in the mind, and are supported by infirmities of the body, do not disappear immediately after death.

"Being then together," says Tuxen, "in company with my wife, my now deceased daughter, and three or four young ladies, my relations, he entertained them very politely, and with much attention, on indifferent subjects, on favourite dogs and cats that were in the room, which caressed him, and jumped on his knee, showing their little tricks. During these trifling discourses,—mixed with singular questions, all of which he obligingly answered, whether they concerned this or the other world,—I took occasion to say that I was sorry I had no better company to amuse him than a sickly wife and her young girls: he replied, 'And is not this very good company? I was always very partial to ladies' society.' After some little pause, he cast his eyes on a harpsichord, and asked whether we were lovers of music, and who played upon it. I told him we were all lovers of it, and that my wife in her youth had practiced, as she had a fine voice, perhaps better than any in Denmark, as several persons of distinction, who had heard the best singers in France, England, and Italy, had assured her; and that my daughter also played with pretty good taste. On this Swedenborg desired her to play. She then performed a difficult and celebrated sonata, to which he beat the measure with his foot on the sofa on which he sat; and when finished, he said, 'Bravo! very fine.' She then played another by Rutini; and when she had played a few minutes, he said, 'This is by an Italian, but the first was not.' This finished, he said, 'Bravo! you play very well. Do you not also sing?' She answered, 'I sing, but have not a very good voice, though fond of singing, and would sing if my mother would accompany me.' He requested my wife to join, to which she assented, and they sang a few Italian duettos, and some French airs, each in her respective taste, to which he beat time, and afterwards paid many compliments to my wife, on account of her taste and fine voice, which she had preserved notwithstanding so long an illness. I took the liberty of saying to him, that since in his writings he always declared that at all times there were good and evil spirits of the other world present with man; might I then be bold to ask, whether now, while my wife and daughter were singing, there had been any from the other world present with us? To this he answered, 'Yes, certainly;' and on my inquiring who they were, and whether I had known them, he said it was the Danish royal family, and he mentioned Christian VI., Sophia Magdalena, and Frederick V., who, through his eyes, had seen and heard it. I do not positively recollect whether he also mentioned the late beloved Queen Louisa among them. After this he retired."

During this visit to General Tuxen, in the course of other conversation, Tuxen produced an autobiographical letter which Swedenborg had written to Hartley, and which began, "I was born in the year 1689." Swedenborg told him that he was not born in that year, as mentioned, but in the preceding. Tuxen asked him if this was an error of the press. He said "No;" and added, "you may remember in reading my writings to have seen it stated in many parts, that every cipher or number has in the spiritual sense a certain correspondence or signification. Now," said he, "when I put the true year in that letter, an angel present told me to write the year 1689, as much more suitable to myself than the other; 'and you observe,' added the angel, 'that with us time and space are nothing.' "

We give these anecdotes as Tuxen relates them. Every one, however, will know from his private experience how little absolute dependence is to be placed upon narrations of conversations, or actions, by even the most truthful. Sir Walter Raleigh, while writing his History of the World, was led to think of the errors into which he might be led, by observing that an affray beneath his prison wall was variously described by several eye-witnesses. If the occurrences of the present are so liable to misstatement, what sort of faith can we place in the history of the past? Wilkinson, commenting on this anecdote of the date of Swedenborg's birth, remarks, in his usual keen style: "We have here a reason for that modification of events according to a context, of which the Gospel histories, so often discrepant from each other, furnish numerous instances. Manifestly it is the plan of the context which regards the events from its own point of view, and paints the narrative in its own colors. It is what all historians do in a lesser way, bending the history to ideas, or shaping it with an artistic force. Taking a certain larger block of time as a period of birth, it is hieroglyphically truthful to play down upon any date contained in the block, according to the subject and signification. There are many kinds of truth besides black and white; and generally, figurative truths require latitude of phrase. At the same time it must be confessed that one would like to know when the writing is pure history, and when it is a base of history, made use of for symbolical purposes, and touched, in part, by spirit. Literal people are apt to be offended otherwise, and we sympathize with them."

Swedenborg arrived in Amsterdam some time in September, 1770, and straightway set about printing his manuscript of the "True Christian Religion." From two letters of a gentleman, named D. Paulus ab Indagine, who seems to have been on familiar terms with Swedenborg, we select the following passages, illustrative of this period of his life. He writes:—"You asked me what this venerable old man,

Swedenborg, is now doing. This I can tell you; he eats and drinks very moderately, but keeps his chamber rather long, and thirteen hours appear to be not too much for him.* When I informed him that his work 'On the Earths in the Universe' had been translated and published, he was much delighted, and his eyes, which are always smiling, became still more brilliant. He is now indefatigably at work; yea, I must say that he labors in a most astonishing and superhuman manner at his new work. Only think! for every printed sheet, 4to, he has to procure four sheets of manuscript; he now prints two sheets every week, and corrects them himself, and consequently he has to write eight sheets every week; and what appears to me utterly inconceivable, he has not a single line beforehand in store.† His work is to consist, as he himself states, of about eighty sheets in print. The title of this work is the following:—'True Christian Religion, Containing the Universal Theology of the New Church, Predicted by the Lord in Daniel viii. 13, 14, and in the Apocalypse, xxi. 1, 2; By Emanuel Swedenborg, Servant of the Lord Jesus Christ.' I could not, in my open manner, conceal my astonishment that he should put himself upon the title page as the servant of the Lord Jesus Christ. But he replied: 'I have asked, and have not only received permission, but have been ordered to do so.' *It is astonishing with what confidence* the old gentleman speaks of the spiritual world, of the angels, and of God himself. If I were only to give you the substance of our last conversation, it would fill many pages. He spoke

*It is not to be supposed that this time was wasted in sleep. In his meditations and spiritual intercourse, he, no doubt, loved the seclusion of his quiet chamber.

†This is quite a mistake. His work he had in contemplation for some years It is probable the revisal, alterations, and additions in the MS. and in the proofs, led Paulus into this misconception.

of naturalists, those who ascribe all things to nature, whom he had seen shortly after death, and amongst them were even many theologians, or such, at least, as had made theology their profession in this life. He told me things which made me shudder, but which, however, I pass by, in order not to be over-hasty in my judgment respecting him. I will willingly admit that I know not what to make of him; he is a problem that I can not solve. I sincerely wish that upright men, whom God has placed as watchmen upon the walls of Zion, had some time since occupied themselves with this man.

"I can not forbear to tell you something new about Swedenborg. Last Thursday I paid him a visit, and found him, as usual, writing. He told me that he had been in conversation that same morning, for three hours, with the deceased king of Sweden. He had seen him already on Wednesday; but as he observed that he was deeply engaged in conversation with the queen, who is still living, he would not disturb him. I allowed him to continue, but at length asked him how it was possible for a person who is still in the land of the living, to be met with in the world of spirits. He replied, that it was not the queen herself, but her *spiritus familiaris*, or her familiar spirit. I asked him what that might be; for I had neither heard from him anything respecting appearances of that kind, nor had I read anything about them. He then informed me that every man has either his good or bad spirit, who is not only constantly with him, but sometimes a little removed from him, and appears in the world of spirits. But of this, the man still living knows nothing; the spirit, however, knows everything. This familiar spirit has everything in accordance with his companion on earth; he has, in the world of spirits, the same figure, the same countenance, and the same tone of voice, and wears also similar garments; in a word, this familiar spirit of the queen, said Swedenborg, appeared exactly as he had so often seen the queen herself at Stockholm, and had heard her speak. In order to allay my astonishment, he added that Dr. Ernesti, of Leipsic, had appeared to him, in a similar manner, in the world of spirits, and that he had held a long disputation with him. What will the learned professor say, when he comes to hear of it? Probably he will say that the old man is in his second childhood; he will only laugh at it, and who can be surprised? I have often wondered at myself, how I could refrain from laughing, when I was hearing such extraordinary things from him. And what is more, I have often heard him relate the same things in a numerous company of ladies and gentlemen, when I well knew there were mockers amongst them; but, to my great astonishment, not a single person thought of laughing. Whilst he is speaking, it is as though every person who hears him were charmed, and compelled to believe him. He is by no means reserved and recluse, but open-hearted and accessible to all. Whoever invites him as his guest, may expect to see him. A certain young gentleman invited him last week to be his guest, and, although he was not acquainted with him, he appeared at his table, where he met Jewish and Portuguese gentlemen, with whom he freely conversed, without distinction. Whoever is curious to see him, has no difficulty; it is only necessary to go to his house, and he allows anybody to approach him. It can easily be conceived, however, that the numerous visits, to which he is liable, deprive him of much time."

About this time, Dr. Ernesti attacked Swedenborg in his Bibliotheca Theologica, and, in reply, Swedenborg published a single leaf, which, in its decisive sharpness, is truly effective. It is as follows :—

"I have read what Dr. Ernesti has written about me. It consists of mere personalities. I do not in it observe a grain of reason against anything in my writings. As it is against the laws of honesty to assail any one with such poisoned weapons, I think it beneath me to bandy words with that illustrious man. I will not cast back calumnies by calumnies. To do this, I should be even with the dogs, which bark and bite, or with the lowest drabs, which throw street mud in each other's faces in their brawls. Read, if you will, what I have written in my books, and afterwards conclude, but from reason, respecting my revelation."

The Landgrave of Hesse Darmstadt now wrote to Swedenborg, requesting information on several subjects. Swedenborg having doubt as to the genuineness of the epistle, did not at first reply to it, until his misgivings were set aside by M. Venator, the minister of that prince. In his reply to the Landgrave, he says: "The Lord our Saviour had foretold that He would come again into the world, and that he would establish there a New Church. But as He cannot come again into the world in person, it was necessary that He should do it by means of a man, who should not only receive the doctrine of this New Church in his understanding, but also publish it by printing; and as the Lord had prepared me for this office from my infancy, He has manifested Himself in person before me, His servant, and sent me to fill it."

The Landgrave again wrote to Swedenborg, inquiring about the "miracle" of his intercourse with the Queen of Sweden's brother, and Swedenborg answered that the story was true, but "not a miracle." He also wrote to M. Venator, "that such matters ought, by no means, to be considered miracles: they are only testimonies that I have been introduced by the Lord into the spiritual world, and that I have been in association with angels and spirits, in order that the Church, which until now had remained in ignorance concerning that world, may know that heaven and hell exist in reality, and that man lives after death, a man, as before; and that thus there may be no more doubt as to his immortality. Deign, I pray you, to satisfy his Highness, that these are not miracles, but only testimonies that I converse with angels and spirits. You may see in the 'True Christian Religion' that there are no more miracles at this time; and the reason why. It is, that they who do not believe because they see no miracles, might easily, by them, be led into fanaticism."

Writing of miracles, Swedenborg remarks in another place, "Instead of miracles, there has taken place, at the present day, an open manifestation of the Lord himself, an intromission into the spiritual world, and with it, illumination by immediate light from the Lord in whatever relates to the interior things of the Church, but principally an opening of the spiritual sense of the Word, in which the Lord is present in his own Divine light. These revelations are not miracles, because every man, as to his spirit, is in the spiritual world, without separation from his body in the natural world. As to myself, indeed, my presence in the spiritual world is attended with a certain separation, but only as to the intellectual part of my mind, not as to the will part. This manifestation of the Lord, and intromission into the spiritual world, is more excellent than all miracles; but it has not been granted to any one since the creation of the world, as it has been to me. The men of the golden age, indeed, conversed with angels; but it was not granted to them to be in any other light than what was natural. To me, however, it has been granted to be in both spiritual and natural light at the same time; and hereby I have been privileged to see the wonderful things of heaven, to be in company with angels, just as I am with men, and at the same time to pursue truths in the light of truth, and thus to perceive and be gifted with them, consequently to be led by the Lord."

CHAPTER XXVII.

The True Christian Religion.

In the early part of 1771, Swedenborg published his "True Christian Religion, or, Universal Theology of the New Church;" and in August of the same year took ship, and left Amsterdam for London. Let us now turn to the consideration of his last great work,—a summary of the doctrines he was commissioned to teach.

"The True Christian Religion, containing the Universal Theology of the New Church," the last work published by Swedenborg, may be looked upon as the summary of his spiritual thought, his theological labors, his heavenly message to mankind. In its ninth English edition, it forms a large octavo volume of 815 pages, and is a complete body of divinity. It is divided into fifteen chapters, a Supplement treating of the states of Luther, Calvin, and Melancthon, the Dutch, English, Germans, Papists, Romish saints, Mahommedans, and the Africans, in the spiritual world; and seventy-seven memorable relations of scenes and representations witnessed in that world, interspersed between the various chapters; altogether forming a volume unique in literature, ancient or modern. At the risk of an occasional repetition of what has before been said, let us take a rapid survey of the contents of this massive and marvellous work.

Chapter I. treats of God the Creator, His Unity, the Divine Esse which is Jehovah, His Infinity or His Immensity and Eternity, the Essence of God which is His Divine Love and Wisdom, His Omnipotence, Omniscience, and Omnipresence, and of the creation of the universe. On these sublime subjects, themes on which, for ages, the weary reason of man has exerted itself with the poorest results, Swedenborg, with a mathematical exactness, sets forth the true doctrine; and with a simplicity of logic which at every step calls the Word of God, and the reason and common sense of man, to witness; leading the reader to wonder why truths so simple, so soul-satisfying, should have been hidden from human eyes so long. Whilst elucidating subjects commonly supposed to transcend human ideas, and yet which humanity is ever restless to discover,—reverence is in nowise deprived of its exercise. It is a great mistake, yet a common one, to associate mystery with true reverence; to talk of "ignorance" as "the mother of devotion." Let any one ask himself whether the reverence of Sir Isaac Newton for that God whose operations in the universe he was favored to discover, was inferior to that of an ignorant devotee, or an illiterate peasant. No. A knowledge of God and His attributes is no destroyer of faith, reverence, or devotion, but the reverse. Our knowledge of Him, however extended, is but the enlargement of a circle, which, as it is enlarged, expands our conception of the infinity beyond. Hence it is that whilst this chapter on God the Creator, goes into details which are the death of mysticism, the truths which it opens to the mind lead to an intelligent and reverential love, to which ignorance can never attain.

Chapter II. is devoted to the consideration of the Lord the Redeemer. It tells how Jehovah God descended and assumed humanity, that He might redeem and save mankind; and how the humanity was united to the Divinity, and thus God was made man, and man God, in one Person; that Redemption consisted in bringing the hells into subjection, and the heavens into order, and in thus preparing the way for a new spiritual Church; and how, without such Redemption, neither could men have been saved, nor could the angels have remained in a state of integrity. Thus Redemption was a work purely divine, and could not have been effected but by God Incarnate. The passion of the cross was in itself alone not Redemption, but was the last temptation the Lord endured in His Humanity; and it was the means of the glorification of that humanity. Hence it is a fundamental error of the Church to believe the passion of the cross to be Redemption itself; and this error, together with that relating to three Divine Persons from eternity, has perverted the whole system of Christian theology.

Chapter III. sets forth the doctrine of the Holy Spirit and the Divine Operation. The Holy Spirit is the Divine Truth, and also the Divine Virtue and Operation, proceeding from the One God, in whom there is the Divine Trinity, thus from the Lord God the Saviour, Jesus Christ. The Divine Virtue and Operation in and on humanity, signified by the Holy Spirit, consists, in general, in reformation and regeneration; and, in proportion as these are effected, in renovation, vivification, sanctification, and justification; and in proportion as these are effected, in purification from evils, remission of sins, and finally salvation. The Holy Spirit being the efflux of Jehovah through the glorified humanity, did not exist until after the incarnation. Hence it is nowhere said in the Old Testament, that the prophets spoke from the Holy Spirit, but from Jehovah God. We have a beautiful and irresistible confirmation of this truth in these words, "for the Holy Spirit was not *yet, because* that Jesus was not yet glorified." John vii. 39.

In this chapter he also speaks of the Trinity. There is a Divine Trinity, consisting of Father, Son, and Holy Spirit; and these three are the three *Essentials* of One God,—which make a One, like soul, body, and operation in man. To conceive of a Trinity of Divine *persons* from eternity, is to think of three Gods; and no amount of word-playing and creed-making can prevent the mind from falling into Tritheism, as long as a Trinity of *persons* and not of *essentials* is spoken and thought of. A Trinity of persons was unknown in the Apostolic Church. The doctrine was first broached by the Council of Nice, and thence received into the Roman Catholic Church, and thus propagated among the Reformed Churches. The Nicene and Athanasian doctrines concerning a Trinity, have, together, given rise to a faith which has entirely perverted the Christian Church; and hence has come that "abomination of desolation, and that affliction, such as was not in all the world, neither shall be," which the Lord has foretold in Daniel, the Evangelists, and the Revelation. For when the Church ceases to know its God, the central point of all faith and doctrine, all subsidiary points must necessarily become involved in darkness. And thus it is that the Athanasian creed has given rise to so many absurd notions about God, and hence, also, to an innumerable brood of heresies and phantasies on every point of doctrine and life; so much so, that had not the Lord effected a Last Judgment in 1757, and established a New Heaven and a New Church, no flesh could have been saved. The "healing of the nations," the new life, light and heat, that have coursed through humanity during the past century, attest the working of Omnipotence for the salvation and restoration of what is most valuable and precious in man.

Chapter IV. is an exposition of the nature of the Sacred Scripture, or the Word of the Lord, proving it to be the Divine Truth itself. The spiritual sense of the Word, and the means by which it is unfolded, together with the law of its composition, are explained at length, and with great perspicuity. It is shown that the spiritual sense is in all and every part of the Word, that hence it is divinely inspired, and is holy in every syllable. Nevertheless the literal sense is not to be disregarded. It is the basis, the continent, and the firmament of the spiritual sense; in it the Divine Truth is in its fullness, its sanctity, and its power; from it the doctrine of the Church is to be drawn and confirmed; and by it conjunction with the Lord and consociation with the angels is effected. The Word is in all the heavens, and the wisdom of the angels is thence derived. The Church exists from the Word, and the quality of the Church with man is according to his understanding of the Word. The marriage of Goodness and Truth, and of the Lord and the Church, is in every part of the Word. Men may collect and imbibe heretical opinions from the letter of the Word; but it is hurtful to confirm such opinions. Many things in the Word are appearances of truth, in which genuine truths lie concealed; and many fallacies arise from the taking of these appearances of truth for genuine or absolute truth. The literal sense of the Word is a guard to the genuine truths contained in it, and in the Word is represented by cherubs. To the wicked, it is a mercy that spiritual truth is thus hidden; for if known and not obeyed, it is profaned, and profanation involves the deepest suffering and distress. The Lord, during his abode in the world, fulfilled all things contained in the Word, and was thus made the Word, that is, the Divine Truth, even in ultimates. Previous to the Word which the world now possesses, there was a Word which is lost, but is preserved in heaven among the angels who lived as men in those times, and is also extant among certain nations in Great Tartary, who, however, have probably no true idea of the treasure they possess. By means of the Word, light is communicated to those who are out of the pale of the Church, and are not in possession of the Word. This is effected outwardly by the communications of commerce, with those nations who have the Word; and internally and insensibly by that community of soul which makes humanity appear before the Lord as one man. There is no thought conceived, no deed done, but which radiates from soul to soul, and produces effects of which the doer is not conscious. Thus it is that the Church—composed of the men who read, love, and obey the Word—benefits the world, and conjoins it with heaven and the Lord. Without the Word, no one would have any knowledge of God, of heaven and hell, or of a life after death, and much less of the Lord. The multiplicity of points involved in these statements, receive, in this chapter on the Sacred Scripture, most copious illustrations, both from the Word itself, and from the common experience of mankind. In reading this chapter, every candid person will feel that, strange and novel as many of the statements are, he is not dealing with a mere theorizer; and that facts and even Revelation itself must be done away, ere the doctrine of the Sacred Scripture here revealed can be overthrown or proved erroneous.

Chapter V. explains the Decalogue, or the Ten Commandments, as to their external and internal sense. The Decalogue, in the Israelitish Church, was the very essence of holiness, and from it the ark and the tabernacle derived their sanctity. In the Ten Commandments are contained all things which relate to love to God, and love towards our neighbor. In its literal sense, the Decalogue contains general precepts of doctrine and life, but in its spiritual and celestial sense it contains all precepts universally. Swedenborg then takes up each commandment singly, and gives an exposition of its literal, spiritual, and celestial application; and when he has done this, we perceive that these Ten Commandments, which every school-boy repeats and feels he understands, nevertheless contain all precepts, and are such as may afford guidance to the wisest angel, and that man can never outgrow them. Taking, for instance, the Seventh Commandment, (the eighth, according to the common numbering,) "Thou shalt not steal," he explains it in the natural sense, after the common acceptation. In the spiritual sense, he shows that to steal means to deprive others of the truths which they embrace in faith, in teaching doctrines known to be false, or teaching for the sake of gain; and in destroying in others, either by word or deed, those truths which lead to salvation. In the celestial sense, to steal is to take away divine power from the Lord, to be vain, to be proud, to arrogate to ourselves the merit and righteousness which are the divine gifts. All who do such things, notwithstanding their seeming adoration of God, do not trust in Him, but in themselves; and likewise do not believe in God, but in themselves; they steal from God; they are spiritual thieves; and every one who knows his own heart, must know how often he must refer to this commandment, in order to govern his life, and restrain his thoughts, before he can know perfect obedience, and be in truth a child of God. As with this commandment, so with all. We need to think of them every day, and to use them in all our states. If we purpose to lead a true and happy life, we must cherish them as constant companions.

Chapter VI. treats of Faith. Faith, it is said, is first in regard to time, and charity is first in regard to end; that is, the use of faith is to lead to charity. A saving faith is a faith in the Lord God the Saviour Jesus Christ, because He is the visible God in whom is the invisible. Faith, in general, consists in a belief that the Lord will save all who live a good life and believe aright; and a man receives this faith in consequence of approaching the Lord, learning truths from the Word, and living a life in conformity with them. Faith without charity is not faith, and charity without faith is not charity; and neither faith nor charity has any life in it but from the Lord. Although a man has power given him to procure for himself faith and charity, and the life of faith and charity, yet nothing of faith, charity, or the life of either, is from man, but from the Lord alone. Charity and faith are together in good works; for charity consists in willing what is good, and good works consist in doing what is good, from and under the influence of a good will; and both charity and faith are merely mental and perishable things, unless they are determined to works, and co-exist in them, whenever there is opportunity. The wicked have no faith, because wickedness is of hell, and faith is of heaven, and all the truth of faith is derived from heaven. Faith cannot dwell with evil, for evil is like fire,—infernal fire being the love of evil, which consumes faith like stubble, and reduces it and all that belongs to it to ashes. Evil dwells in darkness, and faith in light; and evil by means of the falsehood which it loves, extinguishes faith, as darkness does light. And because the world is at this day full of evil, (notwithstanding the morality of life, and the rationality with which faith is spoken and written about,) of true faith there is almost none, because of goodness there is almost none.

Chapter VII. discourses of love towards our neighbor, and good works. It is introduced by the statement that there are three universal loves, the love of heaven, the love of the world, and the love of self. These three loves, when they are in right subordination, make a man perfect; but when they are not in right subordination, they pervert and invert him. The love of self and of the world are not in themselves evil. When the love of heaven, that is, the love of God, of goodness and truth, is supreme in the mind, and the world is loved as a means to do good, and self is cared for that uses to the neighbor may be performed,—then the love of self and of the world are orderly and justifiable. But when the love of God and heaven is dethroned, and the love of self or of the world rules, and a man is religious and just only so far as religion and justice conduce to self-interest and thus God and justice and all things holy are put to vile uses, then the soul of man is inverted,—is a form of hell; and in the light of heaven appears bestial, ugly, and deformed.

Every individual man is the neighbor whom we ought to love, but according to the quality of his goodness or his life. Man considered collectively, that is, as a lesser or larger society, and considered under the idea of compound societies, that is, as our country,—is the neighbor that ought to be loved. The Church is our neighbor, to be loved in a still higher degree, and the Lord's kingdom is our neighbor to be loved in the highest degree. To love the neighbor is not to love his person, but the good which is in him. Charity itself consists in acting justly and faithfully in whatever office, business, and employment a person is engaged, and with whomsoever he has any connection. Eleemosynary acts of charity consist in giving to the poor, and relieving the indigent, but with prudence. There are public, domestic, and private duties of charity. Public duties of charity are, more especially, the payment of imposts and taxes. These are paid with different feelings by those who are spiritual and by those who are natural: those who are spiritual pay them out of good will, because they are collected for the preservation and protection of their country and the church, and as a provision for the proper officers and governors, who must receive their salaries out of the public treasury; therefore those who consider their country and the church as their neighbor, pay such debts cheerfully and with a willing mind, and consider it a wicked act either to withhold them or to use any deceit in the payment; whereas those who do not esteem their country and the church as their neighbor, pay such debts with a reluctant and unwilling mind, and, as often as they have an opportunity, withhold them, or use some fraud in the payment; for they regard only their own house and their own flesh as their neighbor. The domestic duties of charity are of several kinds, as those of a husband to his wife, and of a wife to her husband; of parents to their children, and of children to their parents; likewise of a master and mistress to their servants, and of servants to their master and mistress. There are so many duties relating to the education of children, and the government of families, that it would require a volume to enumerate them. As to what particularly regards the duties of parents to their children, there is an intrinsic difference in this respect with those who are under the influence of charity, and with those who are not, although externally the duties may appear similar. With those who are under the influence of charity, parental affection is joined with love toward their neighbor and love to God, and such parents love their children according to their morals, virtues, pursuits, and qualifications for the service of the public; but with those who are not under the influence of charity, there is no conjunction of charity with parental affection; the consequence is, that such parents frequently love wicked, immoral, and crafty children, more than those who are good, moral, and prudent; and thus prefer such as are unserviceable to the public, before such as are serviceable. Private duties of charity are also of several kinds, such as paying wages to workmen, returning borrowed money, observing agreements, keeping pledges, and other transactions of a like nature, some of which are duties grounded in statute law, some in civil law, and some in moral law. These duties, also, are discharged from different motives by those who are under the influence of charity, and by those who are not; by the former they are discharged faithfully and justly, for the law of charity requires that a man should so act in all his dealings, with whomsoever he may have any connection; but these duties are discharged in a totally different manner by those who are not influenced by charity. Then there are convivial recreations of charity, which consist of dinners and suppers and social intercourse. Every one knows that dinner and supper parties are in general use, and are given to promote various ends; by many on account of friendship, relationship, mirth, gain, recompense, and for party purposes of corruption; among the great they are given on account of their dignity; and in the palaces of kings, for the display of splendor and magnificence. But dinners and suppers of charity are given only by those who are influenced by mutual love grounded in a similarity of faith. Among Christians in the Primitive Church, dinners and suppers had this end alone in view, and were called feasts, being instituted that they might meet together in cordial joy and friendly union. At table, the guests conversed together on various subjects, domestic and civil, but particularly on such as concerned the Church; and as these feasts were feasts of charity, their conversation on every subject was influenced by charity, with all its joys and delights. The spiritual sphere which prevailed on such occasions, was a sphere of love to the Lord and toward the neighbor, which exhilarated every mind, softened the tone of every expression, and communicated to all the senses a festivity from the heart; for from every man there emanates a spiritual sphere, derived from the affection of his love and corresponding thought, which inwardly affects those in his company, particularly at the time of convivial recreations.

The first part of charity consists in putting away evils, and the second in doing actions that are useful to our neighbor. It is believed by many, at the present day, that charity consists only in doing good, and that while a man is doing good, he does no evil; consequently, that the first part of charity is to do good, and the second not to do evil: but the case is altogether the reverse, it being the first part of charity to put away evil, and the second to do good. For it is a universal law in the spiritual world, and thence too in the natural world, that so far as a person wills no evil, he wills what is good; consequently, so far as he turns himself away from hell, whence all evil ascends, he turns himself toward heaven, whence all good descends; and, therefore, so far as any one rejects the devil, he is accepted by the Lord. In performing the exercises of charity, a man does not ascribe merit to works, so long as he believes that all good is from the Lord. Moral life, if it is at the same time spiritual life, is charity. The friendship of love, contracted with a person without regard to his spiritual quality, is detrimental after death. The friendship of love, among the wicked, is intestine hatred toward each other. There is spurious charity, hypocritical charity, and dead charity. There can be no such thing as genuine charity, which is living, unless it make one with faith, and unless both in conjunction look to the Lord. Spurious charity is such as is the charity of those who hold to faith alone for salvation, and who say charity is of no account in leading to heaven. Such charity as these may have is spurious, because not spiritual, and merely performed from selfish and worldly motives. Hypocritical charity is predicable of those who, in public or private worship, bow themselves almost to the ground before God, pour forth long prayers with great devotion, put on a sanctified appearance, kiss crucifixes and bones of the dead, and kneel at sepulchers, and there mutter words expressive of holy veneration toward God, and yet, in their hearts nourish self-worship, and seek to be adored like so many deities. Dead charity is predicable of those whose faith is dead, since the quality of charity depends on the quality of faith. Faith is dead in all who are without works, and in those who believe not in God, but in living and dead men, and worship idols as if they were holy in themselves, after the practice of the old Gentiles.

Chapter VIII. is devoted to the vexed question of Free-Determination, or Free-Will. The doctrines of the Church, as commonly held, are first stated, and then the New Church doctrine on the question is explained under the following heads:—The two trees in the garden of Eden, one of life, and the other of the knowledge of good and evil, signify the free-will which man enjoys in respect to spiritual things. Man is not life, but a recipient of life from God. Man, during his abode in the world, is held in the midst between heaven and hell, and thus in a spiritual equilibrium, which constitutes free will.

From the permission of evil, which every man experiences in his internal man, it is evident that man has free-will in spiritual things. Without free-will in spiritual things, the Word would not be of any use, consequently the Church would be a nonenity. Without free-will in spiritual things, man would have nothing which would enable him to conjoin himself by reciprocation with the Lord; and consequently there would be no imputation, but mere predestination, which is detestable. Without free-will in spiritual things, God would be chargeable as the cause of evil. Every spiritual principle of the Church that is admitted and received in freedom, remains, but not otherwise. The human will and understanding enjoy this free-will; but the commission of evil, both in the spiritual and natural worlds, is restrained by laws, or else society in both would perish. If men were destitute of free-will in spiritual things, it would be possible for all men throughout the whole world, in a single day, to be induced to believe in the Lord; but this would be in vain, because nothing remains with man which is not freely received. Miracles are not performed at the present day because they deprive man of free-will.

Chapter IX. treats of Repentance. It is shown, in the first place, that repentance is the first constituent of the Church in man, and that in proportion as a man practices it, his sins are removed; and as they are removed, they are forgiven or remitted. Contrition, in the sense of a mere lip-confession of being a sinner, and of being involved in the guilt of Adam, without self-examination, is not repentance. Every man is born with a propensity to evils of all kinds, and unless he remove them, in part, by repentance, he remains in them; and whoever remains in them can not be saved. The knowledge of sin, and the discovery of some particular sin in one's self, is the beginning of repentance. Actual repentance consists in a man's examining himself, knowing and acknowledging his sins, supplicating the Lord, and beginning a new life. True repentance consists in a man's examining not only the actions of his life, but also the intentions of his will. Those also do the work of repentance, who, though they do not examine themselves, abstain from evils because they are sins; and this kind of repentance is done by those who perform works of charity from a religious motive. In repentance, confession ought to be made before the Lord God the Saviour, and at the same time supplication for help, and power to resist evils. Actual repentance is an easy duty to those who occasionally practice it, but it meets with violent opposition from those who never practiced it. He that never did the work of repentance, and never looked into, and examined, himself, comes at last not to know the nature either of damnatory evil or saving good.

Chapter X. describes the nature of Reformation and Regeneration. Unless a man be born again, and, as it were, created anew, he can not enter into the kingdom of God. This new birth, or creation, is effected by the Lord alone, through the medium of charity and faith, during man's coöperation. Since all are redeemed, all have a capacity to be regenerated, every one according to his state. The several stages of man's regeneration answer to his natural conception, gestation in the womb, birth, and education. The first act of the new birth, which is an act of the understanding, is called reformation; and the second, which is an act of the will, and thence of the understanding, is called regeneration. The internal man is first to be reformed, and by it the external, and thus the man is regenerated. When this takes place, there arises a combat between the internal and external man, and then whichever conquers has dominion over the other. The regenerate man has a new will and understanding. A regenerate man is in communion with the angels of heaven, and an unregenerate man is in communion with the spirits of hell. In proportion as a man is regenerated, his sins are removed; and this removal is what is meant by remission of sins. Regeneration can not be effected without free-will in spiritual things. Regeneration is not attainable without truths by which faith is formed, and with which charity conjoins itself.

Chapter XI. is devoted to a description of what imputation is, and what it is not. It is shown that imputation, and the faith of the present church, which alone is said to justify, are a one. The imputation which belongs to the faith of the present time is two fold, the one part relating to the merit of Christ, and the other to salvation as its consequence. The faith which is imputative of the merit and righteousness of Christ the Redeemer, first took its rise from the decrees of the Council of Nice, concerning three divine persons from eternity; and, from that time to the present, has been received by the whole Christian world. Faith imputative of the merit of Christ, was not known in the Apostolic

Church, which preceded the Council of Nice, and is neither declared nor signified in any part of the Word. An imputation of the merits and righteousness of Christ is impossible. There is such a thing as imputation, but then it is an imputation of good and evil, and at the same time of faith. The faith and imputation of the New Church can not be together with the faith and imputation of the former Church; and, in case they were together, such a collision and conflict would ensue, that every principle of the Church in man would perish. The Lord imputes good to every man, and hell imputes evil to every man. Faith, with whatever principle it conjoins itself, passes sentence accordingly; if a true faith conjoins itself with goodness, the sentence is for eternal life, but if faith conjoins itself with evil, the sentence is for eternal death. Thought is imputed to no one, but will.

Chapter XII. is a luminous exposition of the uses of Baptism. Without a knowledge of the spiritual sense of the Word, it is shown no one can know what the two sacraments, Baptism and the Holy Supper, involve and effect. The washing which is called baptism, signifies spiritual washing, which is a purification from evils and falses, and thus regeneration. As circumcision of the heart was represented by circumcision of the foreskin, baptism was instituted in lieu of it, to the end that an internal Church might succeed the external, in which all and everything was a figure of the internal Church. The first use of baptism is introduction into the Christian Church, and at the same time insertion among Christians in the spiritual world. The second use of baptism is, that the Christian may know and acknowledge the Lord Jesus Christ the Redeemer and Saviour, and may follow Him. The third and final use of baptism is, that man may be regenerated. By the baptism of John, a way was prepared that Jehovah the Lord might come down into the world, and accomplish the work of redemption.

Chapter XIII. is taken up with a like description of the uses of the Holy Supper. It is shown that it is impossible for any one, without an acquaintance with the correspondences of natural things with spiritual, to know the uses and benefits of the Holy Supper. An acquaintance with correspondences serves to discover the signification of the Lord's flesh and blood, and that the bread and wine signify the same; namely, that the Lord's flesh and the bread signify the divine good of His love, and likewise all the good of charity, and that His blood and the wine signify the divine truth of His wisdom, and likewise all the truth of faith, and that to eat signifies to appropriate. By understanding this, it may clearly be comprehended, that the Holy Supper contains, both universally and particularly, all things of the Church, and all things of heaven. In the Holy Supper the Lord is entirely present, with the whole of His redemption. The Lord is present, and opens heaven to those who approach the Holy Supper worthily; and He is also present with those who approach it unworthily, but does not open heaven to them; consequently, as baptism is an introduction into the Church, so the Holy Supper is an introduction into heaven. Those approach the Holy Supper worthily, who are under the influence of faith toward the Lord, and of charity toward their neighbor, thus, who are regenerate. Those who approach the Holy Supper worthily, are in the Lord, and He in them; consequently, conjunction with the Lord is effected by the Holy Supper. The Holy Supper is, to the worthy receivers, as a signing and sealing that they are sons of God.

Chapter XIV., concluding the doctrinal portion of the work, describes the consummation of the age, the coming of the Lord, and the new heaven and the New Church. The consummation of the age is the last time or end of the Church. The present day is the last time of the Christian

Church, which the Lord foretold and described in the Gospels, and in the Revelation. This last time of the Christian Church, is the very night in which the former Churches have set. After this night, morning succeeds; and the coming of the Lord is this morning. The coming of the Lord is not a coming to destroy the visible heaven and the habitable earth, and to create a new heaven and a new earth, according to the opinions which many, from not understanding the spiritual sense of the Word, have hitherto entertained. This, which is the second coming of the Lord, is for the sake of separating the evil from the good, that those who have believed and who do believe in Him, may be saved; and that there may be formed of them a new angelic heaven, and a New Church on earth; and without this coming no flesh could be saved. This second coming of the Lord is not a coming in person, but in the Word, which is from Him, and is Himself. This second coming of the Lord is effected by the instrumentality of a man, before whom He has manifested Himself in person, and whom He has filled with His spirit, to teach from Him the doctrines of the New Church by means of the Word. This is meant by the new heaven and the new earth, and the New Jerusalem descending out of heaven, spoken of in the Revelation. This New Church is the crown of all the Churches which have existed, to this time, on the earth.

On all these subjects Swedenborg discourses at length, and in a style which, for its combined simplicity and purity, we believe, is unmatched in theological literature. Wilkinson says truly of the volume, that, " viewed as a digest, it shows a presence of mind, an administration of materials, and a faculty of handling, of an extraordinary kind. There is old age in it in the sense of ripeness. If the intellectualist misses there somewhat of the range of discourse, it is compensated by a certain triteness of wisdom. As a polemic, not only against the errors of the Churches, but against the evil lives and self-excusings of Christians, the work is unrivaled. The criticisms of doctrine, with which it abounds, are masterly in the extreme; and were it compared with any similar body of theology, we feel no doubt that the palm of coherency, vigor, and comprehensiveness, would easily fall to Swedenborg, upon the verdict of judges of whatever Church."

We have said nothing of the seventy-six memorable relations strewn through the pages of the "True Christian Religion," because the limits to which we are confined forbid anything approaching to an adequate description of them. They are a great trouble to new readers of Swedenborg, and many who love and delight in the doctrinal teachings of the work, pass over, unread, the memorable relations, and try not to think of them. But this is only for a time. They are only strange and incomprehensible because the principles upon which they are written are not apprehended. The Indian king, who was told that in northern lands water became solid, so that his elephants might walk on it, laughed, and was an unbeliever. But, had the law or principle by which water becomes ice, been made plain to him, his laughter and his unbelief would have ceased. So it is with those who are shocked with Swedenborg's relations of things heard and seen in the spiritual world. Let but the great law of correspondence be understood, and the most marvelous of the relations straightway attain an interest and reality, which none but those who have studied them under the bright light of correspondences can understand, or easily believe possible. A memorable relation, which was to the writer of this, at one time, a thing to cause pity for the man that wrote it, is now the pleasant and practical study of a Sunday afternoon. He knows that his experience in this respect is paralleled by that of most Newchurchmen.

Count Hopken, in a letter to General Tuxen, says, "I once represented, in rather a serious manner, to this venerable man, (Swedenborg), that I thought he would do better not to mix his beautiful writings with so many memorable relations of things heard and seen in the spiritual world, concerning the states of men after death,—of which ignorance makes a jest and derision. But he answered me, that this did not depend on him; that he was too old to sport with spiritual things, and too much concerned for his eternal happiness to give into foolish notions; assuring me, on his hopes of salvation, that no imagination produced in him his revelations, which were true, and derived from what he had heard and seen."

"The True Christian Religion" was the last work Swedenborg published; it was a worthy conclusion of his grand labors. Among his papers, at his decease, was found an incomplete "Coronis" or Appendix to the work. This has been translated and published, and contains an elucidation of several interesting points.

CHAPTER XXVIII.

Anecdotes and Traits of Character.

SWEDENBORG arrived in London, from Amsterdam, in August, 1771, and took up his abode in lodgings he had before occupied in the house of Shearsmith, a peruke maker, at 26 Great Bath street, Cold Bath fields. From Shearsmith we learn several interesting items of intelligence regarding Swedenborg's habits and mode of life.

The dress that he generally wore when he went out to visit, was a suit of black velvet, (made after an old fashion,) a pair of long ruffles, a curiously hilted sword, and a gold-headed cane. In his later years he became less and less attentive to the concerns of the world. When walking abroad, he seemed to be engaged in spiritual communion, and took little notice of things and people in the streets. When he went out in Stockholm, without the observation of his domestics, some singularity in his dress would often betray his abstraction. Once when he dined with Robsahm's father, he appeared with one shoe-buckle of plain silver, and the other set with precious stones,—greatly to the amusement of some ladies of the party. When he lodged with Bergstrom, he usually walked out after breakfast, dressed neatly in velvet, and made a good appearance. In Sweden his dress was simple, but neat and convenient: during winter, he was clad in a garment of reindeer skins; and, in summer, in a study gown: "both well worn, as became a philosopher," according to Robsahm. Mr. Servanté was one of the earliest and most affectionate receivers of New Church doctrine. Before he received the truths of the New Church, he was once passing along St. John's street, London, when he met an old gentleman, of a dignified and most venerable appearance, whose deeply thoughtful, yet mildly expressive countenance, added to something very unusual in his general air, attracted his attention very forcibly. He turned round, therefore, to take another view of the stranger, who also turned around and looked at him. This was Swedenborg; but it was not until some years afterward, on seeing his portrait, that he became aware that the dignified and venerable old gentleman was the author of those works he now so sincerely loved, and so earnestly studied.

In person, Swedenborg was about 5 feet 9 inches high, rather thin, and of a brown complexion. His eyes were of a brownish grey, nearly hazel, and rather small. He had always a cheerful smile upon his countenance. When Collin visited him, he was thin and pale, but still retained traces of beauty, and had something very pleasing in his physiognomy, and a dignity in his erect stature. Ab Indagine tells us his eyes were always smiling; and Robsahm, that his "countenance was always illuminated by the light of his uncommon genius." His manners were those of a nobleman and gentleman of the last century. He was somewhat reserved, but complaisant; accessible to all, and had something very loving and taking in his demeanor. Personally, he left good impressions behind him wherever he appeared.

He did not understand the English language sufficiently well to hold a running conversation in it; and moreover he had an impediment in his speech. He was well acquainted, however, with the principal modern languages, and, of course, was thoroughly familiar with Greek and Latin, and had a sufficient knowledge of Hebrew. All authorities agree that his speech, though not facile, was impressive.

He spoke with deliberation, and when his voice was heard, it was a signal for silence in others, while the slowness of his delivery increased the curiosity of the listeners. He entered into no disputes on matters of religion, but when obliged to defend himself, he did it mildly and briefly; and if any one insisted upon argument, and became warm against him, he retired, with a recommendation to them to read his writings. One day, when Mr. Cookworthy, a member of the Society of Friends, was with Swedenborg in his lodging, a person present objected to something he said, and argued the point in his own way; but Swedenborg only replied, "I receive information from the angels on such things." One day, when dining with some Swedish clergy in London, a polemic tried to controvert the doctrine concerning the Lord, and the nature of our duty to Him; when, according to Mr. Burkhardt, "Swedenborg overthrew the tenets of his opponent, who appeared but a child to him in knowledge."

Swedenborg was practically a vegetarian. Shearsmith said he sometimes ate a few eels, and his servant informs us that he once had some pigeon pie; but his usual diet was bread and butter, milk and coffee, almonds and raisins, vegetables, biscuits, cakes, and gingerbread. The gingerbread he used to take out with him into the area of Cold Bath square, (now covered with houses,) and distribute it among the children as they played around him. He was a water-drinker, but occasionally, when in company, drank one or two glasses of wine, but never more. He took no supper. Of coffee he was a great drinker, which he took very sweet, and without milk. At his house in Stockholm, he had a fire during winter almost constantly in his study, at which he made his own coffee and drank it often, both during the day and in the night.

From the commencement of his illumination, Swedenborg was very particular as to his diet; and his Diary contains many references to his food, and to the spiritual association which various kinds of nutriment induced. In one place we read under the heading of "the Stink of Intemperance," "One evening I took a great meal of milk and bread, more than the spirits considered good for me. On this occasion they dwelt upon intemperance, and accused me of it." Indeed, on the first opening of his spiritual sight, in London, in 1743, when being very hungry from much exercise, he ate with great appetite, the spiritual stranger who appeared, saluted him with the words, "Eat not so much." In his treatise on Heaven and Hell, n. 299, he writes: "It has also been granted me to know the origin of the anxiety, grief of mind, and interior sadness, called melancholy, with which man is afflicted. There are certain spirits who are not yet in conjunction with hell, being yet in their first state, who love undigested and malignant substances, such as food when it lies corrupting in the stomach. They consequently are present where such substances are to be found in man, because these are delightful to them; and they there converse with one another from their own evil affection. The affection contained in their discourse thence enters the man by influx; and if it is opposed to the man's affection, he experiences melancholy, sadness, and anxiety; whereas if it agrees with his affection, he becomes gay and cheerful. Hence was made manifest to me the origin of the persuasion entertained by some who do not know what conscience is, by reason that they have none, when they attribute its pangs to a disordered state of the stomach." Of the killing and eating the flesh of animals, he writes thus in the Arcana Cœlestia, n. 1002. "Eating the flesh of animals, considered in itself, is something profane; for the people of the most ancient time on no account ate the flesh of any beast or fowl, but only grain, especially bread made of wheat, also the fruits of trees, pulse, milk, and what is produced from milk, as butter. To kill animals and to eat their flesh, was to them unlawful, and seemed as something bestial; and they were content with the uses and services which they rendered, as appears also from Genesis i. 29, 30. But in succeeding times, when man began to grow fierce as a beast, yea fiercer, then first they began to kill animals, and to eat their flesh. And because man was such, this was permitted, and at this day also is permitted; and so far as man does it from conscience, so far is it lawful, for his conscience is formed of all those things which he thinks to be true, and so thinks to be lawful: wherefore also, at this day, no one is by any means condemned for this, that he eats flesh."

Swedenborg took snuff, as was the custom in his day. Some of his manuscripts yet bear traces of the dingy powder.

Shearsmith gives the same account of Swedenborg's habits of sleep, as his gardener at Stockholm. He had no regard for times and seasons, days or nights, only taking rest as he felt disposed. This was naturally to be expected, considering the peculiarities of his seership. At first, Shearsmith was greatly alarmed, by reason of his talking day and night. Sometimes he would be writing, and then he would be, as it were, holding a conversation with several persons. But as Swedenborg spoke in a language Shearsmith did not understand, he could make nothing of it. Shearsmith was nevertheless well pleased with his lodger. His servant told Mr. Peckitt, after Swedenborg's death, that "he was a good-natured man, and that he was a blessing to the house, for they had harmony and good business whilst he was with them." A short time before his death, he lay for some weeks in a trance, without any sustenance.

Swedenborg's pension preserved him from all pecuniary cares. Yet in his Diary we read: "I have now been for thirty-three months in a state in which my mind is withdrawn from bodily affairs, and hence can be present in the societies of the spiritual and celestial. Yet whenever I am intent upon worldly matters, or have cares and desires about money, (such as caused me to write a letter to-day,) I lapse into a bodily state; and the spirits, as they inform me, cannot speak with me, but say they are in a manner absent. This shows me that spirits cannot speak with a man who dwells upon worldly and bodily cares; for the things of his body draw down his ideas, and drown them in the body.—March 4, 1748." This experience is worthy of record. Most of us, in our own way, know the truth of it, from heart experience. Whatever his motives were, he would receive back no proceeds from the sale of his theological works, but dedicated the whole to religious subscriptions. To beggars he seldom gave anything. In his writings, he in several places protests against the sham charity which satisfies itself by mere alms-giving. He tells us that habitual beggars lead vicious and impious lives, and that to give them money is rather to curse than to bless them. Swedenborg did not lend money; for that, he said, is the way to lose it; besides, as he remarks, he required it nearly all to pay the expenses of his traveling and printing.

In his later years, Swedenborg had no library but his Bible, in various editions, and his own manuscripts. What need had he of the books of men, when he knew the heavens,—and the glorified authors of earth, in states of wisdom they never dreamed of here?

Swedenborg seldom went to church; for, as he said, he "had no peace in the church, on account of spirits, who contradicted what the preacher said, especially when he spoke of Three Persons in the Godhead, which amounted in reality to three Gods."

Swedenborg's long and arduous labors on earth were now ended. Let us approach his death-bed with reverence, and observe how a good man can die.

CHAPTER XXIX.

Last Days on Earth.

ON Christmas eve, 1771, a stroke of apoplexy deprived Swedenborg of his speech, and lamed one side. He lay afterwards in a lethargic state for more than three weeks, taking no sustenance beyond a little tea without milk, and cold water occasionally, and once a little currant jelly. At the end of that time, he recovered his speech and health somewhat, and ate and drank as usual. Mr. Hartley and Dr. Messiter at this time visited him, and asking him if he was comforted with the society of angels, as before, he answered that he was. They then asked him to declare whether all that he had written was strictly true, or whether any part or parts were to be excepted. "I have written," answered Swedenborg, with a degree of warmth, "nothing but the truth, as you will have more and more confirmed to you all the days of your life, provided you keep close to the Lord, and faithfully serve Him alone, by shunning evils of all kinds as sins against Him, and diligently searching His Word, which, from beginning to end, bears incontestable witness to the truth of the doctrines I have delivered to the world."

At this time Swedenborg seemed to love privacy, and saw but little company. His old friend, Springer, the Swedish Consul in London, called upon him a week or two before his decease. Springer asked him when he believed that the New Jerusalem, or the New Church of the Lord, would be manifested, and if this manifestation would take place in the four quarters of the world. Swedenborg replied: "No mortal can declare the time, no, not even the celestial angels; it is known solely to the Lord. Read the Revelation, chapter xxi. 2, and Zechariah, chapter xiv. 9, and you will find that it is not to be doubted that the New Jerusalem, mentioned in the Apocalypse, which denotes a new and purer state of the Christian Church, than has hitherto existed, will manifest itself to all the earth."

About this time, says Springer, Swedenborg told him that his spiritual sight was withdrawn, after he had been favored with it for so long a course of years. This, of which the world knew nothing, and for which it cared nothing, it was the greatest affliction to him to lose. He could not endure the blindness, but cried out repeatedly, "O my God! hast thou then forsaken thy servant at last?" He continued for several days in this condition, but it was the last of his trials: he recovered his precious sight, and was happy.

About this time he wrote a note, in Latin, to the Rev. John Wesley, to the following effect:—

"GREAT BATH STREET, COLD BATH FIELDS, *February*, 1772.

"SIR,—I have been informed, in the world of spirits, that you have a strong desire to converse with me. I shall be happy to see you, if you will favor me with a visit.

"I am, sir, your humble servant,
"EMANUEL SWEDENBORG."

When the note was handed to Mr. Wesley, he was in company with some of his preachers, arranging their preaching circuits for the year. Wesley read the note aloud, and frankly confessed that he had been strongly actuated by a desire to meet Swedenborg, but he had revealed his wish to no one. He wrote for answer, that he was then occupied in preparing for a six months' journey, but would wait upon

Swedenborg on his return to London. Swedenborg, in reply, stated that the proposed visit would be too late, as he should go into the world of spirits on the 29th day of the next month, (March,) never more to return. Wesley did not call, and they never met. Had he been wise, he would, in spite of engagements, have embraced this opportunity of conversing with that wonderful man, after an invitation of such a character. Had they met, Methodism might have been a different thing from what it is. But let us believe that all such seeming accidents are overruled for the best.

The authority for this anecdote is the Rev. Samuel Smith, a Methodist preacher, who was present when Wesley received Swedenborg's letter. It excited his curiosity to know something of the writings of so remarkable a man; and the result was, a firm conviction of the rationality and truth of the heavenly doctrine promulgated in them, and a zealous activity in their diffusion, throughout the remainder of his life.

Mr. Bergstrom, the landlord of the King's Arms tavern in Wellclose square, at whose house Swedenborg had once lodged, called to see him in his last days. Swedenborg told him, that since it had pleased the Lord to take away the use of his arm by palsy, his body was good for nothing but to be put under ground. Mr. Bergstrom asked him whether he would receive the Sacrament. Somebody present at the time proposed sending for the Rev. Mr. Mathesius, a minister of the Swedish Church. Swedenborg at once declined having that gentleman, for he had sent abroad a report that Swedenborg was out of his senses. (Mathesius himself, in later years, became deranged.) The Rev. Arvid Ferelius, another Swedish clergyman, with whom Swedenborg was on the best terms, and who had visited him frequently in his illness, was then sent for. Ferelius observed to him, that "as many persons thought he had endeavored only to make himself a name, or acquire celebrity in the world, by the publication of his new theological system, he should now be ready, in order to show justice to the world, to recant either the whole or a part of what he had written, since he had now nothing more to expect from the world which he was so soon to leave forever." Upon hearing these words, Swedenborg raised himself half upright in his bed, and placing his sound hand upon his breast, said, with great zeal and emphasis, "As true as you see me before you, so true is everything which I have written. I could say more, were I permitted. When you come into eternity, you will see all things as I have stated and described them; and we shall have much discourse about them with each other." Ferelius then asked him if he would take the Lord's Holy Supper. He replied, "You mean well, but I, being a member of the other world, do not need it. However, to show the connection and union between the church in heaven and the church on earth, I will gladly take it." He then asked Ferelius if he had read his views on the Sacrament. Before administering the Sacrament, Ferelius inquired whether he confessed himself to be a sinner. "Certainly," said Swedenborg, "so long as I carry about with me this sinful body." With deep and affecting devotion, with folded hands, and with his head uncovered, he confessed his own unworthiness, and received the Holy Supper. He then presented Ferelius with a copy of his Arcana Cœlestia, expressing his gratitude to him for his kind attentions.

He knew that his end was near. He told the people of the house on what day he should die, and Shearsmith's servant remarked, "he was as pleased as I should have been, if I was going to have a holiday, or going to some merry-making."

His faculties were clear to the last. On Sunday, the 29th day of March, 1772, hearing the clock strike, he asked his landlady and her maid, who were both sitting at his bed-side, what o'clock it was; and upon being answered it was five o'clock, he said, "It is well; I thank you; God bless you;" and in a little moment after, he gently departed. He was then 84 years, 8 weeks, and five days, old.

His body was taken to the undertaker's, where it lay in state; and then was, on the 5th day of April, deposited in three coffins, in the vault of the Swedish Church, in Prince's square, Radcliffe Highway, with all the ceremonies of the Lutheran faith,—the service being performed by the Rev. Arvid Ferelius.

There the body still lies. No stone, or inscription marks the spot. Swedenborg of all men, least requires monumental commemoration. Every year enshrines his memory in increasing numbers of grateful hearts;—grateful to him, as a medium, whereby the Infinite Wisdom and Goodness might reach its end in blessing mankind by the advent of spiritual truth, and leading them within the gates of the Holy City, New Jerusalem.

CHAPTER XXX.

Progress of the New Church.

SWEDENBORG widely distributed his works during his lifetime, presenting copies to libraries and to distinguished and learned persons everywhere. With the Latin edition of his "Arcana Cœlestia," he issued an English version of volumes I. and II., in numbers, at a very cheap rate. None of his other works were translated into English in his lifetime, with the exception of his little treatise "On the intercourse of the Soul and the Body." This work was translated by his attached friend, William Cookworthy. Six years after Swedenborg's death, in 1778, "Heaven and Hell" was published in English by James Phillips, the Quaker bookseller in George Yard, Lombard street, London. William Cookworthy was the translator of this work also, and defrayed the cost of the whole edition. The Rev. Thomas Hartley revised the translation, and wrote for it an excellent preface, which to this day forms a useful introduction to the work. Book after book was translated by other hands; and the Rev. John Clowes, Rector of St. John's, Manchester, having embraced the doctrines of the New Jerusalem, set about the work of translation in earnest, and gave to the world an excellent and accurate English version of the "Arcana Cœlestia" in thirteen volumes. In 1810, the "Society for Printing and Publishing the Writings of the Hon. Emanuel Swedenborg" was formed, and from that time to this has perseveringly pursued its useful labors, sustained by the contribution of friends. In 1854 a gentleman munificently presented the Society with £3000 to purchase an independent house of publication, and the result was its establishment in a handsome edifice in Bloomsbury street, Oxford street, London. During the past year, the "Swedenborg Society" has reduced the price of its publications one third; and now, quality of workmanship considered, there are no cheaper books in England. It is desirable that works filled with such heavenly thoughts, and capable of so great use and service, should have no bar whatever to a free and wide diffusion.

In the United States of America several editions of Swedenborg's works have been published, and their circulation has been considerably greater than in England. In New York has recently been established an "American Swedenborg Printing and Publishing Society," which, in the few years of its existence, in the public spirit of its management, and the excellence and beauty of its editions, promises to rival and excel its English predecessor. But in such labors of love it is a happiness to be surpassed.

In France, translations of various works of Swedenborg have been executed from time to time. M. Le Boys Des Guays, of St. Amand, Cher, has been, however, the chief laborer in this field. Sustained by some kind friends, but, most of all, by his own ardent perseverance, the Lord's gift, he has executed a uniform translation of the whole of Swedenborg's published theological works. In France, the sale of these works is as yet small, but the dawning of a better day is looked for with confiding faith.

In Germany, Dr. Tafel, librarian to the University of Tubingen, has been the principal worker in the translation and diffusion of Swedenborg's writings. More than this, he has reprinted many of his works in the original Latin, and has been the means of the publication of Swedenborg's

Adversaria and Diarium, from his MSS., thus securing those invaluable records of spiritual experience from all danger of loss. In Germany, as in France, the readers of Swedenborg, as compared with those in England and America, are yet few. In Sweden but little interest, as yet, is taken in his writings. His countrymen seem proud of him, principally on account of his fame abroad. From all that is observed, we are inclined to conclude that Swedenborg can have a fair hearing only in nations where thought and speech are alike free. In the "True Christian Religion," speaking of the "noble English nation," he says: "The English are in the center of all Christians, because possessed of interior intellectual light, derived from the liberty of speaking and writing; while nations, who do not possess such liberty, have this light presented in a confused manner, for it wants an outlet." He also compares free nations, in relation to the Church and theology, to eagles which raise themselves to any height; whilst nations not free are like tame swans in a river. Free nations are also like stags, which range with full license through the plains, groves, and forests; whereas nations not free are like deer enclosed in parks, kept for some prince's pleasure.

It will have been observed, in the course of our narrative, that Swedenborg made no attempt to gather the receivers of the doctrines he was sent to promulgate, into a separate body or sect. When he was attacked by Dr. Ekebom, he defended himself from the Word, the Formula Concordiæ, and the Confessions of the Lutheran Church. When Doctors Beyer and Rosen were charged with heresy, he counseled a like defense. His friends, the Rev. Thomas Hartley, rector of Winwick, in Northamptonshire, and William Cookworthy, a distinguished minister in the Society of Friends, both remained in their old connections until the time of their death, although perfectly confirmed in the doctrines of the New Church. Later, the Rev. John Clowes spent a long life in the Church of England, ministering to a large and affectionate congregation, while alike by tongue and pen he spread abroad the pure faith of the New Jerusalem,—he, with some others, believing that the new doctrines would quietly displace the old, and that no external separation was called for. Others, however, thought differently, and on June 1st, 1788, in Great East Cheap, London, was inaugurated an external organization, calling itself the New Church. One after another, societies in England and Scotland have been formed for the public worship of the Lord Jesus Christ, until in the present year there exist some sixty or seventy such associations. They are most numerous in Lancashire. These societies are represented in an annual conference, which attends to the general business of the Church, and ordains ministers. It has, moreover, prepared a liturgy and book of hymns, and from various grants of money which have been made to it, supports schools in many districts. The conference also possesses, as its organ, a monthly magazine, called the "Intellectual Repository, or New Jerusalem Magazine." The societies of which this conference is composed, possess complete liberty, and manage their own affairs without interference.

In America matters are much the same as in England. There is a general convention, corresponding to the English conference. It also has its organ in a monthly journal, the "New Jerusalem Magazine," published in Boston. In addition, it has lately started a weekly newspaper, "The New Jerusalem Messenger," published in New York. Professor Bush, of New York, likewise edits a monthly magazine with distinguished ability, entitled the "New Church Repository." In America the New Church has made considerably greater visible progress than in England, particularly in the state of Massachusetts.

But it is ever to be remembered that the New Church is a Dispensation and not a Sect; and is to be measured by the goodness and truth in the world, and not by the lip-confession of a creed. The Lord God Almighty, the Creator of heaven and earth, took unto Himself an arm of flesh, in assuming our humanity, and through it has come near to men that He might redeem them from all their foes. Like all Divine works, this has been gradual. The first Christian Church was founded; but, as the centuries glided away, it gradually lost its first purity and innocence, forgot the simplest teachings of its Founder, and fell into evil states, "such as were not since the beginning of the world, no, nor ever shall be." But the Lord "shortened those days; else, no flesh had been saved," and He chose Swedenborg as His servant to bear testimony to the world how such things were, and how, in executing the Last Judgment, He cast down the hells, and swept from the souls of men the myriads of evil spirits which hung like a pall of death around them. Writing in 1771, Swedenborg says: "The reduction of the heavens and the hells to order is not yet accomplished, but has continued in its process since the day of the Last Judgment until now, and still continues."—*T. C. R.*, n. 123. We are beginning to realize the effects of these great changes. In the times in which we live, the nations feel the breath of a new Spring upon their spirits, but faintly conceive the Divine Source from which the inspiration comes. All speak of the new spirit which animates men, and history is in vain appealed to for its cause. History contains no parallel to the things which now are, and the things which are to come. The world has entered upon a new course. The Lord has said: "Behold I make all things new." And in the days which are to come, the Divine will shall be done on earth as in heaven; for the promise of the New Jerusalem is, "Behold the tabernacle of God is with men, and He will dwell with them, and they shall be His people, and God Himself shall be with them, and be their God; and the nations of them that are saved shall wall in the light of it; and there shall be no night there. . . . I Jesus have sent mine angel to testify unto you these things in the churches. I am the root and the offspring of David, and the bright and morning star. The Spirit and the Bride say, Come; and let him that heareth say, Come; and let him that is athirst come; and whosoever will, let him take the water of life freely. . . Even so, come, Lord Jesus. Amen."

"There are five classes of those who read my writings. The first reject them entirely, because they are in another persuasion, or because they are in no faith. The second receive them as scientifics, or as objects of mere curiosity. The third receive them intellectually, and are in some measure pleased with them, but whenever they require an application to regulate their lives, they remain where they were before. The fourth receive them in a persuasive manner, and are thereby led, in a certain degree, to amend their lives and perform uses. The fifth receive them with delight, and confirm them in their lives."—*Swedenborg's Spiritual Diary* 2955.

THE END.

VALUABLE

NEW CHURCH BOOKS

PUBLISHED BY

J. B. LIPPINCOTT & CO., Philadelphia.

*** For sale by Booksellers generally, or will be sent by mail, post-paid, to any address, on receipt of the price by the Publishers.

"Swedenborg's books teem with the grandest, the most humane and generous truths."—*North American Review.*

"Whoever desires to understand modern theology, and the elements which have contributed to its formation, has need to study the writings of Emanuel Swedenborg. Whatever minister desires to understand modern religious thought in his own congregation, must know something of Swedenborgianism, though he has not a Swedenborgian in his parish."—*New York Independent.*

"Swedenborg deserves to be studied as a philosophic writer not often excelled in profundity, acuteness, variety, and consistency of thought."—*Chicago Advance.*

"Swedenborg was a remarkable man in many ways, contributing to scientific knowledge by his discoveries, and making his mark upon the thought of his time. His visions are in striking contrast to the opinions of his age, and in substance are in striking accord with the intuitions of the best minds of our own."—*Golden Age.*

Concerning Heaven and its Wonders, and Concerning Hell. From Things Heard and Seen. By EMANUEL SWEDENBORG. 12mo. Cloth. $1.25. Boards. 50 cents.

"The distinguished author of 'The Heart of Christ' calls this work 'one of the golden books,' and says: 'The time will come when this treatise will be as much read as Milton's Paradise Lost, and enter far more vitally into the popular conception of the life to come. The saintly Oberlin read it and preached it; and the late Mrs. Browning, as we happen to know, was vastly delighted with its ideas, and tried to disseminate them among her English friends, and gain for them a lodgment within what she called 'the husks of the old theology.'"—*Monthly Religious Magazine.*

Heaven and its Wonders, and Hell. From Things Heard and Seen. By EMANUEL SWEDENBORG. From the Latin edition of Dr. J. F. I. Tafel. Demi 8vo. Extra cloth. $2.50.

Angelic Wisdom Concerning the Divine Love and Wisdom. By EMANUEL SWEDENBORG. From the original Latin as edited by Dr. J. F. I. Tafel. Translated by R. N. Foster. Demi 8vo. Extra cloth. $2.00.

" . . . This English version is as nearly literal as the nature of the work and the structure and spirit of our language permit. The principle upon which Mr. Foster has executed it is fully, clearly, and satisfactorily stated by him in an unusually interesting preface, which concludes thus: 'A careful perusal of it (the work) can hardly fail to convince the thoughtful reader that it is the most remarkable combination of philosophy, illumination, and seership which either ancient or modern experience has produced.' "—*Philadelphia Press.*

"From the reading of this book, Christian love and Christian unity will be better understood and appreciated."—*Chicago Evening Journal.*

True Christian Religion. Containing the entire Theology of the New Church, foretold by the Lord in Dan. vii. 13, 14, and Rev. xxi. 1, 2. By EMANUEL SWEDENBORG. From the Latin edition of Dr. J. F. I. Tafel. Translated by R. Norman Foster. 2 vols. demi 8vo. Tinted paper. Extra cloth. $5.00.

*True Christian Religion. By Emanuel Sweden*BORG. 1 vol. 8vo. Cloth. $2.25.

"Swedenborg deserves to be studied. As a philosophic writer he is not often excelled in profundity, acuteness, variety, and consistency of thought. We confess to having read for years past some portion of his works with intellectual and spiritual profit, and we imagine, at least, that we can trace his influence in the conceptions and reasonings of many modern authors of distinction, who do not always give Swedenborg the credit which he deserves. This is especially true on the subject of the devil and evil spirits, the trinity, the relation of the divine to the human in the person of Christ, the atonement, the resurrection, and the future life of heaven and hell. . . .

"Swedenborg's views are quite thoroughly and systematically set forth in the two volumes before us, which have been translated from the Latin into English by R. Norman Foster."—*Chicago Advance.*

"The volumes of Swedenborg already given to the public in this new edition have abundantly satisfied the most exacting critics of the fitness of the translator for his difficult task. . . . Dr. Foster is simply faithful to the Latin original, remarkably happy in the choice of phrases, and of a fine style as a writer. We lack space to point out the place which Swedenborg occupies in the world of religious thought, and the particular office of the work before us. Suffice it therefore to say, that many persons of all sects are greatly interested in Swedenborg's teaching, and that it seems likely to leaven more or less the entire lump of modern religion."—*Chicago Tribune.*

Conjugial Love. By Emanuel Swedenborg. 1 vol. 8vo. Cloth. $1.75.

*Angelic Wisdom Concerning the Divine Provi*dence. By EMANUEL SWEDENBORG. From the original Latin as edited by Dr. J. F. I. Tafel. Translated by R. Norman Foster. Demi 8vo. Tinted paper. Extra cloth. $2.25.

Elements of Character. By Mary G. Ware, author of "Death and Life," etc. 16mo. Cloth. $1.25.

"This work is entitled to a place among the higher productions of American female literature."—*Harper's Magazine.*

Thoughts in my Garden. By Mary G. Ware, author of "Elements of Character," etc. 16mo. Cloth. $1.25.

Death and Life. By Mary G. Ware, author of "Thoughts in my Garden," etc. 16mo. Cloth. $1.25.

Lectures on the Nature of Spirit and of Man as a Spiritual Being. By CHAUNCEY GILES, Minister of the New Jerusalem Church. 12mo. Cloth, $1.25; paper, 60 cents.

"The volume before us is wholly Swedenborgian. We think that nowhere can be found a book from which so clear and so compressed a view of the leading doctrines of this rapidly growing sect can be obtained."—*Historical Magazine.*

"It adheres rigidly to the received principles of Swedenborg's teachings, but it surrounds them with lucid illustrations, clears up their apparent difficulties, enforces their logical applications, and exhibits their practical scope and bearing in a style remarkable for clearness of statement, as well as argumentative force."—*New York Tribune.*

Lectures on the Incarnation, Atonement, and Mediation of the Lord Jesus Christ. By CHAUNCEY GILES, Minister of the New Jerusalem Church. 12mo. Cloth, 75 cents; paper, 40 cents.

Mistaken; or, The Seeming and the Real. By LYDIA FULLER. 12mo. Fine cloth. $1.50.

"The work before us does the highest credit to its author. It is a pure, bright story of every-day life, beautiful in its conception, and charming in its simple yet elegant style. The plot is well conceived, and full of deep and exciting interest, and the tale closes in the happiest manner conceivable. There is nothing of an unhealthy or misanthropical tone in any page of the work. The spirit of the work is excellent, and we wish every success to 'Mistaken.'"—*Star of the West.*

Life: Its Nature, Varieties, and Phenomena. By LEO H. GRINDON, author of "Emblems," "Figurative Language," etc. First American edition. 12mo. Extra cloth. $2.25.

" . . . Mr. Grindon possesses the faculty of *expression.* His prose is full of poetic fancy; and facts which would be as a bundle of dry twigs in another man's hands, are fruitful and beautiful under his pen. He discusses the great and varied mysteries of life in a reflective and instructive manner, and the charm of his poetic style renders his book at once fascinating and of value."—*Phila. Press.*

" . . . Rarely is one met that compasses so much in so brief a space, and still more rarely is such compact condensation of most interesting matter made so very entertaining."—*Cincinnati Commercial.*

In Both Worlds. By Wm. H. Holcombe, M.D., author of "Our Children in Heaven," "The Sexes: Here and Hereafter," etc. etc. 12mo. Tinted paper. Extra cloth. $1.75.

"While likely to prove of the deepest and most thrilling interest to all whose minds are elevated above materiality and the grosser elements of nature, it is in no sense irreverent."—***Boston Evening Traveler.***

The Other Life. By Wm. H. Holcombe, M.D., author of "Our Children in Heaven," "The Sexes: Here and Hereafter," "In Both Worlds," etc. etc. 12mo. Toned paper. Extra cloth. $1.50.

"It is a well-written, thoughtful, and earnest argument in favor of the doctrines of Emanuel Swedenborg concerning the spirit-world. Even those who do not accept these doctrines with the faith of Dr. Holcombe must be struck with the tender piety of its tone and the genuine sincerity of every line of the book."—***Philadelphia Evening Bulletin.***

Southern Voices. Poems by Wm. H. Holcombe, M.D., author of "Our Children in Heaven," "The Other Life," etc. 12mo. Tinted paper. Extra cloth, gilt top. $1.50.

"As the productions of spiritualized sentiment, cultured, refined, devout, and artistic, they will be treasured by many for setting to music thoughts and feelings which nothing but rhythmic measures and poetic language can express."—*Golaen Age.*

"Taste and tenderness are the prevailing characteristics of the volume."—*Philadelphia Age.*

"Dr. Holcombe has a very rich fancy, of which he has afforded evidence in the beautiful volume of poems that lies before us, and which, as the production of a Southern author of high reputation, is entitled to a more marked consideration at our hands than most of the works with which the American book market is nowadays glutted."—***Republican, New Orleans, La.***

Who was Swedenborg? By O. P. Hiller. 16mo. Paper cover, 25 cents; cloth, 50 cents.

Lessons from Daily Life. By Emily E. Hildreth. 12mo. Tinted paper. Extra cloth. $1.00.

*The New Eschatology. Showing the Indestructi*bility of the Earth and the wide Difference between the Letter and the Spirit of Holy Scripture. By J. G. BROUGHTON PEGG. 12mo. Cloth. 75 cents.

Letters to a Man of the World. By J. F. E. LE BOYS DES GUAYS, ex-sous Prefect in Department du cher. Revised edition. 16mo. Cloth. $1.50.

www.ingramcontent.com/pod-product-compliance
Lightning Source LLC
LaVergne TN
LVHW010231110826
845151LV00004B/1262